Strategic Management for Chartered Accountants

Strategic Management for Chartered Accountants

B. Hiriyappa
M.Com., M.Phil., Ph.D.
Associate Professor
KKECS Institute of Management, Bangalore
Sap Consultant
Visiting Faculty of MBA and MHA
for
Padamshree Group of Institutions
Raja Rajeswari Group of Institutions
Bangalore, Karnataka

PUBLISHING FOR ONE WORLD

NEW AGE INTERNATIONAL (P) LIMITED, PUBLISHERS
New Delhi • Bangalore • Chennai • Cochin • Guwahati • Hyderabad
Jalandhar • Kolkata • Lucknow • Mumbai • Ranchi
Visit us at **www.newagepublishers.com**

Published by New Age International (P) Ltd., Publishers
First Edition: 2008

ISBN (10): 81-224-2353-1

ISBN (13): 978-81-224-2353-2

Rs. 200.00

C-08-02-2224

Printed in India at Ramprintograph, Delhi.
Typeset at Inhouse.

PUBLISHING FOR ONE WORLD
NEW AGE INTERNATIONAL (P) LIMITED, PUBLISHERS
4835/24, Ansari Road, Daryaganj, New Delhi-110002
Visit us at **www.newagepublishers.com**

Preface

Strategic management is a stream of decisions and actions with view to develop effective long term and short term planning and policies with technological business forecasting that would help the organization achieve its superior goal. Strategic management includes strategic analysis, strategy formulation, strategic choice, strategy implementation and control strategic decision for an organization to deploy resources into new opportunities.

Strategic management is important for Chartered Accountants, CEO, Directors, Managing Directors, Strategy Planners, Students and Faculty Members of BBM, MBA, M.Com, PGDM, PGDBM, PGDHRM, ICFAI and competitive examinations in India and abroad. I invite suggestions from one and all for improvements in next edition of this book.

Many individuals have rendered their helping hand to me. I take this opportunity to thank all of them. I thank Dr. D.M. Basvaraja, my teacher, guide and supervisor and professor from Kuvempur University for this constant inspiration and support. I also thank Dr. C.M. Thagaraju, Dr. G.T. Govindappa, my teachers, and professors of Kuvempur University. I am immensely indebted to them. I also thank T.N. Suresh, Director of Padmashree group of institutions, Bangalore, Dr. C.N. Aswathnarayan, Chairman of Padmashree group of institutions, Bangalore, Dr. Bakkappa, Coordinator, Shiva Gangothri PG Centre, Davanagere, Dr. A.Venktaraju, Professor, ATNCC, Shimoga, Prof. Sheshchalla, KKECS, Bangalore, Chairman, Principal, HOD and staff of TIMS, Bangalore, and Prof. Shekappa and my friend Nagaraja A.P.

In writing this book I have drawn on a vast amount of literature in strategic management. Naturally, I owe an intellectual debt to numerous authors who have enriched the stream of literature in strategic management by their contributions. My prefounded debt is to American scholars, George Stenier, Ansoff, Newman, Warren, Peter Drucker, Akcoff, Christenson, Kenneth, Bower and Vacil, Acherman, Robinson, Piere, Wheeler and Hunger, Charles W.L. Hill and Gareth R. Jones. In the UK I owe a great debt to Argeni, Hussey, and Barnard Taylor, Thomson and other scholars.

Shri Saumya Guptha, MD, Shri Sudarshan S.P., Marketing manager, the New Age International Publisher, these persons are the main initiators and monitors of this project. I express my sincere gratitude to all of them.

It is my prime responsibility to thank my parents, brother, sisters and friends for put with inconveniences caused during writing of this book.

Dr. B. HIRIYAPPA. Ph. D.

Bangalore

Contents

CHAPTER 1

Business Environment

Contents

- Introduction
- Business
- Objectives of business
- Environmental influences on business
- Environmental analysis
- Characteristics of business environment
- Components of business environment
- The micro and macro environment
- Competitive environment
- Porter's five forces model–competitive analysis

Learning Objectives

The present chapter aims at:

- Definitions and objective of business
- Examine environment analysis, characteristics components of the organisation. Let us know the microenvironment and macro environment
- Understand the competitive environment
- Describe the Porter's five-force model and its limitations.

"Environment factors of constraints are largely if not totally external and beyond the control of individual industrial enterprises and their arrangements. These are essentially the 'givers' within which firms and their managements must operate in a specific country and they vary, often greatly from country to country".

Barry M. Richman and Melvyn Copen

" The environment includes outside the firm which can lead to opportunities for or threats to the firm. Although, there are many factors, the most important of the sectors are socio – economic, technical, supplier, competitors, and government".

Glueck and Jauch

"Analysis is the critical starting point of strategic thinking"

Kenichi Ohmae

"It is not the strongest of the species that survive, nor the most intelligent, but the one most responsive to change".

Charles Darwin

"Strategy is a deliberate search for a plan of action that will develop a business's competitive advantage and compound it".

Bruce D. Henderson

"Awareness of the environment is not special project to be undertaken only when warning of change becomes deafening".

Clifton Garvin, Kenneth R. Andrews

1.1 INTRODUCTION

The concept of strategy has been borrowed from the military and adapted for use in business. This book has reviews of strategy formulation, implementation, controlling and monitoring strategic events, which have to suggest that adopting the concept is easy to business and industry. In business, as in the military, strategy bridges the gap between policy and tactics. Together, strategy and tactics bridge the gap between ends and means. Also this book reviews various issue like business environment and components of business environment, competitive environment, Porter's five forces model, business policy and strategic management, major tasks in strategic management, vision and mission and objectives of the strategic enterprise, strategic analysis in terms of swot analysis, tows matrix, portfolio analysis, strategic planning, marketing, financial production, logistics, research and development and human resources strategy formulation, implementation and control and achieved the strategic edge for the purpose of clarifying the concept and placing it in this context.

In this chapter, we shall discuss about the business, major objectives of business like survival, stability, growth, efficiency and profitability, environmental influence to business, environment analysis, characteristics of business environment, components of business environment, to know the relationship between the organisation and its environment, the micro and macro environment and its elements like customers, competitors, organisation, market, suppliers, intermediaries, demographic, economic, government, legal, political, cultural, technological and global environment impact on business. Companies how to enter into global market, its manifestation trends, strategic response to business, Porter's competitive and five forces model analysis for business enterprises in industry, commerce and services sector.

1.2 DEFINITION OF BUSINESS

The term 'typically' refers to the development and processing of economic values in society. Normally, the term is applied to portion of economic activities whose primary purpose is to provide goods and services for society in an effective manner. It is also applied to economics and commercial activities of institutions which having other purposes.

Business principally comprises of an all profit seeking activities of the organisation which provide goods and services that are necessary to economic system. It is the major economic pulse of a nation, striving to increase society's standard of living. Finally, profits are a primary mechanism for motivating these activities.

Business is in any organisation which makes distribution or provides any article or service to the customers, who are belonging to members of the society. Business may be satisfied customers needs for these purpose customers are able and willing to pay for it.

Business may be defined as "the organised effort by individuals to produce goods and services to sell these goods and services in a market place and to reap some reward for this effort."

Functionally, we may define business as "those human activities which involves production or purchase of goods with the object of selling them at a profit margin".

- The term business refers to the state of being busy for an individual, group, organisation or society.
- It is also interpreted as one's regular occupation or profession or economic activities.
- It deals with particular entity, company, organisation, enterprise, firms or corporation.
- It also interpreted as particular market segment sector like computer business and it included under term business.
- It is wide and willing to use different activities
- It consists of purchase, sale, manufacture, processing, marketing of products, services like manufacturing, trading, transportation, warehousing, banking and finance, insurance and advertising etc.
- It is clearly stated that all business activities main purpose is to earn profit. Profit as a surplus of business and It accrues and distributed to the owners

of the business. Business has to pay wages to workers who works in the business. People invests money in business due to getting a retain. Retain is profit from the business. This is awarded to investor due to be taking the risk.

- Profit is the motive for the investor who serves, runs business and it is the stimulation effort of the business for growth, survival of business.

Profit Is A Main Motive Of Business

- For every kind of business organisation, profit is often regarded as motive for the entrepreneurs and it measure the overall performance of the business.
- Profit is the tool for measuring and evaluation of the business efficiency and productivity at the managerial competence.
- It is helpful to strategic managers how to take well decisions and actions which are turn into effective in the form of able to combine and utilize the available resource and able to sustain the organisation with growth and survival of the business entity.
- Business managers who will take higher efficiency and risk and certainly expect greater volume of the profit from the business entity.
- Business efficiency expressed in terms of percentage of profit to sales volume, to capital employed, to market value of corporate shares.
- Outside investors eager to know the profit of the firm and to make assessment about their commit funds and effective utilization of funds will be in the business entity.

Business According to Prof. R. N. Owens

"Business is an enterprise engaged in the production and distribution of goods for sale in a market or rendering of services for a price".

Business According to L.R. Dicksee

"Business is a form of activity pursued primarily with the object of earning profits for the benefit of those on whose behalf the activity is conducted".

Business According to Urwick and Hunt

"Business is any enterprise which makes, distributes or provides any article or service which other members of the community need and are willing to pay for"

Business According to Haney

"Business may be defined as human activity directed towards producing or acquiring wealth through buying and selling of goods".

Peter F Drucker has drawn some conclusions about what is a business and what are useful from the business and how to understand the term business. His conclusions are listed below:

- Business is created and managed by the people. A group of people who will be taken decisions that will be determined either an organisation is going to prosper or decline, whether it will survive or will eventually perish in market. This conclusion is true in the business.
- Business cannot be explained in terms of profit.

1.3 CHARACTERISTICS OF BUSINESS

- Business is to provide goods and service to the people. It provides the public with the things it needs and wants in order to survive, enjoy life and improve in a material sense. From the point of view of consumer, business is the satisfier of needs and desire of the customer demands which should be provided by business in order to meet people requirements in society.
- Goods that have been produced or procured for sale in retail for price enter the realm of business. This activity of selling results is the creation of the wealth for the society. In satisfying demand, business uses the resources of land, labor and capital. These resources when taken separately have little value; but business combines structures and refines the resources to produce to the value of the society. Further, business employees' people who exchange their talents for wages and salaries. Therefore, these people exchange their compensation for the desired goods and service.
- Business is profit seeking activity firm. It supplies goods and services to customers who are satisfy their demand and desire. It adds to society's value by earning of a profit. Profit is the biggest stimulus for maintains the survival of the business and its future development. Society has permits business to earn profit as a reward for assuming the risks of operating a business.
- Business is also an essential participant in society. For satisfying society demand which supplying goods and services and earning profits. Business involves the most fundamental activities of the society. As a result, Society has looks to business for something more than products, services and profits. It looks to business for leadership and direction in helping to achieve society's objectives. It expects business to assist in the establishment of a better service to the society.

1.4 COMPONENTS OF BUSINESS

Business includes the total enterprise of the country. Business activity has two branches. They are as follows:

- Industry
- Commerce

Industry

In broad sense, industry is the branch of business activity which concerned with raising production, fabrication or possessing of goods and services. In other words, industry is an activity concerned with conversion of raw materials or semi finished goods into finished goods. Industry provides two types of goods namely consumer goods and Industrial goods. Consumer goods are those goods manufactured by industry for ultimate use of a customer. For instance brush, paste, cloth and food products etc., Industrial\Capital goods are those goods produced and used for further production. For instance machineries, tools and raw material etc.,

Types of Industry

Industry is further classified into five broad types. They are as listed below:

1. Extractive industries
2. Genetic industries
3. Manufacturing industries
4. Construction industries
5. Territory\Service industries

Extractive industry

Extractive industry are those industries concerned with extraction of wealth from surface of the earth, soil, forest, water, air etc., for instance agriculture, mining etc.,

Figure 1.1: Components of Business

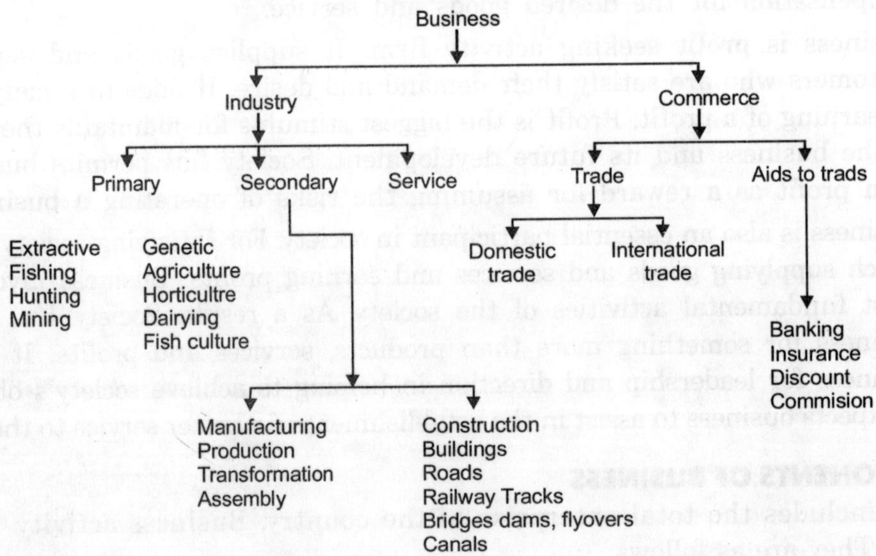

Genetic industries

Genetic industries are those industries concerned with reproduction and multiplication of plants animals for making profit on their sale. For example, Nurseries, cattle building and poultry farming.

Manufacturing industries

Manufacturing industries are engaged in the conversation and process of raw material through separation, combination and transformation into finished goods. Such as machinery and plants of all types, iron and steel, sugar, paper, cotton clothe, electrical appliances, zinc ore, paper pulp water power, etc.,

Construction industries

Construction industries are concerned with the construction of roads, railways, dams, canals, buildings, bridges etc. There are mainly concerned with the manufacture of non-moveable items.

Territory or Service industries

Service industry which produce intangible goods those which cannot be seen or touched included in this category are banking, transport, insurance, communication and services of a professional nature such as lawyers, doctors, dentists, management consultants, advertisers, chartered accountants and engineers, etc.,

Commerce

Commerce has been defined as "the sum total of those processes which are engaged in the removal of the hindrance of persons (trade), Place (transport and insurance), and time (warehousing) in the exchange (banking) of commodities".

Trade

Trade means sale, transfer, or exchange of goods and services, through certain ancillary functions like packing, warehousing, banking, transportation, Insurance, and advertising.

Trade may be

- Domestic Trade
- International Trade

1.5 OBJECTIVES OF A BUSINESS

Business Purpose

Business have some purpose. These purpose are listed below:

- It is to create customers clients in market.
- It is create customers for selling of their products and services.
- It is to create market for redling and buying of product and services.
- Customers determine the main purpose of the business.
- Customers is the basic foundation of the business and keeps its in existence in the market.
- It is due to be catering to material needs and requirement of the society, individual persons, government institutions, company, firms and enterprise.
- Business is running with in the purview of the legal and general public interest.
- It is ultimate result of an economic expansion, growth and change of firm.

In general sense, enterprise pursue multiple objectives rather than a one objective. Strategic manager will be identified a set of main business objectives. These will be pursued by a large cross-section of enterprises. Profitability, productivity, efficiency, growth, technological, dynamism, stability, self reliance, survival, competitive strength, customer services, financial solvency, product quality, diversification, employee satisfaction and welfare and so on are the major objectives of enterprise. Enterprise look for balance of these objectives in appropriate and suitable manner. An important business objectives are listed below:

Figure 1.2: Important Objectives of Business

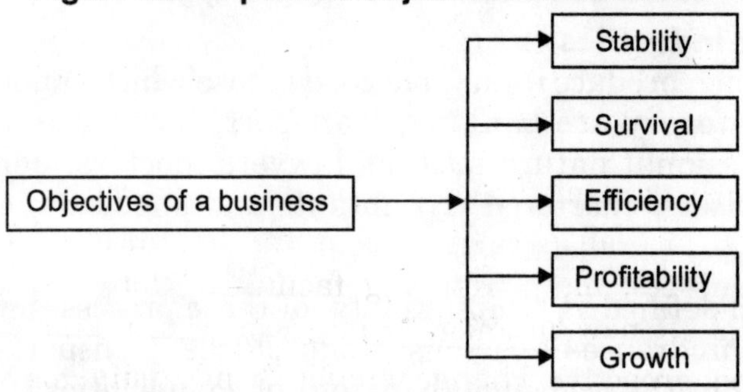

Figure 1.2 has identified the important objectives of business as outlined:

- Survival
- Stability
- Growth
- Profitability
- Efficiency

Survival

- An organisation mission statement reveals the organisation's intention to secure its survival through development growth and profitability of the business.
- It is will and continue the business concern into the future as long as possible perpetuate anxiety strategic managers take more responsibility for survival of the organisation business.
- Therefore, survival is an assumed as goal of the business, if strategic managers often neglected survival, its impact on strategic decisions making for long term.
- It is basic and implied objectives of the most organisations.
- It will be gained more value and important during the stage of the beginning of the business enterprise and during the general economic adversity of business in market.
- The survival refers to the function of the nature of ownership, nature of business competence of management, general and industry conditions, financial strength of the business enterprise or any type of business concern.
- All types of enterprises will be interested in more than mere survival in market.

Stability

- Stability is one of the important objectives of the business enterprise.
- It will be cautious, conservative objective of firm.
- It is a least expensive and risky objectives in form of managerial time and talent and other resources in enterprise.
- A good and steady enterprise always minimizes its managerial tensions and reduces its dynamic nature decisions which are taken from managers for managing business.
- It is least resistance compare to other objectives and hostile to external environment.

Growth

- An organisation growth is closely associated with its survival and profitability and equated with dynamism, vigour, promise, and success of a business.
- Growth refers to overall development of the organisation activities in terms of increase in assets, manufacturing facilities, increase in sales volume in existing or through new product to improve profits and market share.
- Growth may be proactive change and is a necessity for dynamic business environment.
- Growth refers to in terms of expansion business, increase manpower employment, diversification and acquisition of business and create unknown risky paths in this way organisation looks for survival, profitability and growth of the business activities.

Profitability

- Profitability is the vital goals of a business organisation.
- Profit is the sole motive of the business enterprise.
- Private business enterprises are operated on behalf of the owners and its benefits also goes to owners of the enterprise.
- Strategic managers should know how to measure profitability or how to define profitability over the long term or short term of the organisation.
- Profitability clearly indicates of an organisation's ability to satisfy the principal; claims and desires of employees and stakeholder of the organisation.
- Strategic managers analyse interpretations of profit of the organisation, how it impact on survival of the organisation in the future perspective.

Efficiency

- Efficiency is one of objectives of the business.
- It helps to business to achieve goals and success of the business.
- Efficiency refers to best utilization of available and scarce resources and brings the highest productivity in business activities.

- It is useful operation objectives due to effective utilization of economic version of the technical objective which for achieving productivity and designing suitable input and convert into output for effective utilizing of funds, resources, physical facilities and so on in enterprise.

LONG TERM OBJECTIVES OF A BUSINESS

Short run profit maximization is rarely based on the best approach to be achieving the sustained corporate growth and profitability of the firm. It is recognized by the strategic managers of the firm. Therefore, to achieve long term prosperity purpose strategic managers designed long term objectives. Long term objectives of the firm or company or organisation as listed below:

- Profitability
- Productivity
- Competitive position
- Employees development
- Employee relationships
- Public responsibility
- Technological leadership

Profitability

Profitability is an important functional area of the long-term objectives of the firm. The ability of any business to operate in the long run that depends on attaining on acceptable level of profits. Strategically managed firms characteristically have a profit objective usually expressed in terms to return on equity.

Productivity

Productivity is essential need for each strategist in the corporation. Strategic managers try to improve the productivity of their companies. Companies can improve the input–output relationship that results normally increase profitability. Productivity objectives are some times stated in terms of desired to achieve by company. This is an equally effective way to increase profitability.

Competitive Position

Competitive position can increases profitability and productivity of the company. Companies or firms or organisation's competitive position reduces the cost of production of the output. The corporate success depends on the firm's competitive position. It is strongly dominated in the market.

Employee Development

It refers to be experienced employees who are the asset of the organisation. For long-term purposes, the company's employees will be needed training for further course of action that effectively and efficiently managed to produce productivity in the competitive position and market. Therefore, it is one of the major long-term objectives of the organisation.

Employee Relationships

All companies actively seek good employees who have committed relations with organisational environment. Strategic manger should know the employee needs and expectations. Strategic managers take a decision to welfare programme for the employees of the companies. It can be improved the employee's relationship in the organisation.

Technological Leadership

Technological leadership gives clear picture of the organisation goals and objectives. for the long term changes in the business scenario. Many companies state their objectives in terms of their technological leadership.

Public Responsibility

Business recognizes their social responsibilities towards to customer and society. Public responsibility is to be buildup long-term images in the society by through providing social work to public.

1.6 CHARACTERISTICS OF BUSINESS ENVIRONMENT

Business environment characteristics will be indicated that major challenges, opportunities, threat and weakness of the business.

Figure 1.3 : Characteristics of Business Environment

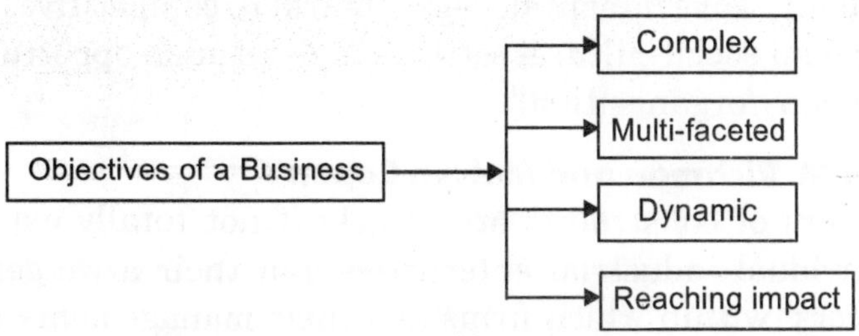

Figure 1.3 indicates the major characteristics business environment as listed below:

Environment is Complex

Business environment principally consists of a number of factors, events conditions. These are influenced to different departmental source in the organisation. These conditions are not exited in isolation and create entirely new set of influences which are interact with each other. If bring comprehensive influence to business environment. This is difficult to influence to organisation. All these factors have to be considered as environment analysis is complex and rigid and totally very difficult to grasp by the functional manager and top level employees in the organisation

Environment is Dynamic

Business and company environment is constantly changing in different nature. Micro and macro environment factors are influenced to business. It impact to change on the business conditions. Dynamic environment is flexible and dynamic nature in company.

This is causing due to change, strategic manager can shape strategy and formulate short term and long term objectives.

Environment is Multi–faceted

Strategic observer can shape and observe different character of environment. Strategic observer to observe a particular change or latest development in the business . It is may be viewed different opinion from different observes in the organisation. These things are frequently seen when the development happens. All are happy to welcome it and think as an opportunity for the company even also as threat to company.

Environment has a far reaching impact

Environment impact is essential ingredients for strategist to study changes and take appropriate decisions at appropriate time. If strategist neglect to take appropriate decisions at the right time which create impact to organisation. Survival, growth, profitability and development of organisation which depends critically in terms of micro and macro factors of the business environment. Environment impact have to be bring new dimensions to business.

1.7 ENVIRONMENTAL INFLUENCES ON BUSINESS

The term Environmental analysis is defined as "the process by which strategists monitor the economic, governmental, legal, market, competitive, supplier, technological, geographic, and social cultural settings to determine opportunities and threats to their firms/company/organisation".

According to Barry M. Richman and Melvyn Copen

"Environment factors of constraints are largely if not totally external and beyond the control of individual industrial enterprises and their arrangements. These are essentially the 'givers' within which firms and their managements must operate in a specific country and they vary, often greatly from country to country."

According to Glueck and Jauch " The environment includes outside the firm which can lead to opportunities for or threats to the firm. Although, there are many factors, the most important of the sectors are soci–economic, technical, supplier, competitors, and government."

These definitions clearly reveals the following important factors:

- Strategist looks on the environment changes while to analyse the threats of the business alongwith searching and offering immense opportunities to business enterprises in the market.
- A successful business enterprise has to identify, appraise and respond to the new dimensions of various opportunities and threats in its internal and external environment.
- Successful business not only recognise business activities even recognise the different elements in the environment.

- These factors are recognised and adopt to their business
- It continuously monitor and adapt to the new environment
- Environment analysis helpful to survival and prosper the business activities.

Environment diagnosis principally consists of managerial decisions which made by strategist for analysing the significance of the data like strengths, weakness, opportunities and threats of the organisation in thin way to design their own strategy for formulation, implementation and controlling the internal environmental factors to firm.

Environmental analysis helps to strategic executive and manager to diagnosis of strategic competitive force and components of strategic management. However, internal environment of the organisation is a quite essential and important from the point of view of the environment analysis. It is the cornerstone of the new and exiting business opportunity analysis too.

Figure 1.4: Environment Forces (Influences) on Business

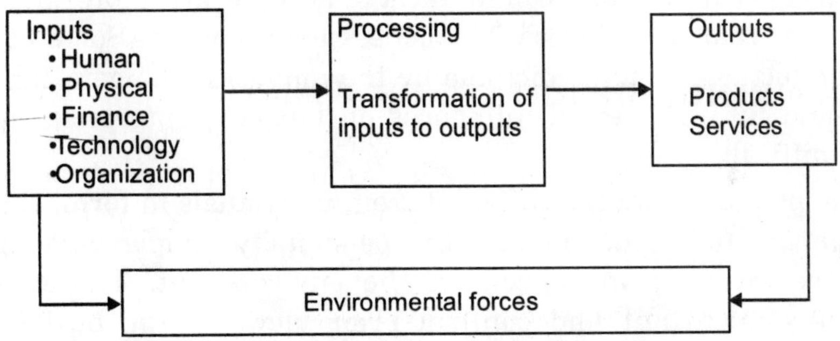

Figure 1.4 indicates the environmental forces on business. For instance, the individual life success depends on his innate capabilities like psychological factors, traits and skills. These are to the cope with the environment then will be got success otherwise failure. The survival is the basic elements and success of the business organisation, it depends on its own strengths in terms of resources like money, men, machinery, materials, market and methods as its command. Organisation success depends on effective utilization of physical resource, financial resources and human resource skills. These are adaptability to the business environment. Environment is the total of several external and internal forces that affects the functions of business.

Every business organisation principally consists of internal environment factors and set of external environmental factors. Environment factors influence to business directly and indirectly that control, manage and administration of business activities in the organisation.

Environment is the basic tool for living all human beings and all living creatures. Human environment consists of family, friends, peers, and neighbors except to natural environment. In additionally includes man–made structures like as buildings, furniture, roads and other physical infrastructure. These are continuously interact with their business environment.

Problem in Understanding the Environment Influences

In strategic business environment, strategic managers have face different problems in different circumstance in their business and have to understand the different environmental influence of business as outlined:

- The environment problems bring different dimensions to strategic managers. Strategic managers are very difficult to make decisions regarding the different diversity of the business. Strategist will list all conceivable environment influences and very difficult to get overall picture of business environment task. These are emerging problems to strategist and influence to business.
- Uncertainty is the second problems encountered by strategic managers. Strategic managers typically claim know the pace of the technological changes and the speed the global network communication. These are more and more faster change now than ever before in business environment. Some of the changes either predictable or unpredictable by the mangers. Mangers can be trying to understand future external influences on business enterprises and this task is very difficult to do so.
- Strategic managers are not different from individuals in form, they are coping with complex and rigid. They tend to be simplify complex and rigid problems which are focusing on aspects of the environment. These problems are historically important and confirm prior views of the business. Strategic managers are trying to take risk and simplify the complex and rigid problems in this way to find to breakout bias in the understanding of their environment. It will be still achieving a useful and usable level of analysis in business environment.

Framework to Understand the Environmental Influences

While understanding of the problems in business environment, strategic managers cannot be ignored the real problems of the business. It will be on opportunity to identify a framework for understanding the business environment of the organisations. Environmental factors influence to identify key issues, find the ways for coping with complex and rigid issues and consider as challenging managerial thinking by mangers.

- First stage is strategic managers is to know the initial structure and nature of the business organisations in terms of uncertainty. This is relatively either static or shows sign of change. Strategic managers should aware of the simple and complex problems and also know the decision skills for focus the rest of the analysis will be taken in the business environment.

- Second stage is the auditing of the environmental that influence to business. During this stage, strategic managers aim to identify different environmental influences are likely to affect the organisation's development or performance. It is done through assessment of external environmental factors like political, economic, social and technological influences. These are factors bearing at the time of audit of the business. It helpful to strategic managers to develop overall pictures or scenario of possible futures and extent to ascertain to change in the business.
- Strategic managers is to move to focus more towards an explicit considerations of the immediate environment of the organisations, it is the last stage of assessment of the strategic managers. It involves competitive environment and its five forces analysis of competitive environment and identify the key forces at work environment. It is also required to analyze the organisation competitive position in form of resources and customers.

1.8 ENVIRONMENTAL ANALYSIS

Strategist should aware of the resource capabilities and how to effective utilization of scarce resource capabilities in the company. Environment analysis is to analysis changes pattern and impact of business for decisions. It will considers to an opportunity to use and time to anticipated the corporate objectives through proper planning and make optional utilization of available resource in the company. These things helps to strategist to form and develop and give warning early system to prevent threats or to develop strategies which can be turn threat into advantages . It clearly indicates future of the company and assessment of the anticipated future.

According to Clifton Garvin, environment analysis as "Positive trends in the environment breed complacency. That underscores a basic point : in change there is both opportunity and challenge".

And it is impact on business. Business environment analysis involves the analysis, diagnosis, and take managerial decisions which are likely to better to company. It reduces to length process and time pressure to manages, board of directors in the company. In the case, strategic manager neglect the environment analysis it impact on business changes and ready to face anticipated problems in future . Therefore, the strategic managers can concentrate environmental influence to organisation or enterprise.

In general sense, Environmental analysis has three basic goals as outlined .

- Environmental analysis must be provided the current and potential changes which are understanding by strategist and bring suitable place in the business environment. Strategist should aware of the existing environment this is must important to company. At the same time, strategist must have to take and consider a long tern perspective about the future.
- Environment analysis basically provide strategic inputs for strategic decision making, It is not mere collection of data and it is not enough to analysis of

the environment. Whatever information collected by the strategist which should be useful to company for making strategic decisions.

- Environment analysis is the basic tool and it should make facilitate and foster strategic thinking in the organisation. It is typically a rich resource capabilities and ideas which are understanding in the context and purview of the business organisation. It should be current challenges, growth, development and opportunities. These wisdoms are bringing by the strategist from the fresh point view of the organisation.

Environment influence On SWOT

Environment influence is a part of SWOT analysis. SWOT is acronym of strengths, weakness, opportunity and threats. Threats and opportunities come under the purview of the external environment of the business. Strengths and weakness come under the purview of the internal environment of the business.. These factors are outlined:

- Opportunity
- Threats
- Strengths
- Weakness

Opportunity

An opportunity is a favourable condition in the business organisation's environment which enables it consolidate to resource and strengthen its position. Increased company's product and services due to demand from the customer. It is the best an opportunity to company to serve products and services to customers

Threat

A threat is an unfavorable condition in the business organisation's environment which causes a risk for, or damage to, the organisation. Emerging the strong and competitors in the market who are likely to offer stiff competition to the existing companies in the industry, trade and business. This is one of the threats to the organisation..

Strength

Strength is an inherent resource capability of the organisation or company which can be use and gain to strategic advantages from their competitors in the market. For example strength is the superior research and innovation which help to development of advance skills which can be used for getting new product, new material, new customer in this way achieved to gain competitive strengths in the business.

Weakness

A weakness is an inherent limitations or constraint or problems of the organisation. It has to create strategic disadvantages to company or organisation. For example a manufacturing company over dependency to single supplier in the market which is potentially risky for company at the time of crisis.

1.9 COMPONENTS OF BUSINESS ENVIRONMENT

Exited Business environment of the firms/company or organisation can be classified into two broad categories

- Internal Environment
- External Environment

Exhibit 1.1: Component of Business Environment

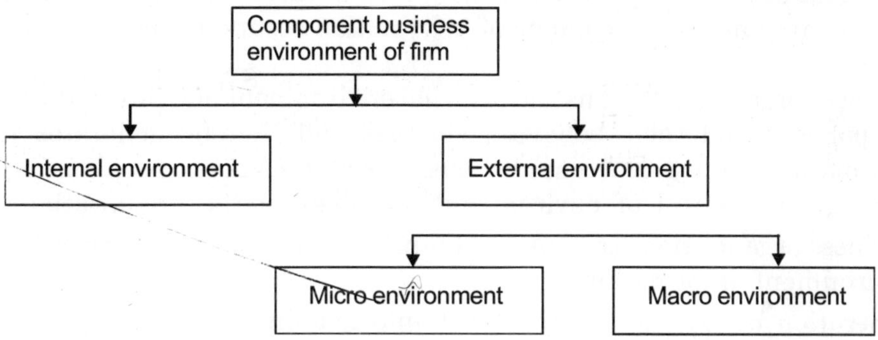

1.10 RELATIONSHIP BETWEEN ORGANISATION AND ITS ENVIRONMENT

Relation of business organisation and its environment is obvious from the point of analysis of strengths, weakness, opportunity and threats of business. Organisation environment consists of internal environment and external environment. Internal environment factors are easily controllable and manage in the organisation. External environment factors are uncontrollable factors due to changes in the legal, social, economic, technical in business enterprise. External environment offers wide range of opportunities, problems, threats and pressures and thereby influence the structure of the business enterprise and its functions. Business enterprise can be treated as subsystem for drawing certain inputs of resource, information and values extracting from the external environmental system. These things transforms into outputs in the form of products and services, goals and satisfactions and exchange of proper ideas and it transmits to business enterprise.

Figure 1.5: Relationship Between Organisation And Its Environment

Figure 1.5 indicates the relation between organisation and its environment as listed below:

- Exchange of Information
- Exchange of Resource
- Exchange of Influence and Power

Exchange of Information

It refers to data or information is exchanged with business enterprise and its internal and external environment . Exchange of information occurs in the following ways are listed below:

- Business organisation scans the external environment and internal environment components and their behavior, changes and thereby generates important information and valuable uses for business and make proper planning, decision making and control of environment variables in the organisation.
- Business organisation structure and functions are adjusted towards the external environment information.
- Generation of external environment information is complex and it is one of the major problem and it involves uncertainty to business organisation.
- A business project look for current information and future information which are relating to demography, competition, technical, legal, political and government policies and procedures.

Apart from the collecting information, a business organisation itself transfer information in the following ways:

- Organisation transfer its own information to several external agencies either voluntarily, inadvertently or legally.
- Other organisations and interest individuals are also approached to business organisation to obtain valuable information which relating with functions, products and services and social responsibility towards stakeholders of the company.
- An organisation collect its own information in form of annual reports, occasional advertisements and media reports etc..
- An business organisation is legally or otherwise bind to supply valuable information to government, society, financial institution, shareholders, creditors, debtors, investors, employees, trade unions, business bodies and the like.

Exchange of Resource

Exchange resource is the second and dominate relationship with the business enterprise and its environment, exchange of resources involves in the following ways in the business:

- Business enterprise receives inputs like finance, materials, manpower, equipment and labor force from the external and internal environment via contractual and other arrangements.

- Organisation employees is very important due to conversion of these inputs (raw materials) into outputs like products and services
- Organisation interacts with supplier for purposefully of getting of inputs. For this purpose, an organisation does not depend on single supplier and collaborates sometimes with other organisation in the process of ensuring a consistent supply of quality inputs.
- An organisation is also dependent on the external environment factors for disposal of its products and services to wide range of clients and customers.
- Disposal of products and services are involved to interaction process to external environment for perceiving the needs of the external environment and catering to them, in this way satisfying the expectations and demands of clients, customers, employees, shareholders, creditors, suppliers, local community, general public and so on.
- These above mentioned groups are tended to press on the organisation due to be meeting their expectations, needs and demands and for upholding their value and interests in organisation resources.

1.11 INTERNAL ANALYSIS OF THE ORGANISATION/COMPANY

Formulation of an effective and efficient strategy has based on a clear definition of organisation mission, an accurate assessment of the external environment and through internal analysis of the organisation. Organisation requires success it needs at least three ingredients. They are as listed:

- Strategy must be consistent with conditions in the competitive environment
- Strategy must place realistic requirements on the organisation/company's internal resources and capabilities.
- Strategy must be carefully formulated, implemented, controllable and executed.

Internal analysis of the organisation is to difficult and challenging one to strategist. An internal analysis has leads to design a realistic organisation profile. It frequently involves tradeoff, value system judgments, educated and skilled guess as well as objective and standardized analysis. A systematic internal analysis leads to main objective of the organisation profile. It is essential to develop strategy and design a realistic mission for achievement of the strategy.

Internal analysis of the organisation must identify the strategically strengths, opportunities, weakness and threats that are based on organisation strategy. Organisational analysis identifies suitable strategy that based on the SWOT analysis.

Internal analysis can be achieved by first identifying key internal factors like value system, mission objectives, management structure and nature, integrated power relationship, human resource, company/organisation image and brand equity, physical assets, R&D, technological capabilities, marketing resource and financial resource factors and secondly by evaluating these factors.

1.12 THE VALUE OF SYSTEMATIC INTERNAL ASSESSMENT

The value system of internal assessment is essential from the point of view of strategy formulation by the experienced strategist of the organisation/company. The value system applies to either large or small business concern. It is critical in developing a successful business strategy. Regardless of the favorable opportunities in the environment, a strategy must be considered the essential internal strengths, weaknesses, opportunities and threats of the organisation if such opportunities are to be maximized for accomplishment of goals.

The value systematic internal analysis is particularly essential in small business organisations. Small business organisations are faced lot of problems like limited resource and markets. These organisations are flexible and capable to capture selected markets and effectively channel their limited resource and maximize these limited market opportunities. Internal analysis is the basis objectives of the organisation.

Steps/Process in the Development of a Organisational / Company Profile

Company/organisation profile focus on determination of strengths and weakness of the strategic environment of the business. Identifying and evaluating strategic internal factors are based to accomplish to organisation future strategy. The major steps are important to development of an organisation / company profile. They are listed below:

Stage one -------------------------------------- Identification of Strategic Factors

Stage two -------------------------------------- Using Value Chain Analysis

Stage three ------------------------------------ Evaluations of strategic internal factors

1.13 IDENTIFICATION OF STRATEGIC FACTORS

An important identification of strategic factors approach as listed below:

1. Functional approach
2. The value chain approach

Functional Approach

Functional approach refers to organisation basic capabilities; characteristics, swot analysis and limitation are the key strategic factors. Functional approach key strategic factors are as follows:

- Marketing
- Finance and accounting
- Production /operation/ technical
- Human resource development
- Organisation of general management

Marketing

Marketing deals with the following issues:

- Organisation's products/service; product life cycle and marketing strategy.
- Concentration of sales in few products or little customer segmentation.
- Ability to be gathered information about the market.
- To know the market share or sub market share.
- Product/service mix and expansion potential: to know the life cycle of key products; to know the profit or loss of the product/service.
- To clearly know the channel of distribution; number, coverage, and control.
- To maintain effective sales organisation: to find out knowledge about the customer needs.
- To improve product/service quality with image and reputation of brand name.
- Efficient and effective utilization of available resource for effective sales promotion and advertising.
- To aware of the pricing strategy and pricing flexibility.
- To effective monitoring and feedback of the marketing functions and expansion of product.
- Effective implementation of after sales service and follow up.
- To keep standards, goodwill and brand loyalty.

Finance and Accounting

Finance and accounting functions are as follows:

- Ability to raise short term and long-term capital: either debt or equity.
- To maintain good corporate level resource.
- To know the cost of capital relative to industry and competitors
- Tax consideration.
- To build up effective relationship with owners, investors, financial institution and stock holders.
- To know the leverage position: capacity to utilization financial strategies, like lease or sale and lease back.
- To aware of the cost of entry and barriers of the entry.
- To know the price earning ratio.
- Present working capital position of the organisation.
- Effective cost control and ability to minimize cost of expenditure for production of goods and service.
- Financial size of the organisation.
- Efficient and effective accounting system for cost, budget, and profit planning of the organisation.

Production/Operation/Technical

Production or operation or technical are as follows:

- To know the present raw material cost and availability.
- Inventory control system of the organisation.
- Location facilities; layout and utilization facilities.
- Technical efficiency and effective utilization of technical resource in the organisation.
- Effective use and implementation of subcontracting.
- Degree of vertical integration in terms of value added and profit margin of the product.
- To know the efficient and cost benefit of production techniques.
- Effective utilization and implementation of operation control procedure: design, scheduling, purchasing, quality control and efficiency.
- To know the costs and technological competencies relative to industry and competitors.
- Research development, innovative, advance ethnological development.
- Patents, trademarks and similar legal protection for their organisation products/ service.

Human Resource Development

Human resource development functions are as outlined:

- Effective management of the human resource in the organisation.
- Improvement of employee skill and morale.
- Labor relations costs compared to industry and competition from present industry scenario.
- Efficient and effective formulation and implementation and controlling of the policies.
- Effective utilization of incentive to motivate employees' performance.
- To know the ability to level peaks and valleys of employment.
- To regulate employee turnover and absenteeism.
- Specialized skills and experience.

Organisation of General Management

Organisation of general management functions are listed below:

- To know the organisation structure.
- Organisation image and prestige to public world.
- Organisation record for achieving goals and objectives.
- Effective utilization of resource and overall organisation control system.

- To effective monitoring organisation cultural climate.
- Effective utilization of systematic procedure and tools and techniques in decision-making.
- To know the top management skills, capabilities and interest.
- Effective implementation strategic planning system.
- To keep and maintain intra organisation synergy (multibusiness)

Some of which would be the focus of internal analysis in most business organisation.

Organisation is not likely to consider all of the factors which are potential strengths or weakness. Strategist has develop or review the factors which are important for successful of the organisation.

For the analysis of the organisation, firstly, a strategist has to analyze the past trends like sales, costs and profitability. These trends are the major importance in identification of the internal factors of the organisation. Further this identification should be based on a clear picture of the nature of the organisation's sales trends. An anatomy of past trends has broken down by product lines channels of distribution of goods and service into different segmentation of key customers, geographical region and sales approach should be developed in detail. A similar anatomy of past trends should focus on costs and profitability. Strategist has to conduct detailed investigation of the organisation's performance history that helps to isolate internal factors influencing to sales, costs and profitability or their interrelationships. The above factors are important in future strategy decisions.

Identification of strategic factors also requires an external focus of the organisation. Strategist isolates key internal factors through analysis of past and present performance like industry conditions/trends and comparisons with competitors. In addition, strategic internal factors are often selected for in depth evaluation due to organisations are contemplating expansion of products or markets, diversification. Strategist carefully scrutinizes the industry under consideration of current competitors. This is a key for identifying strategic factors, if an organisation is evaluating its capabilities more into unfamiliar markets.

The Value Chain Approach

Value chain approach developed by Michael Porter, he wrote a book "Competitive Advantage" which identified the value chain approach of the organisation. A value chain approach is a systematic way of viewing the serious activities of the organisation that performs to provide a product to its customers. Figure 1.6 highlights the typical value chain approach of the organisation. The value chain disaggregate an organisation into its strategically relevant activities in order to understand the behavior of the organisation's cost and its existing or potential source of differentiation. An organisation gains competitive advantage by performing primary and support activities, these activities are more important strategically.

Every organisation can be viewed as value chain approach. Value chain approach as a collection of value activities that are performed to design, produce, market, deliver and support its product. The basic categories of value activities can be grouped into two broad types. They are as listed below:

- Primary activities
- Support activities

Primary Activities

Primary activities are those involved in the physical creation of the product and service in the organisation. Its delivery of goods and service and marketing to ultimate buyer and it's providing after sales support to buyer. These activities are supporting to organisation that provide inputs or infrastructure to the business.

Figure 1.6: Identifying the Primary Activities of the Value Chain

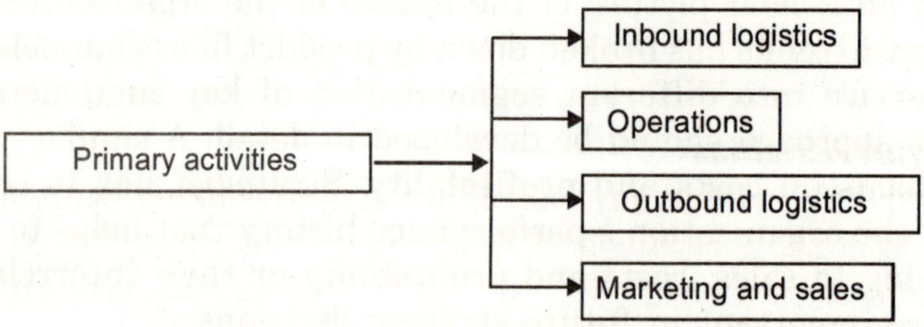

Identifying Primary Activities

Primary activities principally compose of five activities. They are as outlined:

- Inbound logistics
- Operations
- Outbound logistics
- Marketing and sales
- Service

Identifying of the primary value activities requires the isolation of activities that are technologically and strategically distinct in the organisation. They are five basic categories of the primary activities as listed below:

Inbound Logistics

Inbound logistic activities are associated with receiving, storing and dissemination inputs to the product like material handling, warehousing, inventory control, vehicle scheduling and returns to suppliers.

Operations

Operations activities are associated with transforming inputs into the product form, like machining, packaging, assembly, equipment maintenance, testing printing and facility operations in the organisation.

Outbound Logistics

Outbound activities are associated with collecting, storing and physically distributing the product to buyers like finished products warehousing, material handling, delivery vehicle operation, order processing and scheduling.

Marketing and Sales

Marketing and sales activities are associate with providing goods and services to customer can purchase the product and inducting them to do so. Marketing and sales activities are advertising, promotion, sales force, quoting, channel selection, channel relations and pricing strategy of the organisation.

Service

Service activities are associated with providing service to enhance or maintain the value of the product. Service activities are like installation, repair, training, and parts supply and product assessment.

The primary activities most deserving of further analysis depend on the particular Industry.

Identifying Support Activities

Support value activities arise in any one of four activities like procurement, technology development, and human resource management and organisation infrastructure. These categories can be identified or disaggregated by isolating technologically or strategically distinct activities. Identifying support activities often overlooked as sources of competitive advantage. Support activities are listed below:

Figure 1.7: Support Activities Of The Value Chain

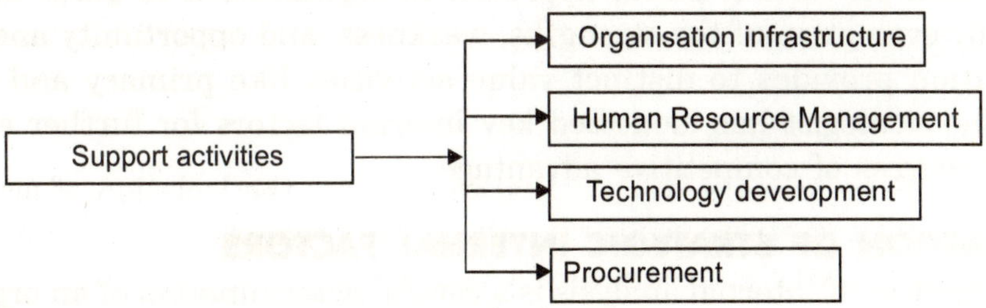

- Procurement
- Technology development
- Human resource management
- Organisation infrastructure

Procurement

Procurement activities are involved in obtaining purchased inputs like raw materials, purchased services and machinery or so on. Procurement stretches across the entire value chain; therefore, it supports every activity-closely relating to be purchased inputs of some kind. Different people typically perform with many discrete procurement activities in an organisation.

Technology Development

Technology development activities are involved in desiring the product like creating and improving quality of the products and service. Technological development is closely relating to innovation of new products and service of the organisation. We shall tend to think of technology in terms of the product or manufacturing process. However, every activity of the organisation performs and involves a technology. Organisation has developed own research and development department for performing to innovation of new product and service.

Human Resource Management

Human resource management activities are necessary to ensure the recruitment, training and development of employees in the organisation. Every activity involves human resources. Therefore, human resource management activities can control and mange across the entire chain.

Organisation Infrastructure

Organisation infrastructure activities are such activities as general management, accounting, legal, finance, strategic planning and all others developed organisation specific primary activities or support activities but essential to the entire chain's operation.

Using Value Chain In Internal Analysis

The value chain provides a useful approach to organisation to guide and monitor systematically evaluation of the strengths, weakness, and opportunity and threatens. An organisation provides to distinct value activities like primary and supporting activities. The strategist has identified key internal factors for further examination as potential sources of competitive advantage.

1.14 EVALUATION OF STRATEGIC INTERNAL FACTORS

The major objective of internal analysis is a careful determination of an organisation's strengths and weakness. An internal analysis generates a long list of resources and capabilities have provided little to help in strategy formulation. Instead, internal analysis must identify and evaluate a limited number of strengths and weaknesses relative to the opportunities targeted in the organisation's present and future competitive environment.

Strategist evaluates the key internal strengths and weaknesses. He has considered four important basic perspectives. They are as follows:

- Comparison with organisation's past performance

- Stages of product/market evolution
- Comparison with the competitors
- Comparison with key success factors in the organisation's industry

Comparison with Past Capabilities and Performance

Strategist has taken more care about the comparison with past capabilities and performance. However, the historical experience of the organisation as a basis for evaluating internal factors. Strategic managers are most familiar with the organisation internal capabilities and constraints. Therefore, they have been immersed over time in managing the organisation's financial, marketing, production facilities, sales organisation, financial capacity, control systems, and key personnel. Organisation has developed own strategy on the basis comparison with past capabilities and performance.

Stages in Product/Market Evolution or Product Life Cycle

Product life cycle is the second factor to ascertainment of strengths and weakness of organisation. Stages in product life cycle are essential from the point of view of successful of the organisation. As a result, strategist can use changing patterns associated with different stages in product lifecycle/market evolution as a framework for identifying and evaluating the organisation's strengths and weakness.

There are four major stages of product life cycle/market evolution. They are as below:

- Introduction
- Growth
- Maturity
- Decline/Saturation

And typical changes in functional capabilities often associated with business success at each stage of the development of product/market cycle.

Strengths are needed in the growth stage because of rapid growth brings competitor into the market. This stage involves with brand recognition, product or market differentiation and the financial resources to support both heavy marketing expenses and affect the price competition and effective cash flow can be key strengths at this stage.

As the product/market moves through a "shakeout" phases and into the maturity stage, this stage market growth continues but at a decreasing rate the number of market segments begins to expand, while technological change in product.

While the products markets move toward a saturation decline stage, this stage strengths and weakness center on cost advantages, superior supplier or customer relationships and financial control.

Comparison with Competitors

A major focus in determining organisation strengths weaknesses is the comparison with potential competitors. Organisation in the similar industry often have different marketing potential skills, financial resources, operating facilities and locations, technical know how, brand image, levels of integration, managerial talent. And so on. These different internal capabilities can become relative strengths or weaknesses depending on the strategy of the organisation to select. In selection strategy, strategist should compare the organisation 's key internal capabilities with those of its rivals, thereby isolating key strengths or weaknesses.

Exhibit 1.2 : Comparison with Competitors Growth in Software Industry
With the wave of consolidation sweeping the software industry and small and medium sized software vendors needing scale to survive, Netkraft's sell-out was anticipated. When queried earlier, both company executives and its VC partners had brushed aside any such happening, saying that there was space for small and medium sized companies to survive in the current highly competitive market place. Medium sized software vendors, who have recently succumbed to the merger wave, include Kshema Technologies, which was acquired by MphasiS, and iVega which merged with the Kolkata-based TCG Software of the The Chatterjee Group. Adea Solutions, which has a development centre in Hyderabad, has emerged as a global player with a comprehensive portfolio of services including solutions development and delivery in domains like consulting, retail, finance and healthcare. The firm, which has a widespread global presence, employs around 1,500 people. Adea chief executive Abid H Abedi was awarded the Ernst & Young Entrepreneur of the Year award in 2003. Abedi had earlier stated that, with the expansion of the company's labs in Dallas and Hyderabad, its delivery capabilities are bound to be substantially effective in this competitive marketplace. Netkraft, which has managed to overcome its financial crisis and earn profits, is said to have made around $8 million last fiscal and is expected to touch the $10 million revenue figure this fiscal. The company started operations in 1998 and presently earns around 50 per cent of its revenues from the retail vertical. It recently joined the growing band of Level 5 CMMI certified companies.BANGALORE: US-based Adea Solutions, a global provider of business process and technology consulting services, has pipped a few international software firms to acquire Bangalore-based Netkraft. Netkraft, which focusses on retail, healthcare and banking and finance solutions, is currently owned by private equity firm Actis, US technology fund Jumpstart and employees. Sources said that Ernst & Young was the advisor for Adea on this deal. The deal size could not be confirmed. While Actis holds around 45 per cent, Jumpstart owns around 20 per cent of Netkraft with the employees holding the balance. Netkraft had been in the news when its original promoters, Prashanth Prakash and Atul Jalan, left the company, though they still have a stake in the company, a year ago. Sources added that a Texas-based software multinational firm too was keen to acquire the company. When contacted by The Economic Times, Anand Sudarshan, CEO of Netkraft, declined to comment.

Source: Times news net work, June 10,2004

Success Factors in the Industry

The key determinant success factor in the industry may be used to identify the internal strengths and weaknesses of the organisation. By scrutinizing industry competitors, as well as customer needs, vertical industry structures, channels of distribution costs barriers to entry, availability of substitutes, and supplier. A strategist seeks to determine whether organisation's current internal capabilities represent strengths or weakness in the new competitive factors.

Quantitative Versus Qualitative Approaches in Evaluating Internal Factors of the Organisation

Numerous quantitative tools are available for evaluating selected internal capabilities of a term. Ratio analysis is useful for evaluating selected financial, marketing and operating factors. The organisation's balance sheet and income statement are important sources from which to derive meaningful ratios.

Quantitative tools cannot be applied to all internal factors and the normative judgments of key planning participants may be used in evaluation.

1.15 EXTERNAL ENVIRONMENT

The concept of external environment is important for every kind of business operation. External environment is an attempt to understand the outside forces of the organisational boundaries that are helping to shape of the organisation. External environment clearly considerable bearing on that which transpires will in. The external environment can provide both facilitating and inhibiting influences on organisational performance. Key dimension of the external environment principally consists of a micro environment and a macro environment.

Exhibit 1.3: External Environment

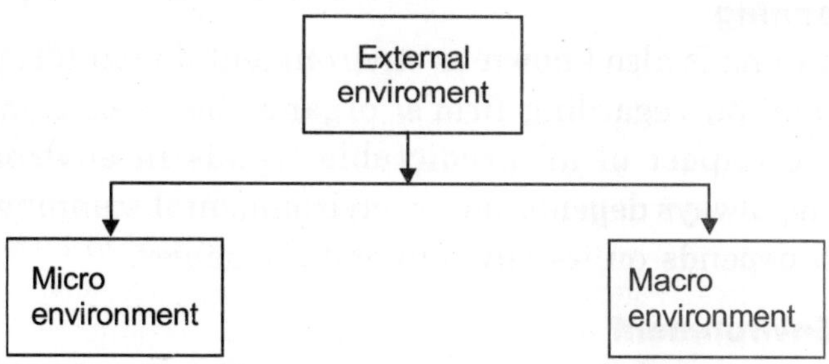

External environment of the business can be categorized into two broad categories as outlined

- Micro Environment
- Macro Environment

Micro environment of business enterprise refers to study on small area or immediate periphery of the business organisation. Micro environment directly or regularly influence to business organisation. It analyses the following important factors:

- Human resource (Employees) of the firm, their characteristics and how they are organized in the firm.
- It analyses the customer base of firm who are major and minor clients of business.
- It analyses the way of raising of finance of the firm.
- It analyses who are the suppliers of raw materials and how are the supply chain network between the supplier and firm being developed?
- It analyses the local communities of firm where its operating.
- It analyses the direct competition from the competitors and how they perform in business.

Macro environment study the overall issues of firms and broader dimensions. It principally consists of economic, technological, political legal and socio-cultural. Macro environment issues are as outlined:

- It analyses the who are their competitors in the competitive world in which how they are operate and know what are threats from the competitors.
- It analyses which areas of technology become pose a threat to current product and services and find the reasons for threat.
- To analyses the bargaining power of suppliers and customers.
- It analyses nature of competition and how to face the threat and weakness of the firm.

Environmental Scanning

Environmental scanning is also known as environmental monitoring. It is the process of gathering information regarding firm's/ organisation's or company, analyzing it and forecasting the impact of all predictable trends in environmental changes. Successful marketing always depends on its environmental scanning and its marketing programmes which depends on its environmental changes.

Micro/Operating Environment

The micro / operating environment consists in the organisation or company's immediate environment that affects the performance of the organisation/company. These include as listed below:

Exhibit 1.4: Micro Environment Elements

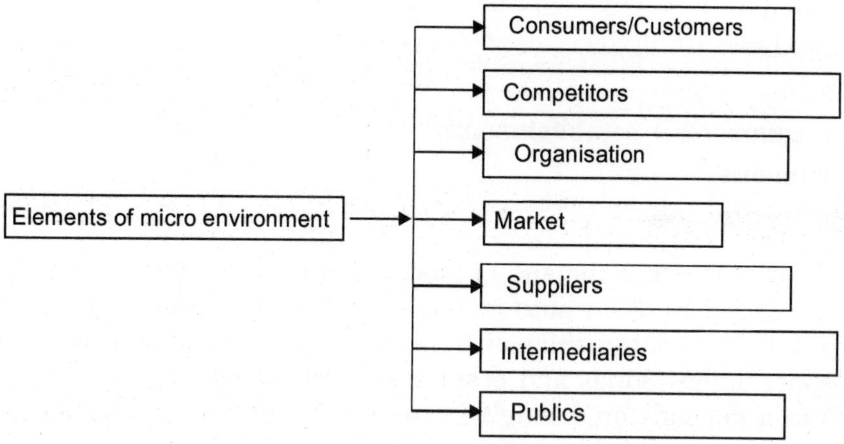

It is quite important that micro/operating environment factors are more intimately linked with organisation or company than macro/remote environment factors. The micro/operating forces need not necessarily affect all organisations in a particular industry. Some of the micro factors particularly affect an organisation. For instance, an organisation that depends on a supplier may have a supplier environment that is quite entirely different from that of an organisation whose supply source is also different. When competing organisations in an industry have the same microelements, the relative success of the organisation depends on their relative effectiveness in dealing with these elements.

Suppliers

Supplier is the important force of the micro/operating environment of an organisation or company i.e., the supplier are those who supply the inputs like raw materials and components to the organisation. The major and important of reliable source / sources of supply to the smooth function of a business is very important. Uncertainties are generated due to the several supply problems like maintenance of inventory, delay of supply of inventory to organisation.

Many organisations give high importance to vendor development, vertical integration for solve the supply problem. Organisation has depended on a single supplier is a risk factor due to a strike, lockout or any other production problem of the supplier. Always an organisation has depended on several supplier of the same raw material. Similarly, a change in attitude or behavior of the suppler may also affect the organisation. Hence, multiple sources of supply often help reduce such risks. The supply management assumes more importance in a scarcity environment.

Customers

The major task of business is to create and development of customers. A business can exist only because of its customers. Customers are the people who pay money to acquire or buy an organisation products in the form of goods and services. Monitoring the customer's behavior is a prerequisite for the business success. Consumer is the one who will ultimate use of company's products and services.

Organisation may have different kinds of customers. They are listed below:

- Individual
- Households
- Industries
- Other commercial establishments
- Governments
- Other institutions

According to Peter Drucker the aim of business is to create and retain customer. For instance, the customers of an auto-mobile sphere parts manufacturing organisation may include individual automobile, owners, automobile manufactures, public, private sector transport undertakings and other transport operators.

Organisation depends on a single customers is often much difficulty and risky task. Organisation cannot survival without survival. Therefore, it may place the organisation in a poor bargaining position, apart from the risks of losing business result to winding up of business by the customer or due to the customers switching over to the competitors of the organisation.

The strategic choice of the customer segments should be made by considering a number of factors including the relative profitability, dependability, and stability of demand, growth prospects and the extent of competition.

Firms should know about who are their customers, expectations and buying patterns.

Competitors

An organisations competitor includes not only the other organisation which market the same or similar products but also those who compete for the discretionary income of the customers. For instance, the competition for a organisation's televisions may not come from other televisions manufactures but also from two -wheeler, refrigerators, cooking ranges, stereo sets and so on and from organisations offering saving and investment scheme like banks, unit trust of India, companies accepting deposits or issuing shares or debenture etc. This competition among those products maybe described as desire competition as the primary task here is to influence to the basic decision of the consumer. Such desires competition is generally very high in countries characterized by limited disposable incomes and many unsatisfied desires because of human wants are unlimited.

If the consumer decides to spread his discretionary income and recreation he will still be confronted with a number of alternatives to select from such computer, stereo, two in one, three in one. The competition among such alternatives that satisfy a particular category of desire is called generic competition.

An implication of these demands a marketer should strive to create primary and selective demand for his products and services.

Marketing Intermediaries

The immediate environment of a organisation may principally consist of a number of marketing intermediaries which are "organisations that aid the organisation in promoting, selling and distributing its goods to final buyers". In many cases, the customers are not aware of the manufacturer of the products and services they want buy. They want to buy products and services from the local intermediaries.

The marketing intermediaries are as outlined:

- Middlemen
- Agents
- Merchants
- Marketing agenesis
- Advertising agencies
- Marketing research firms
- Media
- Consulting firms

Publics

Public is the one important marketing intermediaries for promoting, advertising, channeling, selling the organisation's product into different segmentation. If public accept the product of the organisation, definitely it will successful in the market, suppose product is rejected by the public definitely it will close the company.

Organisation

- Organisation involves the group of employees who are working different positions and different nature of jobs. These employees come from the outside. And individual employee interest is different and varied.
- An organisation has consist of several non specific factors in the organisation's environment which are affecting its activities. Owners, Board of Directors and employees are likely to influence to organisation.
- Owners are individuals, shareholders, groups, or organisations who have a major stake in the organisation. Owners are vested interest in the well being of the company.
- Board of directors are originate in companies formed under the companies Act,1956. The board of directors is elected by the shareholders. Board of directors are responsible and in charge of the organisation, also overseeing the general management of the organisation. In this way, board of directors have to ensure that run business in best serves to the shareholders' interest.
- Employees are the asset of the organisation who are intended to work in an organisation. Employees are the major force of the organisation. Work culture, values and goals of the organisation are important to employees. Therefore, they differs in terms of beliefs, education, attitudes, and capabilities. When

there is difference with employee goals and manager's goals that time entire organisation will be suffered due to different attitude and reactions about in organisation.

Market

Market is to essential and important to organisation. The market structure is to be studied in the form of its actual and potential size, its growth and also attractiveness of product and services of the organisation. Strategist should be studied the trends and development and key success factors of the market. The major marketing issues are outlined:

- What is the cost structure of the market?
- What is the price sensitivity of the market?
- What is the existing distribution system of the market?
- Is the market growing/mature/decline?

Macro/Remote Environment

Macro environment is largely external to the business enterprise. Macro environment factors are uncontrollable factors and beyond the direct influence and control of the organisation. Its factors are powerfully influence to its functions. External environment consists of individuals, groups, agencies, organisations, events, conditions and forces. These are frequently contacted by the organisation for its functions. It establishes good interaction and interdependent relations in form of conducts business transitions. Proper designing and administration of macro environment enable appropriate strategies and policies to cope with and make changes. Other wise negotiates and buildup its future by using of the macro environment factors.

Exhibit – 1.5: Macro Environment Elements

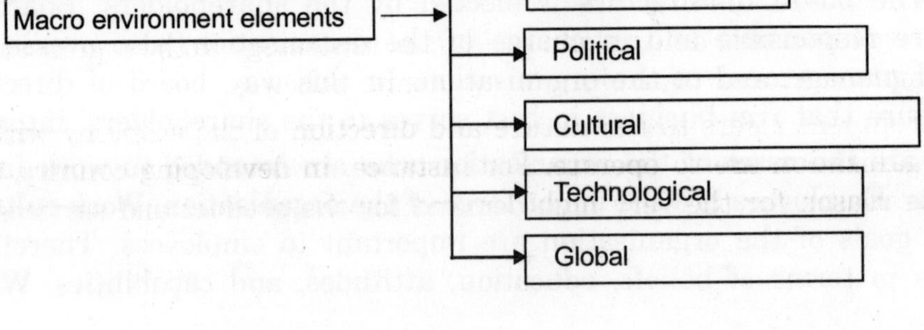

The macro/remote environment principally consists:

- Economic environment
- Political environment
- Legal environment
- Socio-cultural environment
- Demographic environment
- Natural environment
- Physical and technological environment
- Technological Environment
- Global or International environment

Macro environment force is uncontrollable i.e. uncontrollable factors of business organisations.

1.16 ECONOMIC ENVIRONMENT

The economic environment constitutes to economic conditions, economic polices, and the economic system that is important to external factors of business.

The economic conditions of the country include:

- Nature of the economy of the country.
- The general economic situation in the region, conditions in resource markets like money, material, market raw material components, services, supply markets and so on which influence the supply of inputs to the organisation, their costs, quality, availability and reliability of supply of products and services.
- It determines the economic strength and weakness in the market.
- Purchasing power of the individual depends upon the economic factors like current income, price, savings, circulation of money, debt and credit availability.
- People income distribution pattern analyses the market possibilities and impacts on enterprise.
- Development process of the country.
- Availability of economic resources of the country.
- The level of the economic income of the country.
- The distribution of income and assets of the country.
- Public finance of the country.

These are the very important determinants of business strategy in the organisation for formulating, implement and controlling of economic policies.

Economic environment refers to the nature and direction of the economy within which business organisation are to operate. For instance, in developing country, the low income may be reason for the very high demand for the product and services of the business.

In countries where the investments and income are steadily and rapidly rising, business prospects are generally bright and further investments are encouraged.

In developed economics, replacement demand accounts for a considerable part of the total demand for many consumers durables where as the replacement demand is negligible in the developing countries.

Money is the lifeblood of any business organisation and the economic system. The economy consists of micro-economics and macroeconomics. Micro and macro elements are important from the point view of strategic decisions. Strategist must scan, monitor, forecast, and assess the following critical elements of the macro and micro economic environment:

- Economic system
- Nature of the country economy
- The monetary and fiscal policies
- Autonomy of the economy
- Functions of economics
- Factors of productions
- Economic trends and structures
- Economic policy statements and structure
- Economic legislation
- Economic problems
- Import and export policy
- Tax rates
- Interest rates
- Government budget deficit
- Consumption pattern
- Price fluctuations
- Global movement of labour and capital
- Stock market trends
- Coalitions of countries and regional states
- Availability of credits
- Inflation trends in country
- Unemployment trends
- Foreign country economic conditions
- Company of Petroleum Exporting Countries (OPEC)) policies.

Economic environment encourages liberalisation, privatization and globalization of the economic policies in the business environment. Every country's development is based on the economic environment activities that focus to the development process of the country.

1.17 POLITICAL-LEGAL ENVIRONMENT

Political environment refers political and government and legal environment. It has close relationship with the economic system and economic policy. For instance; the communist countries had a centrally planned economic system. Communist government countries laws are control investment and related matters. There are number of law that regulates the conduct of the business. These laws cover such matter as standards of business and its production and service.

- The democratic governments countries law's / act are passed in the parliament. Then they are regulating rules and regulation of business according to the act.
- Political stability, responsibility, political ideology and level of political morality, the law and order situation, and practice of the ruling party and major purposefulness and efficiency of the government agencies.
- Political agency's nature, its influence to economic and industrial act ivies in the country.
- Government policies like fiscal, monetary, industrial, labour, and export and import policies which are influenced to specific legal enactments and framework towards the business organisation political legal function and degree of the effectiveness which are influenced to formulate and implement policy in the legislature.

The political environment is based on the uncertainty, therefore, demographic countries consist of number of political parties. Political parties aren't got clear majority to form a government. In this situation, industry and commerce collapsed their business activities due to hung government. The political parties are unable to formulate stable government, it affect and fluctuate the government policies. Therefore, business organisation and public are needed to the stable government.

Elements of Political and legal Environment

There are three important elements are associated with the political and legal environment as listed below:

- Government
- Legal
- Political

Government

- Government policies, rules and regulation are controlling and monitoring the business enterprises and its activities in the state.
- Secondly, the type of government administration of the state and what is the business policy of state? These things should be evaluated by the strategist from point of view of business.
- Strategist should study about the changes in the regulatory framework of the government and impact on the business.

- Government tax policies are critical and affect to the business organisation in the state.

Legal

- Sound legal system is the basic requirement for running of the business operating with in the state.
- Strategist should aware of various business laws which are protecting consumers, competitors, and organisation.
- Business organisation should aware of the laws which relevant to companies, competitors, intellectual property, foreign exchange, labor and so on.

Political

- Political system is also influenced to business and its activities.
- Political pressure groups influence to government and in this way some extent to control and regulate business activities with in the country.
- Recently, special interest groups and political action committee put pressure to business organisation and to pay more attention towards consumer's rights, minority rights and women rights.
- Apart from the sporadic movements against certain products and services and some business organisation in the state.

1.18 SOCIO–CULTURAL ENVIRONMENT

Socio-cultural environment is an important factor that should be analyzed while formulating company business strategies. If company's is ignoring the customs, traditions, tastes and preferences and education. There factors affect to business. It consist of factors which are related to human relationships and the impact of social attitudes and cultural values. These are bearing on the business of the organisation.

Business organisation is a successful due to appropriate strategies effective utilization of socio-cultural environmental factors. Social cultural environment is an important for MNC. Therefore, MNC should study of the social cultural activities of the region, where there are introducing their own business. Even when the people so different cultures use the same basic product, the mode consumption, conditions of use or perceptions of the product attributes may very so much so that the product attributes method of presentation, promoting product may have to varied to suit the characteristic of different market segmentation. Socio-cultural factors are beliefs, values, norms and traditions of the society determine how individuals and organisations should be interrelated.

The difference in language sometimes poses a serious problem, even necessitating a change in the brand name. The value and beliefs associated with colour vary significantly between different cultures. For instance, white indication death and mourning in china and Korea; but some country it expresses happiness and is the colour of the wedding dress of the bride.

Some of the socio-cultural factories are influenced to operating environment of organisation as outlined:

- Social issues like the role of the business in the society, environment pollution, corruption, use of mass media and consumption of products and services which are offered by the company.
- Social attitudes and values issues like social customs, beliefs, rituals and practices, changing life style patterns and materialism are expectations of society from the business.
- Family structure, values and attitudes towards the family and these changes also influence to business and its operation.
- Role of the women, position, nature of responsibilities in society is also influenced to business and its operation in market.
- Educational levels, awareness and consciousness of rights and work ethics of the society can be influenced to business and its operation.

Social practice, beliefs and associated factors are helpful for promotion of the certain products, services or ideas, the success of marketing depends to a vary large extent, on the success in terms of changing social attitudes or value systems.

1.19 DEMOGRAPHIC ENVIRONMENT

Demography refers to study of the population. Demographic factors are as below:

- The population size
- Growth rate of population
- Age composition of the population
- Family size
- Economic stratification of the population
- Education levels
- Language
- Caste
- Religion
- Race
- Age
- Income
- Educational attainment
- Asset ownership
- Home ownership
- Employment status and location

These factors are the relevant to the business for formulating and implementing of strategy for controlling and accomplishment of the objectives of the organisation.

Demographic factors like size of the population, population growth, rate, age, composition, life expectancy, family size, spatial dispersal, occupational status, employment pattern etc., affect the demand for goods and service.

The growth of population and income result increases demand for goods and services. A rapidly increasing population indicates that a growing demand for many products. For instance, developing countries like India, Pakistan, etc; high population growth rate indicates an enormous increase in labor supply.

The occupational and spatial nobilities of population have implications for business. Labor is easily mobility between different occupations and regions. Its supply will be relatively smooth and this will be relatively and this will affect the wage rate.

If a labor is highly heterogeneous in respect of language, caste and religion, ethnicity, etc., personal management is likely to become a more complex task. The heterogeneous population with its varied tastes, preferences, beliefs, temperaments, etc, gives rise to different demand patterns and calls for different marketing strategies.

Business organisation needs to study different demographic issues which are particularly address the following issues as listed below:

- What democratic trends which will affect the market size of the different types of industry?
- What democratic trends will represent opportunities or threats?

Interested Domestic Environment Factors To Business

We shall briefly discuss a few demographic factors which are interest of business:

- Population Size
- Geographic Distribution
- Ethnic Mix
- Income Distribution

Population Size

Size of population is important either small or large to business organisation. Companies use population size for critical assessment for customer behavior and changes of the customer behavior and its impact on business. Important issues are outlined which are relating with population:

- It study the changes in a nation's birth rate and family size.
- It study the increase and decrease in the total population.
- It also study the changes effects in terms of rapid population growth on natural resources or food supplies.
- It also study the life expectancy of infants, youth and old age people.

These issues are very important to company for analysis of demand and supply of products and services. Healthcare companies role is needful for assessment of the product requirement for infants, youth, middle age and old age people.

Geographic Distribution

It refers to geographic region and population that shifts from one region of a nation to another or from village/rural areas to urban areas. This is may be an impact on a company's strategic competitiveness in market. Geographic Distribution issues are outlined:

- Location advantage and government support is also very important to company.
- In the case, population is shifted from one region to another region. This is the significant impact on company's qualified workforce and company consider relocation of its skilled human resources.
- Today, working at home concept and electronically on the information highway have also begun in India in an very small level.

Ethnic Mix

Ethnic mix is also important to company and know eager know changes in ethnic mix in population. Assessment and implications of ethnic mix is useful for company and its works force. Ethnic issues are outlined:

- Company should know the changes in the ethnic mix and its impact to company's product and services.
- Company should know the new products demand or existing products and services from the different ethnic groups.
- Company ready to face challenges, treats from ethnic and try to make solutions for these ethnic challenges and treats.

Income Distribution

Income distribution is also one of the important factors of demographic environment. Company is planning to measure changes in incoming distribution, savings patterns for different level of individual. This purpose, company can forecast and assess the changes in income patterns and ready to identify new opportunities for companies.

1.20 NATURAL ENVIRONMENT

Natural environment is the study of an important component of the nature i.e., natural environment. Natural environment includes geographical and ecological factors areas as below:

- Natural resource endowments,
- Weather
- Climate conditions
- Topographical factors
- Location aspects in the global context
- Port facilities are relevant to business.

Difference in geographical conditions between markets may sometimes call for changes in the marketing mix. Geographical and ecological factors also influence industries which help material index tend to be located near the raw material sources. Climate and weather conditions affect the location of certain industries like the often textile industry.

Ecological factors have recently assumed great importance. The depletion of natural resources, environmental pollution and the disturbance of the ecological balance has caused great concern. Government policies aimed at presentation of environmental purity and ecological balance, conservation of non replevisable resources etc., have resulted in additional responsibilities and problems for business, and some of these have to affect of increasing the cost of production and marketing, externalities also become an important problem of the business has to confront with.

1.21 TECHNOLOGICAL ENVIRONMENT

Technological factors some times pose serious problems. A firm that unable to cope with technological changes may not be survived. Further, the differing technological environment of different markets or countries may be called for product modifications.

Technology is the most important elements of the macro environment. Technology is the human being innovation and it literally wonder. Technology helps to human being go to moon, travelling the spaceships, other side of the globe with few hours.

Advances in the technologies have facilitated product improvements and introduction of new products and have considerably improved the marketability of the products.

The fast changes in technologies also create problems for enterprises as they render plants and product obsolete. Today adopt changes in technology to achieve successful in business and industry.

Internet and telecom system is the part of technological development in the world. These things today changed whole world. It changes people and business operation. It leads to many new business opportunities apart from the many existing systems. Technological environment characteristics are outlined:

- The find of technological change
- Opportunities are arising out of technological developments.
- Risk and uncertain is the major feature of the technological developments.
- Research and development role to country

Technology and business activities are to be highly considerable, interrelated and interdependent. Technology output/fruit's available to society through business activities in this way improve the quality of life in the society. Therefore, technology nurtured by business.

Technologies issues relating with companies are listed below:

- Access to the internet communication facilities which is enable to connect large numbers of employees to work from one place/ home to another place in the globe. Information Highway provide opportunity to strategist to access to richer source of information..

- It helps to business for sales and exchange of goods and services.
- It provide opportunity to customers with accessing to online shopping through the internet technology.

Key Issues Of Technology

- Strategist should know what of type technology used by company?
- Strategist should know the which type of technologies are used in the companies business, products and its services?
- To know the critical issues in technology and know the operating skills in technology related products and services.
- To know the availability of technology to organisation. And its procedure to get external technology to company for its operations.
- To know the cost of technology, alternative technology, competitors, design structure T of the technology and production implementation services of the company.
- To know the companies business applications which are relating to technology.
- To know the additional technologies which required to companies business. And how to get these additional technologies in the world market.
- Technology is help to business for formulation of strategy, implementation of strategy and control of the company performance.

Exhibit 1.6: Technological Environment of the Company

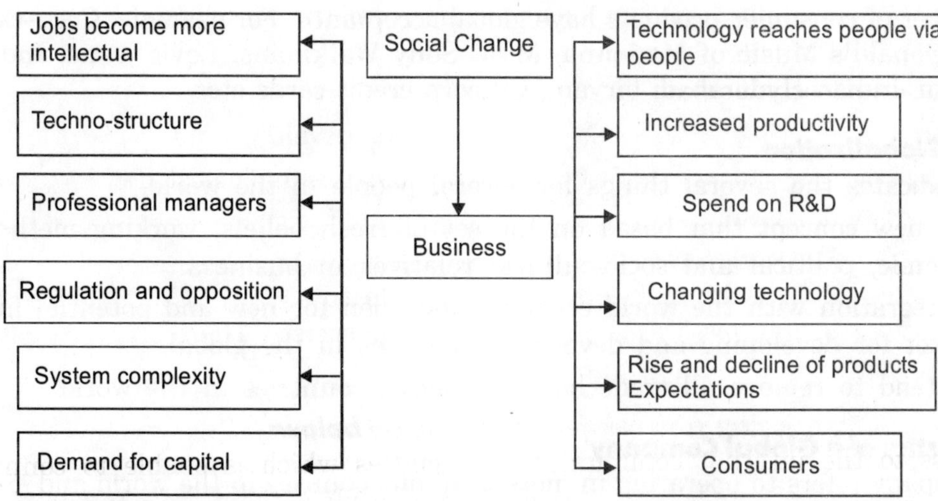

1.22 GLOBAL ENVIRONMENT

Global environment is one of the important elements to macro environment of the business. Today competitive scenario changes rapidly and its impact on business of company. For this, reasons, strategist should understand the global environment, its characteristics, functions and merit and demerit to company. Global environment treated as whole world just as village and has changed how individuals and organisations relate to each other. Nowadays, increased offshore operations and changes business operation. These are influenced to organisation to get project from global clients.

Assessment Of The Global Environment Factors

Assessment of the global environment factors are outlined:

- To know the potential positive and negative impact of significant international events like a sport meet or a terrorist attack.
- To identify both emerging global markets and global market which are ensuring changing. It includes newly industrialized countries like in Asia. In developing countries that imply the opening of new markets for new products, that's result is to be increased competition from emerging globally competitive companies in India and South Korea and China.
- To know the difference between in cultural and institutional attributes of individual global markets.

Globalization of markets refers to the process of integrating and merging of the distinct world markets into a single market. This process involves the identification of some common norm, value, taste, preference and convenience and slowly enables the cultural shift towards the use of a common product or service.

A number of consumer products have global acceptance. For example, Coca–Cola, Pepsi, McDonald's Music of Madonna, MTV, Sony Walkmans, Levis jeans, Indian masala dosa, Indian Hyderabadi biryani, Citicorp credit cards etc.

Nature of Globalization

- It indicates the several things for several people in the world.
- It is new concept that based on the set of fresh beliefs, working methods, economic, political and socio-cultural relatives in business.
- It integration with the world economy and open for new and potential huge market for developing and developed countries in the global.
- It intend to remove all trade barriers among countries in the world.

Characteristics of a Global Company

Global company refers to operating in more than one country in the world and gains its R&D, production, marketing and financial advantages in terms of costs and reputations that are not available to domestic competitors. Global company is one that has the world market. Minimizes the importance of national boundaries, sources, raises capital and market in this way it will be done the best job.

Global company major characteristics are outlined

- Global company is a firm which having multiple units that are located in different parts of the world but all linked by common ownership umbrella.
- Global multiple units draw on a common pool of resources like money, credit information, patents, trade names and control systems.
- Global company can be follow common strategy for sell its products in most countries and manufactures in many. Another important fact is that its shareholders and human resources are also based on different nations.

Reasons for Globalisation

- Large-scale industrialisation enabled mass production. Consequently, the companies found that the size of the domestic market is very small to suffice the production output and thus opted for foreign markets.
- Companies in order to reduce the risk diversity of portfolio of countries.
- Companies globalise markets in order to increase their profits and achieve goals.
- The adverse business environment in the home country pushed the companies to globalise their markets.
- To cater to the demand for their products in the foreign markets.
- The failure of the domestic companies in catering the needs of their customers pulled the foreign countries to market their products.

International environment is the very important from the point of view of certain categories of business. It is particularly important to industries which are directly depending on imports or exports and import competing industries.

Advantages of Globalisation

- Free flow of capital and increase in the total capital employed
- Free flow of technology from developed countries to developing countries
- Increase in industrialisation
- Spread production facilities throughout the global
- Balanced development of world economies
- Increased in production and consumption of outputs
- Commodities available at lower price with high quality
- Cultural exchange and demand for a variety of products in foreign market
- Increased in jobs opportunities and income
- Balanced in welfare and prosperity of the country's economic

Disadvantages of Globalisation

- Globalisation kills domestic small business firms
- Exploits human resources in global firms
- Leads to unemployed and underemployment in developing countries
- The customer demand decline in domestic products
- Decline the income because of unemployment
- Widening gap between rich and poor
- National sovereignty at stake
- Leads to commercial and potential colonialism to poor countries

Why do companies go global?

There are Important reasons for companies go to global as outlined:

To Gain Access to New Customers

This is the first reason to companies expand into foreign market. It offers potential for increased revenues, profits and long-term growth and becomes an especially attractive option when a company's home markets is mature. Mature industries plan to enter new market, therefore, to access to new customer for their products and service.

To Achieve Lower Cost Enhance the Firms Competitiveness

This is the second reason to domestic companies opt to be expanding their market in outside countries. Many companies are driven to sell their products and service in more than country because the sales volume achieved in their own domestic markets is not large enough to fully capture manufacturing economies of scale and experience curve effects and thereby substantially improve a firm's cost competitiveness.

To Capitalise on it's Core Competencies

This is the third factor to companies expand their domestic market into international market. A company with competitively valuable competencies and capabilities may be able to leverage them into a position of competitive advantage in foreign market as well as just domestic markets.

To spread its Business Risk across a Wider Market base

This is the last reason opt companies to expand their domestic market into international market. A company spreads its business risk by operating in a number of different foreign countries rather than depending entirely on operations in its own domestic market.

Except in a few cases, companies in natural resource – based industries such as oil and gas, minerals, rubber and lumber often to find it necessary to operate in the international arena because of attractive raw material suppliers are located in foreign countries.

Speed And Faster Communication Network

Globe thanks to faster communication, speedier transportation, growing financial flows and rapid technological changes due to advanced communication network development.

Reduce transportation costs

Companies often set up overseas plants and machinery to reduce transportation costs. The following development are also responsible for transportation operation of companies:

- It happens when increasing emphasis on market forces and growing role for the private sector in all developing countries.
- Globalisation of firms and industries
- The rise of the services sector. It constitute the one of the largest single sector in the world economy.
- Rapidly changing technologies which are transforming in the originate nature, organisation, an location of international production.

Manifestation Of Globalization

Exhibit 1.7: Manifestation Of Globalisation

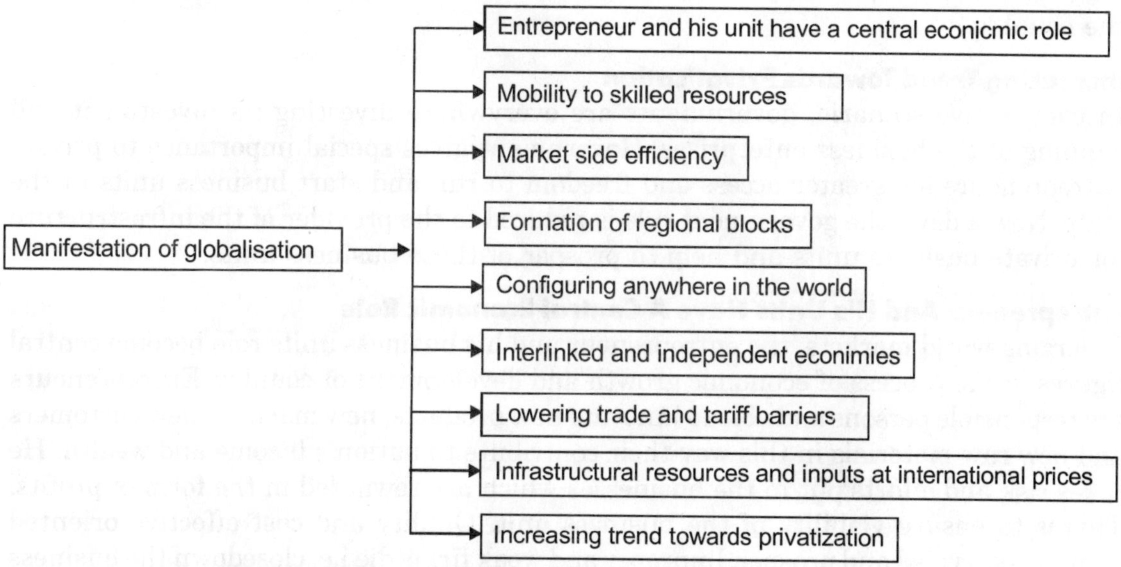

Important manifestation of globalisation are outlined:

Configuring Any Where In The World

An global organisation can be located in different place in the world and its different types of operations in different countries for supply of raw material, look for consumer markets and low cost labor and manufacturing of products and services in the world.

Interlinked And Independent Economies

Globalisation refers to economic welfare of the state and its people for uniquely economically interdependent international environment. Each country's prosperity is dependent on the interlink with the rest of the world. No nation can be survival any longer time without existence of the international market and domestic market.

Lowering Of Trade And Tariff Barriers

Global environment brings lowering of trade and tariff barriers to global enterprises in the world. It proposes a new global co-operative arrangements and redefined the role of the state and its industry status. It help towards privatisation of manufacturing, services sectors, and less government interference in business decisions and help to private sector to buildup the value added sector in this way to gain market place and competitiveness in the global market. When the lowering of trade and tariff barriers in state which results in available products and services at lower cost with abundant supply of goods and services to ultimate customers.

Infrastructural Resources And Inputs At International Prices

When global firms are entering into global market, it ensure that infrastructural inputs must be available at competitive prices due to availability of cheap labor and other valuable resources like physical facilities, raw material etc, a global firms take high level risk particularly continuous inflation and high infrastructural costs in the country.

Increasing Trend Towards Privatisation

In competitive scenario, governments are everywhere divesting its investment and running of the business enterprises. Government gives special importance to private entrepreneurs for greater access and freedom to run and start business units in the state. Now a days, the government role is reduced to the provider of the infrastructure for private business units and help to prosper of these business units.

Entrepreneur And His Units Have A Central Economic Role

Emerging world markets, the entrepreneur and his business units role become central figures in the process of economic growth and development of country. Entrepreneurs are responsible persons and able to innovate new products, new markets, new customers and new raw materials in this way their contribute to nation's income and wealth. He takes risk and efforts put in the businesses which are rewarded in the form of profits. This is to ensure viability of the business unit. Quality and cost effective oriented firms are survived and prosper. Improper and weak firms die i.e. closedown the business units due to loss.

Mobility Of Skilled Resource

Skilled resources is also one of the important manifest of the globalisation. It refers to experience, trained and educated labor in the company. Skilled labors are highly mobile from one place to another location in the world with freely mobile.

In the case, labors are unskilled that time management will be spent some money for training and education of their employees in this way enhances the skills of the unskilled labor. Factors of production like land and capital also mobile. In the case of developing country, it have long on land and short on capital it can invite by foreign investment and make good deficiency. Similarly, a developed country which have long on capital and short on land it can be used by developing country as a base for its business operations.

Factors of production like land, labor and capital can be mobile anywhere in the world.

Make-side efficiency

Integration of global market implies in terms of costs, quality processing time, these terms of business become dominant competition drivers in the global market. Customers will get a maximum choice of products and services on the basis of maximum value of money. State monopolies are unable to provide quality and value products to customers. Apart from this, consumers are searching the quality products and services from the global market.

Formation of Regional Block

A final result of globalization is to formation of trade blocks. Formation of regional block is obvious. Major reasons for formation of regional block are outlined:

- To form strategic alliance to reduce economic and technological threats and leverage their respective comparative and competitive advantages.
- Important regional blocks are NAFTA (North American Free Trade Area), European Union, ASEAN, SAARC

South Asian Association for Regional Co-operation (SAARC) SAARC consist of seven South Asian Countries with Bangladesh, Bhutan, Maldives, Nepal, Pakistan and Srilanka and India. SAARC encourages and promotion of economic growth in the region. It also promote and develop social progress and cultural development in the region, it helps to active collaboration and mutual assistance in the form of economic, social, cultural, technical and scientific fields and strengthen of co-operation among the member states in the international forums on matters of common interest.

1.23 STRATEGIC RESPONSE TO THE ENVIRONMENT

It is very difficult to define, when business environment is commenced and when it will be ended in business. It is very difficult to determine the exactly environment response in the business. Strategic manager, very efforts to exploit the opportunity and reduce to weakness. Different strategic responses approaches to the environment are listed below:

- Least resistance
- Proceed with caution
- Dynamic response

Least Resistance

Few business just involves to manage and survival by the way of coping and adjusted with their dynamic external environment. These are simple and goals maintained. These are very passive behavior and are solely guided and supervise by the signals of the external environment.

Proceed With Caution

It is next level of strategic response to the environment, strategist are responsible to take an intelligent interest to adapt with the changing environment. Strategic managers in the company promptly seek and monitor changes in the environment, its analysis, impact on their own goals and activities will translated for assessment in terms of specific strategies survival, stability and strength. These are regarded as the pervasive complexity and turbulence of the external environmental elements as prescribed with the framework of which they have to function like adaptive organic sub systems. It is an admittedly to suitable and modern strategy and wait for changes in business. And take corrective adaptive in nature.

Dynamic Response

This level is highly sophisticated level. In this level, external forces in business are efficiently and partially manageable and controllable by their actions in company. Feed system is highly dynamic and powerful system adopted in organisation. These things not only recognise threats and weakness and ready to convert into their threats into opportunities in business environment. These are highly conscious and confident of their strengths and weaknesses of the external environment constraints. Dynamic response have to generate a contingent set of alternatives course of action which are picked up in tune with the changing shape of business environment.

Shaping External Environment

- Shaping environment is one of the major problem of the business enterprise.
- It generate the powerful dominating behavior of command organisations may generate powerful countervailing pressure and forces in the real environment.
- It is more inclusive apart from the individual action in business enterprise.
- Its values and interests are much broader than internal environment of the business.
- Adopt a innovative and autonomous in organisation.
- It happens with certain limitation of the company.

1.24 COMPETITIVE ENVIRONMENT

"Only firms who are able to continually build new strategic assets faster and cheaper than their competitors will earn superior returns over the long term".

C.C.Markides and P.S.Williamson

"Organisation succeed in a competitive market place over the long run because they can do certain things their customers value better than can their competitors".

Robert Hayes, Gary Pisano, and Daid Vpton

- Strategy formulation is coping with the competition. This is basic requirement of the strategist in business.
- Intense competition is neither a coincidence nor bad luck to business organisation.
- All type of business enterprise have competition with competitors in the market.
- Multinational company offered different product and services which are clash directly on every level of product and services offered by the similar Multinational companies.
- In a competitive environment, a business enterprise competition which spells out freedom of entry and exit in the matter and affects its price and scale of operations in market.
- Business enterprise have to consider their competitor's strategies, profits levels, products and services that are required for preparing and implementing their business plans.
- Nature and extent of competition of business, this is facing in the market and it is one of the major factors that are affecting the rate of growth, income distribution and consumer welfare.
- While formulating business policy, enterprises have to identify separately and concentration on the competitors who are significantly affecting the business in the market.
- Competitors are ready to satisfy the needs and requirement of the customer.

Nature and Extent of Competition

Nature and extent of competition is important to multinational companies and its customers. For better understanding, we shall know the following important questions that are relating to completion:

(a) Who are the competitors in the market?
(b) What are their product and services in the market?
(c) What are their market share?
(d) What are their financial positions?
(e) What is the cost of products and services in the market?
(f) Who are the potential competitors ?
(g) What are the future products and services which are offered to customers?
(h) What is the target market?

Co-operation In A Competitive Environment

- Small number of only manufactures/sellers of a product may form association in this way achieve cooperation in a competitive environment.

Major purpose of Cooperation in a Competitive Environment

- It is the association of manufacturer or sellers.
- It is coordination and unification of trade practices and the determination of the best means of safeguard their interest in the form of individually an collectively
- It helpful to decide the price of the products and service for example OPEC
- It may be form for deciding market share, prices and profits etc.
- It may be witnessed in highly competitive business environment.
- For example, various credit card and finance companies are entering agreements the other business to launch co-branded credit cards and debit cards. This type of arrangements help in reaching greater number of customers.

Co-operation On Account Of Family Ownership

- Cooperation is the primary tool for family owned business
- It generates automatically in business enterprise owned by a same family.
- Family is directly responsible for control, management and ownership of business.
- Family ownership group is nothing but a family and its kin and kith.
- Major and minor decisions made by the family ownership groups in business.
- It influence to managerial decisions and activities of the enterprise.
- It is identify the goals and needs of the family and its business operations
- Family members are amicable settlement their business constraints like properties and ownership issues.

Non Co-operation On Account Of Family Ownership

- Quarrels with family members.
- Conflict among the family members.
- Family matters tend to distort their behavior in managing the business enterprise and also thereby damaging its functions.
- Succession problems.

1.25 COMPETITIVE ADVANTAGE

Competitive advantage refers to organisation or companies how much benefit from the point views of cost and benefit analysis. Every organisation has strategically competitive advantage for their business. For example, India's competitive advantage as listed below:

Case 1.1: Competitive Advantage Of The Satyam Edge

Satyam: The preferred IT services provider

With nearly a decade-and-a-half of experience in servicing global MNCs and Fortune 500 clients with end-to-end IT services, solutions and products, Satyam has come a long way, emerging as the preferred IT services provider for major global business corporations. An innovative organization, Satyam has been a pioneer-of-sorts in the Indian IT industry.

Landmarks

- Pioneered the IT Offshore Development concept in India
- First established a satellite link for communicating with client sites
- Developed the unique RightSourcing delivery model
- Established India Development Centers for clients
- First to have acquired BVQI's ISO 9001:2000 certificate
- Developed eSCM model for ITES/BPO space with Carnegie Mellon University and Accenture
- **Satyam Infoway (Sify)** India's first Indian Private ISP; India's first Internet firm listed on the NASDAQ (NASDAQ: SIFY)

Advantage Satyam

- World class processes (SEI CMM® Level 5, ISO 9001: 2000, eSCM)
- Global presence (Operations in 45 countries across 6 continents)
- Long lasting customer relationships (Nearly 80 % of repeat business)
- Flexible engagement models (RightSourcing delivery model, IDCs, GDCs, JVs)
- Evolved competency and solution-based services
- Technology-led innovator
- Experience in serving top-notch customers that include four of Top 10 Fortune 500 corporations
- Strong Domain knowledge
- Highly qualified IT professionals
- State-of-the-art infrastructure
- Offshore advantage

Questions:

1. Explain the business environment of the Satyam Edge.
2. Describe the competitive scenario of Satyam Edge.

Source: Satyam Company Website (www. Satyam.com)

Exhibit 1.8: Competitive Advantage India

"Companies around the world are gaining competitive advantages by using Indian software services that offer high quality, cost effectiveness, time savings, state-of-the-art technologies and above all reliability".

The World Bank funded study compared India with many other countries to analyse India's position vis-a-vis cost and quality. Its findings proved that India is the **best** positioned as a high-quality and cost-effective country for software development. The advantages India offers are tremendous.

They include:

• A virtual 12-hour time zone difference between India and USA offers cost and time savings provides the client with a virtual 24-hour office environment.

• A huge pool of English speaking and computer literate graduate workforce who can continue to cater to the growing demand of professionals for IT Enabled Services.· India offers the ultimate quality advantage with relatively less costs. India has more than 137 ISO 9000 certified and 147 more companies are in the pipeline to be ISO certified by March 2001. As many as 32 Indian companies already have SEI-CMM certification, with six of them having reached Level 5. It must be noted that worldwide, only 12 companies have reached that level, and just six of them do not belong to India.

• India enjoys very strong brand equity in major markets, thanks to its growing and globally competitive software industry.

• Indian software companies believe in highest adherence to delivery schedules and customer satisfaction by using state-of-the-art technologies.

• E-Business and web based solutions : Indian companies offer the most cost-effective, innovative and extensive web-based solutions. They also offer varied solutions for E-commerce and E-Business applications. Hotmail, Junglee, who where are some of the examples of Indian innovativeness.

Other Global advantages

One of the unique methods used by Indian software companies to deliver competitive advantage to its clients involves using high-speed (64 kbps, 2 Mbps and above) datacom links, which in turn allow computers situated anywhere in the world to be used by programmers in India on a real-time and on-line basis.

Large Pool of Professionals

Just as the Gulf has its crude oil and South Africa in diamonds, India's natural resource in today's knowledge economy is its abundant technically skilled manpower. India has the second largest assembly of English-speaking scientific professionals in the world today, second only to the US. It also has a growing bank of 4.1 million technical workers, supplied by, among others, over 1,832 educational institutions and polytechnics, which train more than 67,785 computer software professionals every year. This includes the graduates passing out of the prestigious Indian Institute of Technology (IIT), where the quality of technical training is comparable to the best of the educational institutes in the world.

NASSCOM every year undertakes a survey to understand the manpower requirements of the industry. The study undertaken in 1999, highlighted the following facts:

- The number of software professionals employed have increased to 250,000 in 1999 compared to 2,00,000 in the preceding year.
- This includes software professionals in non-commercial organisation as well as software development units in user organisation.
- Almost 67% of the software professionals employed in the industry were in software development and operations, 3% in domain expertise development, 11% in marketing and relationship development, 15% in client support and 4% in other activities.
- The overall median age of the software professionals was about 26.2 years.
- 77% of software professionals in software companies were men, whereas 18% were women. However, this ratio is likely to be 65:35 (male : female) by the year 2003.

- Half of the software professionals possessed 5 years of working experience.
- There was an average of 21% rise in basic salary in 1998 over the previous year.

However, rise in total compensation was supported by issuance of stock options to employees. During 1999, as many as 41 software and solutions companies announced employee stock options plans.

- In 1999, although the attrition rate was controlled at 16% (from the earlier turnover rate of 25% in 1992), but it still remained high, fuelled by 50% growth in the revenue for the software industry in 1998-99.
- This caused the HRD market to tighten considerably.
- Our software professionals were highly rated by their employers for their quality. Most gave an average of close to a 9 on a 10 point rating scale, with 1 being the lowest and 10 being outstanding.
- The skills in demand were in the area of business applications of software development, E-Commerce, Euro, software engineering, Java, ERP, CRM/ ERM, Interactive Integration Services, Datawarehousing, Internet, Client-Networking, BPR, OOPS, client-server, GUI, Windows, project management, quality assurance, technical writing, telecommunications, networking and RDBMS

Question:

1. Explain the competitive advantage of India .

Source: NASSCOM.

FIVE FORCE MODEL

Organisation offering products and services which are close substitute for each other. Close substitute are products and service. They are satisfied the essential consumer needs and desire. The task facing strategic managers is to analyze competitive force in an industry environment in order to identify the strengths, weakness, opportunities and threats confronting an organisation. Michael E.Porter, professor of the Harvard School of Business Administration has developed a framework, which is known as Five Forces Model. It appears in figure 1.8 helps to managers in their analysis of competitive force of the organisation. This model focuses on five forces which shape to create competition within an industry. Five forces are as below:

- The risk of new entry by potential competitors
- Risk of entry by potential customers
- The degree of rivalry among established companies within an industries
- The bargaining power of supplier
- The closeness of substitute to the industry's product

Porter argues that the stronger each of these forces, the more limited is the ability of established organisation to raise prices and earn greater profits. Within Porter's framework, a strong competitive force regards as a threat since it depresses profits. A weak competitive force views as on opportunity for an organisation to earn greater profits. Because of these forces beyond an organisation's direct control like industry evaluation, the strength of five forces may change through time. In such circumstances, the task facing strategic managers is to recognise opportunities and threats in order to develop and to formulate appropriate strategic opportunities.

Figure 1.8: The Five-Force Model

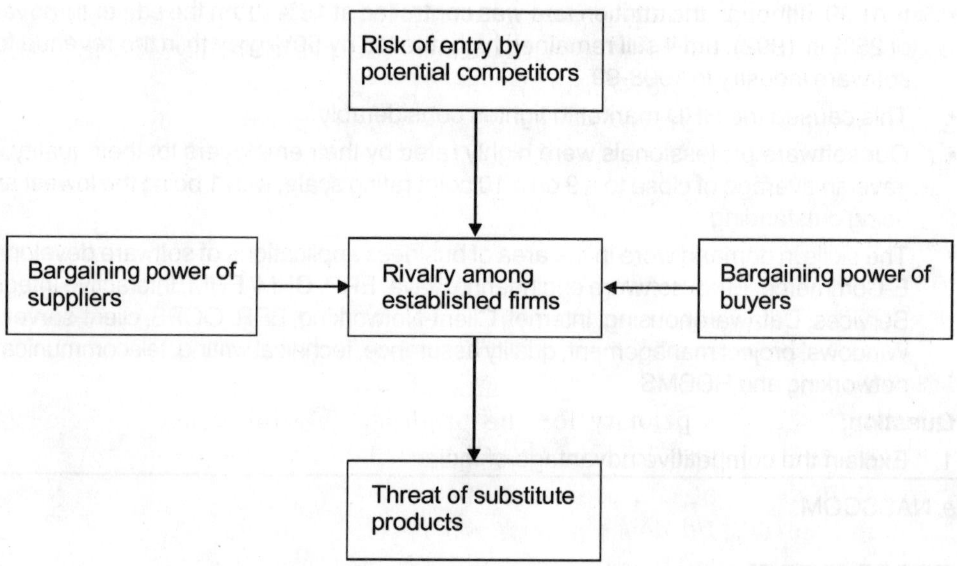

The character, mix and subtleties of competitive forces are never the same from one industry to another. Five force model is a powerful and widely used tool for systematically diagnosing the principles competitive pressures in a market and it should be assessing the strength.

The five force model determine competitive scenario in different industry as outlined:

Identify the specific competitive pressures associated with each of the five forces

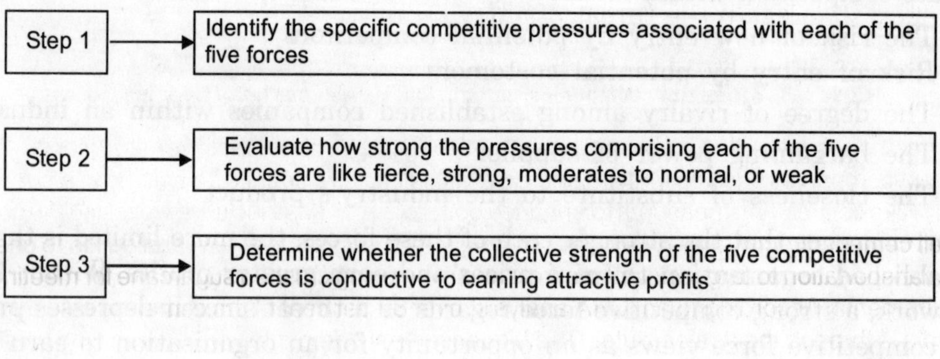

Potential Competitors

Potential competitors are organisations which currently are not competing in an industry but they have the capability to do if they choose. Established organisations try to discourage potential competitors from entering to the industry. Since the more organisations enter an industry, it is the very difficult for the established organisations to hold there share of the market and generate to profits. Thus high risk of entry by potential competitors represents a threat to the profitability of the established organisations. On the other hand, if the risk of new entry is low, established organisations could take advantages of this opportunity to raise prices and earn greater returns.

Economist Joe Bain who identified three main sources of barriers to new entry:

- Brand loyalty
- Absolute cost advantage
- Economies of scale

Brand Loyalty

Brand loyalty is buyer's priority for the products of established organisations. An organisation create brand loyalty through continuous advertising of brand and organisations names, patents protection of products, products innovation through organisation research and development programmes, an emphasis on high product quality and providing goods after sales service. Significant brand loyalty makes it difficult for new entrants to take market share away from well established organisations. Thus it reduces the threat of entry by potential competitors.

Absolute Cost Advantages

Absolute cost advantages can be achieved from superior production techniques. These techniques arises due to past experience, patents, hidden process; control of particular inputs required for production like labor, materials, equipment or management skills; These access to cheaper funds because exiting organisation represent low risks than established organisations. If established organisations have an absolute cost advantages, than again the threat of entry decreases.

Case -1.2:Cement companies adopt innovative cost-cutting measures

FOR cement companies innovation may be the key to cost competitiveness. Hence, larger cement companies such as Grasim and Gujarat Ambuja are seen to be shifting to a number of innovative cost-cutting measures to enhance bottomlines. These include bypassing the dealers to sell cement directly to the customer, shifting from the traditional rail-road option to cheaper sea transportation to target distant markets and even using crushed sugarcane for meeting fuel requirements. According to an ICRA analysis, over 80 per cent of the cement is sold currently in India is through the dealer route. "The bigger cement companies are now shifting towards a dealer-free route to supply to bulk consumers, including builders and infrastructure companies to save on the dealer margin," an industry source said. Customers are encouraged to contact the cement companies directly with their requirements, following which the manufacturer delivers the requisite quantity of cement to their doorsteps. The move also gives the companies better price competitiveness as compared to those servicing customers through the dealer route, industry players said. Bigger players are also saving on logistics expenses, which is one of the major operating costs faced by the industry. Companies such as Gujarat Ambuja are extensively relying on the coastal transportation route to service the southern market, rather than on rail or road, according to industry analysts. Several cement companies are also using high capacity Volvo trucks for road transportation to cut down on costs, industry sources said. In order to bring down energy costs, most of the cement companies have already shifted entirely to captive power stations and are using a variety of fuels, including pet coke and lignite. Gujarat Ambuja, in fact, has partially replaced coal with crushed sugarcane as a fuel for its Gujarat plant, according to analysts. Cement companies are also tracking the international polypropylene prices to strike deals with manufacturers of polypropylene bags, used as packaging material in the country, according to ICRA. The scope for saving through this route is enormous, since in India cement is almost entirely sold in 50 kg bags, as opposed to it being sold in bulk in most other countries. Some of the domestic cement companies are also reportedly considering the bulk-sale route to optimise costs, industry sources said.

Question:

1. Explain the Cement companies adopt innovative cost-cutting measures

Source: Business Line, dated June 29,2004

Economies of Scale

Economies of scale are the cost advantages associated with large organisation size. Sources of scale economies include cost reductions gained through mass producing a standardized out put, discount on bulk purchase of raw material inputs and components parts, the spreading of fixed costs over a large volume. A new entrant faces the dilemma of either entering on a small scale and its result suffering a significant cost advantages or taking a very large risk by entering on a large scale and bearing significant capital costs. A further risk of large-scale entry results to increase the supply of the product will reduce the prices.

Rivalry Among Established Companies

It is the second of Porter's five competitive forces, it is the extent of rivalry among established organisation within the industry. When this competitive force is weak, business organisation have an opportunity to raise prices to earn greater profits. But if it is strong, business organisation have an opportunity to reduce prices to earn fewer profits. It is significant due to price competition, including price wars, may result from the intense rivalry. Price competition limits reduce the profitability the on sales. Thus intense rivalry among established organisations within industry is largely a function of three factors are listed below:

- Industry competitive structure
- Demand conditions
- The height of exist barriers in the industry

Competitive Structure

Competitive structure refers to the numbers size, and distribution of products and service in the organisation in an industry. Different competitive structures have different implications for rivalry. Fragmented industries consist of a large number of small or medium sized organisations, none of which is in a position to dominate the industry. A consolidated industry dominates by small number of large organisation or, in extreme cases, a monopoly (by just in one organisation). Fragmented industries included agriculture, video-rental, health clubs, real estate and pharmaceuticals etc.

Low entry barriers and commodity-type products are hard to differentiate characterize many fragmented industries. The combinations of these characteristics tend to result in boom and bust cycles of the industry. Low entry barrier indicates whenever demand is strong and their impacts on profits are high. In this circumstance, there will be a flood of new entrants to cash in the boom.

In the case consolidated industry, the competitive action of the organisation has directly affects the market share of its rivals, forcing to response from them. The result of the competitive interdependence can be dangerous to competitive spiral with rival companies. They are trying to undercut each other's prices of the products and service is pushing to industry and their profit down in this process. More typically, when price wars are threat, organisation competes on nonprime factors like product quality and design characteristics. This type of competition constitutes an attempt to build brand loyalty and minimize the likelihood of a price war.

Demand Conditions

Industry demand conditions are another important determinant of the intensity of rivalry among the established organisations. Growing demand trends provides expansion and greater expansion of the production activity. When demand is growing ultimate result is a searching of entrants of customers or if existing customers are purchasing more of an industry products. When demand is growing, organisation can increases revenues without taking a market share away from other companies.

Therefore, declining demand result in more competition from rivalry organisation. It is very difficult to maintaining revenue and market share of the organisation. Consumers are leaving marketplace or when individual consumer buying less. Therefore, declines the demand, declining demand constitutes a major threat to organisation.

Exit Barriers

When industry demand is declining because of exit barriers are serious competitive threat for organisation. Economic, strategic and emotional factors are treated as exit barriers. It keeps organisation competing in an industry even when returns are very low. Organisation can become locked into an unfavorable industry when exit barriers are high. Excess productive capacity tends to lead to intensified price competition, with companies cutting prices in an attempt to obtain the orders needed to utilize their idle capacity.

Exit barriers include the following

- Investment in plant, machinery and equipment that have no alternative uses and cannot be sold off if the organisation wishes to leave the industry; it has to write-off the book value of the assets.
- High fixed cost of exists like severance pay to workers who are being made redundant.
- Emotional attachments to an industry, as when a company is unwilling to exist from its original industry for sentimental reasons.
- Strategic relationships between business units. For instance, within multi-industry organisation, a low return business unit may provide vital inputs for a high return business based in another industry. Thus the company may be unwilling to exist from the low return business.
- Economic dependence on the industry, as when company is not diversified and so relies on the industry for it income.

The Bargaining Power of Buyers

It is third of Porter's five competitive forces; it is the bargaining power of buyer. Buyers can be influenced as competitive threat when they force down prices of the products and service. It means that when buyer demand is higher quality and better service which increasing operating costs of the products and service of the organisation.

According to Porter's buyers are more powerful in the following situations:

The supply industry which consists of many small organisations and the buyers are few in number and large. These situations allow the buyers to dominate supply organisations.

- The buyer purchase in bulk in such situations, buyers can be bargained for price reductions of the products and service organisation.
- The supply industry depends on the buyers orders, buyers can bargained for price reductions of the products and service of the organisation.
- The buyer can switch orders between supply organisations at a low cost, thereby playing off organisations against each other to force down prices.
- It is economically feasible for the buyers to purchase the products and service from the several organisations at once.
- The buyer causes threat to supply their own needs through vertical integration, its impact on the price reducing of the products and service organisation.

The Bargaining Power of Suppliers

The bargaining power of suppliers is the fourth of Porter's competitive force. Supplier influenced as a threat when they are capable to force up the price that organisation must pay for products and service or reduced the quality of goods supplied thereby, reducing the organisational profitability.

In other words, weak supplier gives opportunity to organisation to force down the prices and demand higher quality. As with the buyer, the capability of supplier to make demands on an organisation depends on power relative to organisation. According to Porter's suppliers are most powerful in the following cases:

- The product suppliers have to sell substitutes and is important to organisation.
- The organisation industry is not an important to customer to the suppliers have does not depend on the organisation's industry, and supplier have little incentive to reduce prices or improve quality of the products and service.
- The suppliers of the respective products are differentiated which is to more expensive for organisation to switch from one supplier to another. In such circumstance, the organisations depend on its supplier and cannot play them off against each other.
- To raise prices, suppliers use can threat of vertically integrating forward into the industry and competing directly with the organisation products and service.
- Buying organisation cannot use the threat of vertically directly with the organisation product and service.
- The buying organisation cannot use the threat of vertically integrating backward supplying their own needs as a means to reduce the product and service.

The Threat of Substitute Products

The fifth and final force in the Porter's model is the threat of substitute products-the product of industries that serve identical consumer needs as those of the industry being analysis.

For instance, organisations in the coffee industry compete directly with those in the tea and soft drink industries. In the case of substitute products, if the price of the coffee rises too much relative to that of tea or soft drinks, than coffee drinkers will switch from coffee to those substitutes. The existence of close substitutes creates a strong competitive threat, limiting the price an organisation.

CHAPTER 2

Business Policy and Strategic Management

Contents

- Introduction
- Business policy as a discipline
- What is a strategy
- Generic strategic alternatives
- The dynamics of competitive strategy
- Strategic management
- Strategic decisions making
- The tasks of strategic management
- Value, mission and objectives
- Strategic levels in organisation

Learning Objectives

This chapter aims to be provided: business policy as discipline, What is a strategy, Generic strategic alternatives, The dynamics of competitive strategy, Strategic management, Strategic decisions making, The tasks of strategic management, Value , mission and objectives ,Strategic levels in organisation ,Characteristics of strategic management decisions at different levels, Benefits of strategic management and risks of strategic management.

"Strategic management is not a box of tricks or a bundle of techniques. It is analytical thinking and commitment of resources to action"

Peter Drucker

"Without a strategy the organisation is like a ship without a rudder"

Joel Ross and Michael kami

2.1 INTRODUCTION

Strategic management and business policy is a stream of instructions, guidance, directions for decisions and actions with view to develop effective long term and short term planning of the organisation. Strategic management and business policy decisions help to organisation for accomplishment of goals and objectives of the business. Forecasting the strategic decisions would help the organisation to achieve its superior goal. Strategic management and business policy includes strategic analysis, strategy formulation, strategy implementation and strategic controlling and monitoring of all events of the organisation. Strategic decisions might to be to deploy resources in the organisation into new business opportunities. Strategy decisions normally representation of the environment analysis, value chain concept and analysis, integration, diversification, mergers and acquisitions, new product development, product redesigning, up gradation, strategies for marketing, technology, new customers, finance, geographic areas and entry into new markets. Strategic management decisions help to survival, growth and development of organisation.

2.2 BUSINESS POLICY AS A DISCIPLINE

According to Glueck

"Development from business policy arose from the use of planning techniques by managers. Starting from day to day planning in earlier times, managers tried to anticipate the future through preparation of budgets and using control systems like capital budgeting and management by objectives. With the inability of these techniques to adequately emphasize the role of the future, long range planning came to be used. Soon, Long range planning was replaced by strategic planning, and latter by strategic management:, a term that is currently used to describe the process of strategic decision making".

According To Christensen And Others

Business policy is "the study of the functions and responsibilities of senior management, the crucial problems that affect success in the total enterprise, and the decisions that determine the direction of the organisation and shape its future. The problems of the policy in business, like those of policy in public affairs, have to do with the choice of purposes, the moulding of organisational identity and character, the continuous definition of what needs to be done, and the mobilization of resources for the attainment of goals in the face of the competition or adverse circumstances".

- It tends to focus on the rational analytical aspect of strategic management
- It presents a design framework for understanding for strategic decision making.
- Strategic framework enables a individual to make preparations for handling general management responsibility effectively and efficiently.
- Business course introduced by the Harvard Business School and origin of its business policy traced back to 1911.
- It is integrative course in management and aimed to the creation of general management capability.
- This course was based on interactive case studies that had been use at the school for instructional purposes since 1908.
- It is intended to enhance general manager capability of students.
- The introduction of business policy is the curriculum of business schools and management institutes came much later, in 1969.
- The American Assembly of Collegiate Schools of Business is a regulatory body for business schools. It made that the course of business policy is a mandatory requirement for the purpose of recognition.
- This course spread to different management institutes across different nations and become an integral part of management curriculum.
- It is considered as a capstone, and integrative course offered to business students who have previously been through a set of core functional area business course.
- The term 'Business Policy 'had been traditionally used in the business schools in world which though new titles for the course have begun to be introduced in recent years in India.

2.3 IMPORTANCE OF BUSINESS POLICY

- They tend to serve as precedents and thus reduce the repetitive rethinking of all the factors of individual decisions which they save time.
- Policies aid in co-ordination, if a member of individuals are guided by the same policies, they can predict more accurately the actions and decisions of others.
- Policy provides the stability in the organisation, a certainty of action is assured even though the top management may any change. The policies continue and this continuity promotes stability in the organisation and thus reduces frustrations of members.
- Clear policies encourage definite individual decisions. Each functional manger has clearly understanding the range policy within the organisation which helpful to make decision and thus feel less uncertain as to whether he\she can

give answers to subordinates without "getting into trouble".

- Policies clearly specify routes towards the related goals of the organisation. Policies serve as a standard or measuring yard for evaluation performance in the organisation. The actual results can be compared with the policies of the organisation which is to determine how well the members of an organisation have lived into their professed and intentioned to what extent goals have been achieved in an organisation.
- Sound policies help to build up employee enthusiasm and loyalty for the organisation. This is specifically true when they reflect established principles of fair play and justice and when they help people to know that within an organisation.
- They setup the pattern of behavior and permit to participants to plan with a greater degree of confidence and lead to better co-operation in the organisation.
- Policies are monitored and controlling of the organisation which guides for delegated decision-making. They seek to ensure consistency and uniformity in decisions relating to problems that recur frequently and under similar. But does not happen at identical circumstances in an organisation.
- Policies always with clarity, relevance and reasonableness and enable a firm to make the optimum utilization of scarce available resources and thereby bring about an efficient level of operations because wastage must be avoided.
- Corporate policies always buildup an image of the business in the eyes of the public and this brings in more reputation, goodwill; sale and profits so that more and more acts of social responsibilities may be undertaken by organisation.
- Proper administration and implementation of policies that encourage initiative in the employees so that they act with full responsibility with in the framework of the policies of the organisation. This naturally improves the working environment like very good-labor management relations within the organisation.

2.4 CLASSIFICATION OF BUSINESS POLICY

Figure 1.2 indicates the classification of business policy. Different types of business policy as follows:

- On the basis of level of management
- On the basis of functional areas
- On the basis of expression
- On the basis of nature of origin
- On the basis of scope of organisation
- On the basis of nature of management function

Figure-2.1: Classification of Business Policy

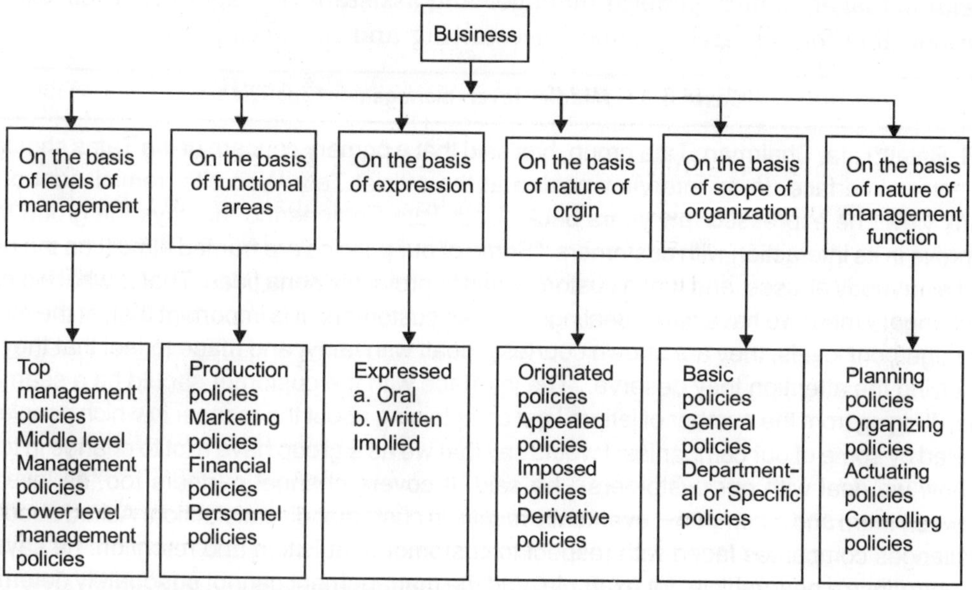

On The Basis of Level of Management

Business policies are framed at different levels of the management, and accordingly these may be classified as:

Top Management Policies

These policies are derived from the top management planning. The top management principally comprises of the Board of Directors, chairman /president, vice president/ vice-chairman, managing director, general manager etc, and the top management frames the policies by themselves and it is, therefore, responsible for these. These people are the ultimate level of authority in the operation of the enterprise. The policy makers plan to set up the objectives, define the goals, establish the policies, see that these policies are put into effect and judge the results.

The top management policies involves with the long range product selection extent of its diversification, a acquisitions and mergers of two or more units, spin-offs-their nature, extent and liability-sales forecasting sizing the enterprise, process of selection, machine selection, determining site, location and needs of the plant, decisions regarding investment of available resources in capital and human research development, settlement of problems of executives regarding their promotion, transfer, retirement etc., and accomplishment of the organisation objectives/goals.

Middle Level Management Policies

These policies are the out-come of the deliberations of the executives at the upper middle and middle level. The upper middle management consists of the head of the personnel administration department like Production manager, sales manager, marketing manager, financial manager, deputy general manager and assistant manager etc, their executives are responsible for research, finance, accounting and marketing etc,

Case 2.1: Middle level management policies

MR. Ratan Tata, Chairman, Tata group, has said that a primary concern of the Tatas should be customer interface. In an interview posted at the official Tata Web site, reminiscent of the frank views he expressed few years back about Tata Engineering, he says the group must improve in its interaction with customers. "Some of our policies are framed almost on the basis that everybody abuses, and that a customer has to prove his bona fides. That is what we need to change. Where we have direct dealings with our customers, it is important that, at the middle management levels, they are shown courtesy, dealt with fairly, and made to feel that they are receiving the attention they deserve. "The interface with the customer should be a seamless one. Judging from the number of letters I get complaining about the manner in which people are treated by some of our companies, I would say that we as a group have a lot to change in terms of how we deal with our customers," he said. It covers channel partners too, as love lost between them and a company, eventually results in customer dissatisfaction. Asked about the challenges companies faced with respect to customer acquisition and retention, he says, "If you introduce a new vehicle, for example, and the management cannot adequately determine what the market wants, the company is in trouble. Theoretically, the top managers of a company should take up the role of that ideal customer. They should be driving their competitors' vehicles, they should be driving the best-of-breed vehicles, and they should be making cost comparisons. "While a top manager should be the ideal customer, he should also be the greatest critic of his company's products. If the CEO compromises, or is only looking at the margins, then even if he is successful, the company's success will be shortlived." Further, "Market feedback is very important, but it has to be stripped of its colour. You have to be able to strip away the vested interest or the bias that sometimes comes in. You have to view it objectively, not defensively." On how to enthuse CEOs and employees to create value for shareholders and customers, he says, "We need to make it our responsibility to expose employees to the company holistically. "I often tell some of my colleagues, `You don't have to face the shareholders when you make a loss. I do. May be you should stand up one day and face the shareholders for what you've deprived them of.' Selectively involving people in shareholder meets, investor conferences, and dealer meets will help in exposing them to different situations that they may face. We have been doing that at Tata Engineering." What would the Tata differentiator be in a market with so many competing brands and products? He says, "I would like the customer to say that the next product he buys will also be a Tata product because of everything that he experienced. That is really what customer retention is all about."

Question:

1. Explain the middle level strategic management policies in TATA.

Source: Business line, Dated March19, 2003

They lay down the policies regarding upon the establishment of organisation, selection of the best-suited executives staff and employees to carry out the plans, installation of proper departments, designing of operating policies and operating routines, deciding processes, methods and techniques of production which exploration of new markets and decisions about channels of distribution for assignment of duties to each department and to each individual, who are deciding about source of manpower, resources and their selection, deciding about wage, salary and incentive plans for them, obtain necessary finances, controlling costs and solving problems of actual sales activities etc.,

Middle management consists of the deputy heads of the various sections under different functional departments-employment and training, industrial relations, labor welfare and social security. Junior executive, superintendents of departments divisions etc., these executives are the deputy head of the functional department like sales, production, research, finance and accounting divisions of the organisation. They frame policies are known as middle management polices.

Lower Level management Policies

The lower level management people are men and women who have direct supervision over the working force in office, factory, sales field, and other areas of activity of the organisation. They are directly related to the accomplishment of the task for the small sub-divisions of the whole enterprise. They chalk out policies or the assignment of the jobs to the best suited persons in the organisation. The lower level management policies guidelines of the provision of adequate tools, raw materials, training of the workers, issuing of orders, maintenance of quality, improving working conditions, morale, maintaining discipline and controlling absenteeism etc.

Operating Force Policies

These are the rules or a code for doing the job which enriched to a particular worker performance. These are usually written down in the note books of the organisation. Operating policies notice to the worker how long each job work should take a time, what tricks of the trade are required, and what quality feature are emphasised.

On The Basis of Functional Areas

On the basis of functional areas business policies may be classified as production policies, marketing and sales polices, financial policies and human resource development policies

Production Policies

Production policies are framed and concerned with the following issues:

- The product to be produced (product line, type of product).
- The type of technology, processes, equipment and tools, to be used.
- The selection of factory\office\plant site, location and layout.
- The decisions regarding scale of production.
- Making of production budgets manufacturing costs and deciding about total cost and cost of installation and its maintenance.

- The selecting of junior executives;
- Inventory control.
- Collective bargaining and labor relations.
- Organisation and co-ordination of their activities.
- Selection of systems of quality, cost production control.
- Production policies are the basic determinants of the total policy making procedure.

Marketing and Sales Policies

These policies relate to policies in market analysis, business law, display, salesmanship and advertising etc, i.e. they are concerned with total process of marketing which covering both 'product mix' and 'market mix'. The product mix includes decisions regarding the type, quantity and quality of product design, contents shape, methods and techniques of production etc. Market mix covers the issues like price, place, promotion, channels of distribution, advertising policies, packaging and branding decisions, consumer psychology and behavior and pricing of the product etc.

Since the modern concept of market has treated as 'consumer as a king', every product is brought to satisfy customer needs. Hence its gamut is very fast. The policies in this field, therefore, deal with the following issues:

- Spotting out of the present and potential markets, the size and nature of consumers.
- The degree of competition in the market and how best could it be met.
- The location of prospects and persuading them to purchase.
- Fixing price of product, offering rebated, discounts and other concessions.
- compensating salesman adequately; and providing them with training and developmental opportunities.
- Selecting channels of distribution or employing representatives and agents.
- Dividing the total market into branch or dealer areas.
- Establishing advertising policies like:
    - i. Setting up sales control policies.
    - ii. And establishing sales volume and expense budgets.

Financial Policies

Financial policies may be regarded as the most important business policies of the organisation. It depends on the entire success and failure of a business unit of the organisation. Properly and careful framed financial policies help to effective utilisation of the resource like men, machine, market, method, materials and long term survival of the business while improper framed financial policies are ruin to business activities of the organisation.

Financial policies are essential to organisation. They are as listed below:

- To know the capital requirement of the organisation in terms of short, medium and long term-and know the how to procurement and effective utilization of finance in the organisation.
- The method of raising funds and the ratio between the various types of sources of funds, particularly the proportion of owned funds to borrowed funds.
- Utilisations of the funds and the ratio between different types of asset.
- The credit policy, declaration and distribution of dividend to the shareholder.
- Profit policy, provisions for taxes, renovations and modernisation of plants and machinery.

Costing policy includes the policy for selecting the method of costing, the method of allocating, apportioning, reapportioning and absorbing overheads.

Accounting policy includes the following areas:

- The basis of valuation of stock in trade at the year end; whether at total cost, or at direct cost or at works costs.
- The issue price of the raw material; whether to follow first in first out method or last in first out method or average cost or any other methods of issue of raw materials
- Depreciation policy; whether straight line method or reducing balance method or mileage method or any other method.
- The treatment of deferred revenue expenditure, intangible asset, fictitious assets and preliminary expenses.
- Capitalization of expenditure during construction period.
- The policy for provision of bad and doubtful debt, investment losses, etc.

Human Resource Development Policy

Personal policy are concerned with human resource utilization, its recruitments and selection, source of supply, training of employment, training of the employees at whole cost; the promotion and transfer policy, the issues regarding compensation to the employees, wage incentive and other perks, benefits and services etc.

On the Basis of Expression

On the basis of expression policy may be classified into express policies, oral policies and written policies.

Express Policy

Express policies are those policies, which expressed in terms in clear words either orally or in writing.

Oral Policies

Oral policies are those, which are issued or stated by the management in terms of words of mouth to their subordinates. Such policies are generally adopted when an organisation is small and face-to-face communications is desired. Since they are direct, they are more effective and, hence can be bettering understood and implemented. They are more flexible and can be adjusted to be different organisational conditions.

Limitation

First is the main drawback of such policies are not written as such. Second is the interpreted in any way by the persons receiving them. Thirdly they are often not remembered for long time and easily forgotten, especially when there are number of policies and where their frequency of issues is great. Therefore, usually oral policies are not in popular use.

Written Policy

Written policies are those, which are normally, pull in black and white and stated in clear terms so that persons whom they are addressed to easily understand them. For putting the policies in written, much care has to be taken, for instance;

- Policy is always written in terms of words which neither vag nor unnecessarily academic, nor in any way offensive to those for whom it is meant.
- Words, sentence and paragraphs should be short and statement of policy should be complete and precise.
- It should not contain irritating words are expression antagonistic or cast as persons on others.
- The tone should be warm, without use of any legalistic phraseology
- The frame should be convenient and handy for management reference and application.

Written policies are desirable in the following situations:

- The subject matter on which a policy is to be formulated, But it is of a very controversial nature.
- The distance between the top and lower levels of management is so wide as to make personnel/informal contact and communications rather difficult in an organisation.
- Consistent treatment all is needy and certainly of action desired.
- Preciseness and complete understanding is needed to convoy to the employees at the different levels.

Advantages

There are distinct advantages of written policies are as follows:

- The writing of policies makes commitments on the part of an organisation.
- Writing ensures uniformity of application and assures continuity of action even when the management is changed.
- It limits freedom of action on the part of the management, for it is worked within the boundary of policies.

- The written policies provide something concrete on which to base an appeal if there is any disagreement about what is the organisation's policy.
- Writing helps to ensure that the professed policies are right for organisation tries to put its best foot forward.
- The likelihood of wrong interpretation or misunderstanding is very much lessened.
- Written policies facilitate easy and smooth compliance.
- The results in greater convenience both to the policy frame worse and implementers

However, written policies cannot be easily changed and perfect secrecy, when desired cannot be maintained and writing of good policies needs fluency in english that every person does not possess.

Even then, in all large organisations, written policies are a rule rather than exception.

Implied Policies

These are the policies, which are implied from the code conduct or from mode of behavior of business executives; but they are not stated in terms of orally. They generally flow from philosophy of the business, it is social values and even traditions, for instance, smoking and drinking may be prohibited not in writing but it implied by the conduct of superior executives who refrain from these habits while on the duty.

Originated Policies

Originated policies emanate from the company objectives which are determined by the top management, who are primarily responsible for shaping business policies to guide and direct them and the subordinate in the attainment of organisation's objectives these are framed by the board of directors the president and general manager etc, and passed on to the executives in hierarchy for implementation.

The subordinates usually readily accept such policies because they have been framed by higher ups in power that entrusted with the shaping of business policy for concern.

Appealed Policies

Appealed policies are often known as "suggested policies". Because they are framed on the suggestions of the subordinates or those who are implement the policies. The idea is to make a policy is more effective so that particular problems could find solutions under it. Such policies also have general acceptance as that of the originated policy because, they have already got the approved from the top management.

2.5 DEFINITION OF STRATEGY

The term strategy is derived from the Greek word 'strategia' which means "generalship." In the military concept, strategy often refers to maneuvering troops into position before the enemy is actually engaged war in the war field. According to in this concept, strategy refers to the deployment of troops in the war field. Once the enemy has been engaged war, attention shifts to tactics how to win war. Here, the employment of troops is central point of strategy formulation, implementaion and controlling of war. And this concept transfer to the business world which begins to take form in terms of formulation, implementation and controlling business policy to achieve strategic goals of the business enterprise.

Strategy also refers to the means by which policy is effected; according to Clauswitz' famous statement as 'war is the continuation of political relations via other means'. Given the centuries-old military origins of strategy, it seems sensible to begin our examination of strategy relationship within the military view.

Strategy According to B. H. Liddell Hart

In his book, *Strategy* Liddell Hart examines wars and battles from the time of the ancient Greeks through World War II. He concludes that Clausewitz' definition of strategy as "the art of the employment of battles as a means to gain the object of war" which is seriously flawed. In this view, strategy intrudes upon policy and makes battle the only means of achieving strategic ends. Liddell Hart has observes that Clausewitz later acknowledged these flaws and then points to what he views as a wiser definition of strategy set forth by Moltke: "the practical adaptation of the means placed at a general's disposal to the attainment of the object in view." In Moltke's formulation, military strategy is clearly a means to political ends.

Concluding his review of wars, policy, strategy, and tactics, Liddell Hart arrives at this short definition of strategy as "the art of distributing and applying military means to fulfil the ends of policy." Deleting the word "military" from Liddell Hart's definition makes it easy to export the concept of strategy to the business world.

Strategy According to George Steiner

George Steiner is the father of strategic planning in the business and industrial world. George Steiner, a professor of management and one of the founders of *The California Management Review which* generally considers a key figure in the origins and development of strategic planning. His book, *Strategic Planning* closes to being a bible of the strategic planning. Yet, Steiner does not bother to define strategy except in the notes at the end of his book, Strategic Planning. There, he notes that strategy enters the management literature as a way of referring to what one did to counter a competitor's actual or predicted moves. Steiner also notices that there is very little agreement as to the meaning of strategy in the business and industry world. Some of the definitions in use to which Steiner pointed have outlined:

1. Strategy of the top management which is the greatest importance to the organisation.
2. Strategy refers to basic directional instructions and set of decisions which relates to purposes and missions.

3. Strategy consists of the important actions and moves which necessary to realize these directions.
4. Strategy always answers to the question: What should the organisation be doing?
5. Strategy answers the problem: What are the ends we seek and how should we achieve them?

Strategy According to Henry Mintzberg

Henry Mintzberg wrote a book *"The Rise and Fall of Strategic Planning"* in 1994. It has points out that people use "strategy" in several different ways, the most common being these four as outlined:

1. Strategy is like a plan, a "how," a means of getting from here to there.
2. Strategy represents a pattern in actions over time; for example, a company has regularly markets very expensive products is using a "high end" strategy.
3. Strategy represents position; it reflects decisions to offer particular products or services in particular markets.
4. Strategy represents perspective like vision and direction of the company.

Mintzberg has argues that strategy emerges over time as intentions collide with and accommodate a changing reality. Therefore, one might start with a perspective and conclude that it calls for a certain position, which is to be achieved by way of a carefully crafted plan, with the eventual outcome and strategy reflected in a pattern evident in decisions and actions over time. This pattern in decisions and actions defines what Mintzberg called "realized" or emergent strategy.

Strategy According to Kenneth Andrews

Kenneth Andrews is a professor of Harvard Business School and for many years editor of the Harvard Business Review. Kenneth Andrews wrote a book. "The concept of Corporate Strategy". It has presents this lengthy definition of strategy as.

"Corporate strategy is the pattern of decisions in a company that determines and reveals its objectives, purposes, or goals, produces the principal policies and plans for achieving those goals, and defines the range of business to company and how it is to pursue the kind of economic and human organisation it is or intends to be, and the nature of the economic and non-economic contribution it intends to make to its shareholders, employees, customers, and communities."

Andrew's definition obviously anticipates Mintzberg's attention to pattern, plan, and perspective. Andrews also draws a distinction between "corporate strategy," which determines the businesses in which a company will compete, and "business strategy," which defines the basis of competition for a given business. Thus, he also anticipated "position" as a form of strategy. Strategy as the basis for competition brings us to another Harvard Business School professor, Michael Porter, the undisputed guru of competitive strategy.

Strategy According to Michael Porter

Another Harvard Business School professor, Michael Porter is the undisputed guru of "competitive strategy". Michael Porter has argues that competitive strategy is "about being different." He adds, "It means deliberately choosing a different set of activities to deliver a unique mix of value." In short, Porter argues that strategy is about competitive position, about differentiating yourself in the eyes of the customer, about adding value through a mix of activities different from those used by competitors. In his earlier book competitive Strategy, Porter defines competitive strategy as "a combination of the ends (goals) for which the firm is striving and the means (policies) by which it is seeking to get there." Thus, Porter seems to embrace strategy as both plan and position. (It should be noted that Porter writes about competitive strategy, not about strategy in general.)

Strategy According to Kepner-Tregoe

In *Top Management Strategy* Benjamin Tregoe and John Zimmerman, of Kepner-Tregoe, Inc., define strategy as "the framework, which guides those choices that determine the nature and direction of an organisation." Ultimately, this boils down to selecting products (or services) to offer and the markets in which to offer them. Tregoe and Zimmerman urge executives to base these decisions on a single "driving force" of the business. Although there are nine possible driving forces, only one can serve as the basis for strategy for a given business. The nine possibilities are listed below:

- Products offered
- Market needs
- Technology
- Production capability
- Method of sale
- Method of distribution
- Natural resources
- Size/growth
- Return/profit

It seems Tregoe and Zimmerman takes the position that strategy is essentially a matter of perspective.

Strategy According to Michel Robert

Michel Robert takes a similar view of strategy in, *Strategy Pure & Simple*, where he argues that the real issues are "strategic management" and "thinking strategically." For Robert, these boils down to decisions pertaining to four factors are listed below:

- Products and services
- Customers
- Market segments
- Geographic areas

Like Tregoe and Zimmerman, Robert claims that decisions about which products and services to offer, the customers to be served, the market segments in which to operate, and the geographic areas of operations should be made on the basis of a single "driving force." Again, like Tregoe and Zimmerman, Robert claims that several possible driving forces exist but only one can be the basis for strategy. The 10 driving forces cited by Robert are listed below:

- Product-service
- User-customer
- Market type
- Production capacity-capability
- Technology
- Sales-marketing method
- Distribution method
- Natural resources
- Size/growth
- Return/profit

Strategy According to Treacy and Wiersema

The notion of restricting the basis on which strategy might be formulated has been carried one step farther by Michael Treacy and Fred Wiersema, authors of *The Discipline of Market Leaders*, Treacy and Wiersema assert that companies achieve leadership positions by narrowing, not broadening their business focus. Treacy and Wiersema identify three "value-disciplines" that can serve as the basis for strategy: operational excellence, customer intimacy, and product leadership. As with driving forces, only one of these value disciplines can serve as the basis for strategy. Treacy and Wiersema's three value disciplines are briefly defined below:

- Operational Excellence
- Customer Intimacy
- Product Leadership

Operational Excellence

- Strategy is predicated on the production and delivery of products and services. The objective is to lead the industry in terms of price and convenience.

Customer Intimacy

- Strategy is predicated on tailoring and shaping products and services to fit an increasingly fine definition of the customer. The objective is long-term customer loyalty and long-term customer profitability.

Product Leadership

- Strategy is predicated on producing a continuous stream of state-of-the-art products and services. The objective is the quick commercialization of new ideas.

Each of the three value disciplines suggests different requirements. Operational Excellence implies world-class marketing, manufacturing, and distribution processes. Customer Intimacy suggests staying close to the customer and entails long-term relationships. Product leadership clearly hinges on market-focused R&D as well as organisational nimbleness and agility.

Strategy According to Igor H. Ansoff

"The common thread among the organisation's activities and product–markets that defines the essential nature of business that the organisation was or planned to be in future".

Strategy According to William F. Glueck

"A unified, comprehensive and integrated plan designed to assure that the basic objectives of the enterprise are achieved".

What Is Strategy?

What is strategy? Is it a plan like short term or longterm? Does it refer to how we will obtain the ends we seek? Is it a position taken any decision? Just like as military forces might take the high ground prior to engaging the enemy; might a business take the position of low-cost provider? On the other hand, does strategy refer to perspective, to the view of the matters, to the purposes, directions, decisions, and actions stemming. Lastly, does strategy refer to a pattern in our decisions and actions? For example, does repeatedly copying a competitor's new product which offerings signal a "me too" strategy? Just what is strategy?

Strategy is all these-it is perspective, position, plan, and pattern. Strategy is the bridge between policy and high-order goals on the one hand and tactics or concrete actions on the other. Strategy and tactics together straddle the gap between ends and means. In short, strategy is a term that refers to a complex web of thoughts, ideas, insights, experiences, goals, expertise, memories, perceptions, and expectations that provides general guidance for specific actions in pursuit of particular ends. Strategy is at once the course we chart, the journey we imagine, and, at the same time, it is the course we steer, the trip we actually make. Even when we are embarking on a voyage of discovery of facts, with no particular destination in mind, the voyage has a purpose, an outcome, and an end to be kept in view.

Company/Corporate Strategy

- A company strategy is the game plan management.
- It can be using to stake out market position.
- It consciously considered and flexible designed long term plan and intent to achieve goals for this purpose to mobilize resource, to direct effort and behavior, to handle events and problems, to perceive and utilize opportunities, and to meet challenges and find threats to corporate survival and success.

- It will be conducted operations in terms of attracting and please to customers.
- It will be competed successfully in competitive market.
- Its achieve company goals and objectives.
- Company's strategy consists of the combination of competitive moves and business approaches that managers employ to please customers compete successfully and achieve organisational objectives.
- Company strategy is a long-range blueprint of an organisation's desired image, direction and destination what it wants to be, what it wants to do and where it wants to go.

Strategy, then, has no existence apart from the ends sought. A general framework provides guidance for actions to be taken and, at the same time, which is shaped by the actions taken. This means that the necessary precondition for formulating strategy is a clear and widespread understanding of the ends to be obtained. Without these ends in view, action is purely tactical and can quickly degenerate into nothing more than a flailing about.

When there are no "ends in view" for the organisation writ large, strategies still exist and they are still operational, even highly effective, but for an individual or unit, not for the organisation as a whole. The risks are not having a set of company-wide ends clearly in view include missed opportunities, fragmented and wasted effort, working at cross purposes, and internecine warfare. A comment from Lionel Urwick's classic *Harvard Business Review* article regarding the span of control is applicable here listed below:

"There is nothing which rots morale more quickly and more completely than . . . the feeling that those in authority do not know their own minds."

For the leadership of an organisation to remain unclear or to vacillate regarding ends, strategy, tactics, and means is to not know their own minds. The accompanying loss of morale is enormous.

One possible outcome of such a state of affairs is the emergence of a new dominant coalition within the existing authority structure of the enterprise; one that will augment established authority in articulating the ends toward which the company will strive. Also possible is the weakening of authority and the eventual collapse of the formal organisation. No amount of strategising or strategic planning will compensate for the absence of a clear and widespread understanding of the ends sought.

Concept of Strategy

A strategy is a long-term plan of action designed to achieve a particular goal. Strategy applies to many disparate fields such as: Military strategy, strategy, economic strategy, environmental strategy, corporate strategy, business strategy, industry strategy, commerce, science, grand, stability Expansion, retrenchment, combination, modernization diversification, integration, turnaround, divestment hybrid, alliance merger and acquisition strategy etc.

Strategy is essentially linked with military science. It implies facing the enemy under war conditions that are to one's advantage. A policy when given a particular meaning under a prevailing situation and in view of the enemy or competitor policy becomes strategy. So, strategy can be defined as interpretative planning. Strategy includes the determination and evaluation of alternative paths to an already established mission or objectives, and eventually choosing the right alternatives, In common sense, a strategy outlines how management decides and plans to achieve its goal and objectives. Management formulates strategy to shade out the effect of other polices and compared to overall plan and programs of the competitors, policy to avail of competitive advantage.

Characteristics of Corporate Strategy

As listed below are the important strategy characteristics. They are:

- It is long range planning, apart from also to be consider and cope with the short term planning.
- Strategies are specific actions suggested to be achieving the objectives.
- Strategies are action oriented.
- It can be formulated at the top level management and delegate and associate powers to middle level and low level for policy formulation, implementation and control of strategy.
- It copes with a competitive and complex setting in corporate environment.
- It goals and objectives are translates them in reality in corporate.
- It concerns with perceiving opportunities and deployment of resources and threats and seizing initiatives to cope with them.
- Everyone is empowered to implement the strategy.
- Strategies are means to an end.
- Strategies are concerned with uncertainties with competitive situations like risk etc, which are likely to take place at a future date.
- Strategy is deployed to mobilize the available resources in the best interest of the company.
- It gives special importance to combination, sequence, timing, direction and depth of various moves and action initiatives taken by managers to handle environment uncertainties and complexities.
- It is flexible and dynamic.
- It provides unified criteria for managers in function of decision making in corporate.
- It is multipronged and integrated with objectives and goals of corporate.

2.6 GENERIC STRATEGIC ALTERNATIVES

According to William F Glueck and Lawrence R Jauch

There are four generic ways in which strategic alternatives can be considered: these are outlined:

Exhibit 2.1: Generic Strategic Alternatives

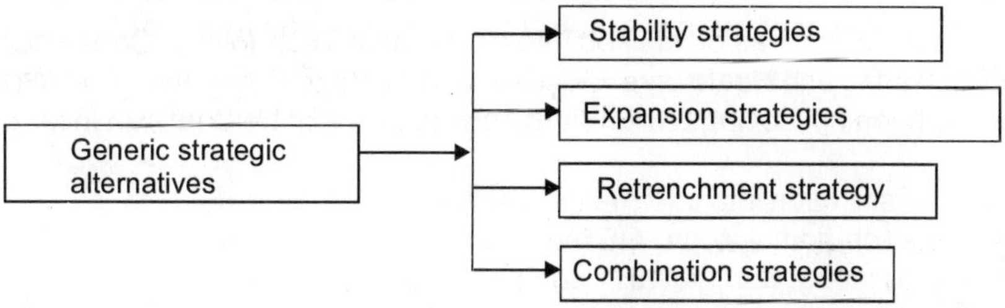

An organisation may have to find the best possible strategy from different types of strategic alternatives. The major types of strategies are normally related to industrial business organisation. They are as follows:

Stability Strategy

Stability strategy refers to the maintaining status quo of the existing business operation. Stability strategy aims at slow growth rate. It is followed as a matter of principle when an organisation attempts incremental growth of its functional performance in terms of its customer groups, customer functions, and alternative technologies, whether in combination or individually. Thus when organisation decides to serve the same target customer groups with same products service and follows the same objective to maintain the stable business status, it can be termed as stability strategy.

Stability strategy is pursued by a corporate when

- It continues to serve in the same or similar markets and deals in same products and services.
- The strategic decisions focus on incremental improvement of functional performance of business firm.

It involves keeping track of the new developments to ensure that the strategy continues to make real sense. In small business organisations, it will also frequently use stability as a strategic focus to maintain comfortable market or profit position.

Expansion Strategy

When an organisation desired to expand extents its business network widening the scope of its customer groups, customer functions and state of the art technologies, we have the making of an expansion strategy. Expansion or growth strategy is principally adopted when an organisation enhance its level of objectives with high target. Intensive expansion is a fundamental approach to safeguard and develop the organisations product market and thereby increased the volume of scales, profit, market share and total business network very rapidly.

Expansion through diversification

Case - 2.2: Expansion through diversification of Wipro
Founded in 1945, Wipro has diversified into Information Technology, Consumer Care and Lighting, Engineering and Healthcare. Our diversification into IT happened in 1980 and since then there has been no looking back. Wipro had revenues of USD 902Mn in March 2003. Milestones 1980 : Diversification into Information Technology. 1990 : Incorporation of Wipro-GE medical systems. 1992 : Going global with global IT services division. 1993 : Business innovation award for offshore development. 1995 : Wipro gets ISO 9001 quality certification, re-certified twice for mature processes. 1997 : Wipro gets SEI CMM level 3 certification, enterprise wide processes defined. 1998 : Wipro first software services company in the world to get SEI CMM level 5. 1999 : Wipro's market capitalization is the highest in India. 2000 : Start of the Six Sigma initiative, defects prevention practices initiated at project level. 2001 : First Indian company to achieve the "TL9000 certification" for industry specific quality standards. 2001 : World's first PCMM Level 5 company 2001:Ranked 87 among 100 best performing technology companies globally (BusinessWeek, June 2001). 2002 : World's first CMMi ver 1.1 Level 5 company. 2002 : Ranked the 7th software services company in the world by BusinessWeek (Infotech 100, November 2002).
Questions 1. Describe the expansion strategy of wipro. 2. Explain the diversification strategy of wipro.

Source. www.wipro technologies

Diversification strategy refers to diverting the business focus from the existing traditional areas to new promising areas like new products, new product lines, new services, or new markets, involving substantially different skills, technology and knowledge. Diversification means of utilizing their existing facilities and capabilities a more effective and efficient manner.

Since technology is changing day by day, it is based on the customers expectations and to draw their attention to organisation. Organisations focus to produce or manufactured new and substitute products and services for attract and draw attention of customers. These changing attitudes have been opening more and more new areas of promising business. Diversifications can be changed business focus may be either in terms of customer function, customer group and or new alternative technologies.

Vertical Integration Strategy

Case 2.3: Reliance Industries Limited
Reliance Industries Limited, This Group's principal activity is to produce and distribute plastic and intermediates, polyester filament yarn, fibre intermediates, polymer intermediates, crackers, chemicals, textiles, oil and gas. The Group has its manufacturing facilities at Patalganga in Maharashtra, Ahmedabad, Surat and Manager in Gujarat. The brands include Recron, Relpet, Relene, Reclair, Repol, Reon, Relab, Vimal, Harmony, SlumbeRel, Ruerel and Reance. Refining accounted for 53% of fiscal 2003 gross revenues; Petrochemicals, 45% and Others, 2%.
Question 1. Explain the grand strategy of RIL

Source: http://www.ril.com/

Vertical integration refers to diversification into new production line to produce items required as inputs for other main products of the same company. This may be undertaken by an organisation with the purpose of either maintaining continuous flow or serving as a customer for outputs for marketing and selling the organisation products by opening its own sales and marketing division and showroom instead of selling through agents or distributors. Producing input items may be necessary in case of unreliable suppliers letting down the company production with erratic and irregular supply of inferior inputs; or to have total control over the input supply and output distribution also. Vertical integration is of two types:

- Backward integration strategy
- Forward integration strategy

Backward integration strategy

- Backward integration strategy refers to diversifying the business operations towards some of the raw material or inputs supply.

Forward integration strategy

- Forward integration strategy refers to diversifying business operations for marketing, sales and distribution of products and services and taking up those activities to bring the organisation closer to the ultimate customer.

Expansion through acquisitions and mergers

A company is to entry into a new business area through acquisition. It involves purchasing an established company's all facilities like plant and equipment, human resource and financial resource. Entry into new business area through internal new venturing, it means that starting a business from scratch; building facilities, purchasing equipment, recruiting personnel, operating and opening up distribution outlets.

- The company immediately gets the ownership and control over the acquired firm's factories, employees, technology, brand names and distribution network in this way expansion of business.

- The company can formulate suitable strategy and generate more revenues for expansion of business.
- If the industry already reached the stage of optimum capacity level or overcapacity level in the host country. This strategy helps the economy of the host country.

Retrenchment Strategy

- When an organisation decides to reduce its business operation by reducing the scope of customer groups or customer functions or alternative technologies with view to have better control for better performance, retrenchment strategies are accepted.
- In retrenchment strategy, unattractive and unwanted areas of business are sequenced gradually.
- It is a not matter of failure of business planning, rather well planned exercise to get rid of unprofitable parts of business which will help the organisation concentrate its total attention to the most profitable and promising areas of business only.
- In cases of temporary and partial setbacks, the enterprise can endeavor to cut back on its capital and revenue capital and revenue expenditure in terms of administrative blocks, replacement of worn-out machinery, advertising, R&D activities, employee welfare subsidies, community development projects, executive parks so on.
- The nature and timing of retrenchment are matters of enterprise and have to be carefully decided by management. It involves to enterprise may think of withdrawing from some marginal markets, withdrawal of some brands and sizes of products, withdrawal of even some slow moving products, winding up some branch offices, abolition of some executive positions and so on.
- An enterprise may resort to sale of some manufacturing facilities and individual product divisions which are drag on the enterprise resources. In this stage, enterprise may also seek retirement neither from the production or the marketing stage retrenchment.
- An enterprise also thinks of offering itself for take over by another more viable enterprise. As a last option an enterprise may seek liquidation which means that corporate death.

Combination Strategy

In changing business environment, an organisation may also find it beneficial to adopt a unique combination of stability, expansion and retrenchment indifferent levels related areas of business which depending on the business environment. In other words, combination strategy refers to the combination of the stability, expansion and retrenchment strategy in different levels of the organisation. It is possible to adopt a mix of above strategy which are to be suited particular situations.

2.7 THE DYNAMICS OF COMPETITIVE STRATEGY

- Strategic management thinking involves orientation of the enterprise's internal environment with the changes of the external environment in business operations.
- Competitive strategy evolves the company strengths and weakness, industries opportunities and threats like economic and technical which are based on the internal and external factors of the company. These are considered valuable tool for competitive strategy is formulated.
- Economic and technical component of the external environment are considered as the major factor that leading to new opportunities and closing threats to the business enterprise.
- Strength and weakness are the internal factors of the firm which are determine to competitive strategy in business world.
- Competitive strategy is analyzed and finds out the functional area like marketing, R&D, operations, etc. these are superiority over the competitors.
- The opportunities arising from the external environment that are to be considered in the context of major strengths.
- Strategist is also play dominant and major roles in formulating the competitive strategy.

Figure 2.2: Context in which Competitive Strategy formulated

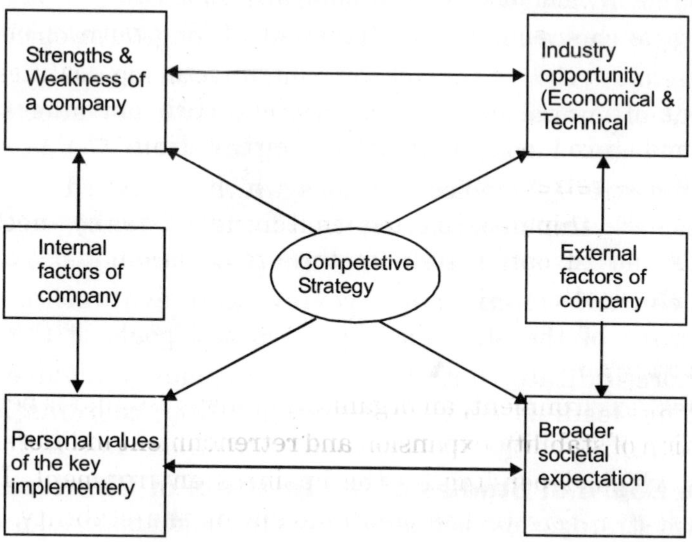

2.8 MEANING OF STRATEGIC MANAGEMENT

Strategic management is a stream of instructions, guidance, directions for decisions and actions with view to develop effective long term and short term planning of the organisation. Strategic management decisions help to organisation for accomplishment of goals and objectives of the business. Forecasting the strategic decisions would help the organisation to achieve its superior goal. Strategic management includes strategic analysis, strategy formulation, strategy implementation and strategic controlling and monitoring of all events of the organisation. Strategic decisions might to be to deploy resources in the organisation into new business opportunities. Strategy decisions normally representation of the environment analysis, value chain concept and analysis, integration, diversification, mergers and acquisitions, new product development, product redesigning, up gradation, strategies for marketing, technology, new customers, finance, geographic areas and entry into new markets. Strategic management decisions help to survival, growth and development of organisation.

Strategic management is defined as "The set of decisions and actions resulting in formulation, implementation of strategies designed to achieve the objectives and goals of an organisation". This definition reveals the following factors:

1. Determining the mission of the organisation which consists of broad statements about its purpose, philosophy and goals.
2. Developing a company profile which reflects internal environment conditions and capabilities of the organisation.
3. Assessment and appraisal of the external environments of the organisation in terms of growth, competitive and general contextual factors.
4. Analysis of strength, weakness, opportunity and threatens of the organisation.
5. Identifying the desired options of the organisation like uncovered possibilities are considered in the light of the company mission.
6. Set of strategic choice for the achievement of long term objectives and grand strategies.
7. Development of annual/short term objectives with out affecting of long-term objectives and grand objectives of the organisation.
8. Implementing strategic choice decisions which are based on budget resource allocations and emphasizing the matching of tasks, people, structure, technologies and reward system of the organisation.
9. Strategic control, monitoring, review and evaluation represent the accomplishment of the strategic objectives and goals of the organisation.

All these factors indicate that strategic management involves the planning, directing, actuating, leading, communication, staffing, coordination, motivation, budgeting and controlling of the strategy related decisions and actions of business.

According to Board of Studies of the Institute of Chartered Accountants of India: The term strategic management refers to the managerial process a strategic vision, setting objectives, crafting a strategy, implementing and executing the strategy, and then overtimes initiating whatever corrective adjustments in the vision, objectives, strategy, and execution are deemed appropriate.

Framework of strategic Management

Exhibit 2.2: Framework of Strategic Management

Stage one	Where are we now? (Beginning)
Stage two	Where are we want to be? (Ends)
Stage three	How might we get there? (Means)
Stage four	Which way is best (Evaluation)
Stage five	How can we ensure arrival? (Control)

Stage One

- Stage one is the starting point of strategic planning. It involves the situational analysis of the firm in the environment context.
- Firms find out its relative market position, corporate image, its strengths and weakness and also environmental threats and opportunities.

Stage Two

- Second stage is the important stage of strategy framework of the firm.
- It involves the goal settings for the firm and after it finalised its vision and mission.
- A strategic vision is a road map of the firm's future, it specific focus on technology and customer, geographic and product markets to be pursued.
- It capabilities to plans and develop and design the suitable goal and objectives of the firm.
- Firm's mission clearly indicates that what customers it serves, what need it satisfies, and what type of product it offers to ultimate users.

Stage Three

- It deals with the various strategic alternatives find outs in firm environment.

Stage Four

- During this stage, out of all alternatives generated in the earlier stage of the organisation selects the best suitable alternative in line with its SWOT analysis.

Stage Five

- This stage involves the implementation and control stage of a suitable strategy of organisation.
- It again involves the organisation continuously does situational analysis and repeat the stages again in business enterprise.

Importance of Strategic Management

- It provides the major framework for all the major business decisions of an organisation like decisions on businesses, products and markets, manufacturing facilities, investment and organisational structures.
- It provides alternative strategic choice to business enterprise.
- To find out the strengths and opportunities in business.
- To determine the mission and vision of the firm.
- To determine the core competencies and competitive advantages for an enterprise its survival and growth.
- It ensure to good future for the firm.
- It seeks to prepare the corporation to face the future and even shape the future in its favor, and working into the environment and shaping it, instead of getting carried away by its turbulence or uncertainties.
- It determines the environmental unconditional and make suitable business strategy to frame in critical environment of the firm.
- The success of the firms depend on the strategic management and its factors like the vision, insight, experience, quality of judgment and the perfection of methods and measures of the firm.
- Strategy formulation, implementation and control and changes to the environment which requires that strongest strategic policy for survival, growth and development of the entity.
- It is searching for tool, techniques for converting of loss into winning position of the organisation.

Characteristic/Nature of Strategic Planning

- **It is an entrepreneurial Function**

  This function is related to overall business activities like manage and administration of the organisation. It is an implication of the strategic management which is felt by the results is positive or negative of the organisation.

- **Changing orientations**

  According to Anthong Pats that "strategic management is a process having to do with the formulation of long range strategy and grand strategic policy type plans that change the character direction of the organisation".

- **Long term nature**

  Generally a strategic management involves long-term prospective. Strategic management requires considerable commitment and expertise gained out of the experiences of several experts in the field from within and outside the organisation for long-term without affecting the short term planning goal with sense future business prophecy.

- **It is an Intellectual process**

  Intellectual process involves analytical thinking, formations of the set of decisions, selection of long-term strategy for effective utilization of scarce available resource in which without affecting the internal and external environment of the organisation. Strategy implementation and strategy monitoring and controlling is an intellectual process. The executives are utilized well efficient skills for judgment of the project. And they study about all areas of the project like policies, strategic decisions, programmed resource, business environment etc., to integrate them into suitable for achieving the objectives of the company/organisation/firm.

- **Continuous process**

  Strategic management is not a one-time exercise and it is a dynamic process in the organisation. It requires special skills for implementation of strategies and to know the different policies of the organisation for analysis, interpretation of strength, weakness, opportunity, and threaten from the internal and external environment. One cannot be expected at any time to set a time table. Strategic management should always ensure to proper changes in the organisation.

Scope of Strategic Management

Strategic management as a process is concerned with directing the efforts of human activities at all levels and all types establishment-whether they are profit making or service rendering organisation, whether they are big or small, whether government or private sectors. The scope of strategic management is quite broad and includes within its fold almost all aspects of business operations. How ever the following are included in it:

- **Subject matter of management**

  Strategic management includes strategy analysis, its choice, its formulation, its implementation, and control.

- **Functional areas of strategic management**

Functional areas of strategic management issues are listed below:

1. Strategic and business policy–it includes strategy, concepts, characteristic, functions, business policy and types of business policy.
2. Strategic management overview–it includes strategic management nature and scope, characteristics, process, components and limitations.

3. Strategic environment–it includes micro, macro, internal and external environment–political, social, cultural, technological, legal, demography, and demand and competitive environment.
4. Types of strategy–it includes grand strategy, stability strategy, expansion strategy, retrenchment strategy, and combination strategy.
5. Value chain concept and analysis–it includes organisational analysis, process of organisational analysis, company profile analysis, industry analysis, strategic analysis and choice.
6. Integration, diversification, mergers and acquisitions–it includes horizontal integration, vertical integration, factors influence to diversification, horizontal and vertical merger strategy.
7. Strategic change management–it includes strategic change, power and conflict.
8. Training strategy–it includes strategic use of marketing variables, product development strategy, marketing mix strategy, customer and channel strategy.
9. Implementation and control–it includes corporate culture, leadership, culture guiding and evaluating strategy
10. Current issue of strategic management–it includes strategic audit and managing technology.

- **Strategic management is an interdisciplinary Approach**

  For the correct application of the strategic management to study of commerce, science, economics, statistics, psychology, and mathematics is very essentials.

2.9 DIMENSIONS OF STRATEGIC DECISIONS

Decision making is a managerial process and important function of selecting a particular course of action out of several alternatives courses for the purpose of achievement of the organisational goals. Decisions are programmed and non programmed decisions. They may be major or minor. Strategic decisions dimensions are listed below:

- **Top Management Decisions are based on the strategic issues**

  Strategic decisions consist of several areas of organisation like marketing, production, finance, accounting, human resource management and research and development operations. Top management involves in decision making is an obvious factor for business activities of the organisation. Only at this level is for understanding and anticipating broad analysis, implication and ramification and power to authorize the resource allocations necessary for implementation of strategic issues.

- **Strategic Issues Involve the Allocation of Huge Amount of Organisation Resource**

  Strategic decisions involved substantial resource allocation for functional department of the organisation. Money, material, men, machine, method and markets are essential resource of the business. These are secured internally and externally from the organisation's environment.

- **Strategic Issues are Likely to Make a Significant Role on the Long Term Prosperity, Survival and Growth of the Organisation**
  The strategic decisions are committed the organisation for a long period of time typically for five years or more. Once an organisation has been committed itself to particular strategic options. It has developed competitive image and advantages are usually tied to committed strategy, therefore, organisation become known in certain markets, for certain products with certain characteristic. Therefore strategic decisions have enduring effects on organisation for positive or negative results performance oriented.
- **Strategic Issues are Future Oriented**
  Strategic decisions are based on future forecast made by the strategic manager of the organisation. Special importance is on developing projections which will enable the organisation to select the most promising options. In the complex and competitive free environment has build up a successful organisation in most proactive stance toward changes.
- **Strategic decisions usually have Major Multifunctional or Multi-busines Consequence**
  A strategy decision is co-ordinative decisions like customer mix, competitive emphasis or organisational structure which necessarily involve a number of organisation's business unit, functions, divisions, programme units. These areas will be affected by allocation and reallocation of responsibilities and resource related to the functional department decisions.
- **Strategic Decisions Consider external environmental Factors of the Organisation's**
  All business organisation exists in an open market system. Strategic manager has beyond their control of the external environmental factors like legal, economic, cultural and competitive force. Therefore, the strategic manager is to accomplishment of organisation objectives and goal in it future competitive situations. The strategic manager look beyond the limits of organisation's own operations and considers the competitors, customers, suppliers, creditors, government and labor.

2.10 TASKS IN STRATEGIC MANAGEMENT

Strategy formulation and implementation process consists of five interrelated managerial tasks as are outlined:

Setting Vision and Mission

- It is the first important task in strategic management.
- Strategic vision and mission formulation is the basic stage of the company.

- It determines long term direction towards the its operations like products and services, technology and quality etc,
- It decides what kind of enterprise the company, it also is trying to become and infuse the organisation with a sense of purposeful action oriented in future.

Setting Objectives

- Setting objectives involves to the converting the strategic vision and mission into specific performance outcome for the company to achieve it.

Crafting strategy

- Crafting the strategy is to achieve the desire and expected outcomes in the company.

Implementation

- Implementation and execution on suitable strategy is efficiently and for effectively implementation of project in an organisation

Control and Evaluation

Control and evaluation performance and initiating corrective adjustments are relating in terms of vision, long-term direction, objectives, goals, strategy execution in light of actual experience, changing conditions, new ideas, and new opportunities for business enterprise.

2.11 STRATEGIC MANAGEMENT MODEL

Strategic management model provides three major functions as listed below:

- It provides a visual representation of the major components of the entire strategic management process. This model also show the how the components are related and how they are related throughout the process.
- This model provides the general over view of the strategic management process of the organisation.
- This model recommends the strategy formulation, implementation and control, monitor, guide and evaluation of the organisation objectives.
- It is the best be studied and applied using a model.
- This model widely accepted and is comprehensive.
- It's identifying the vision, mission, objectives, strategic analysis and its choice for each goal.
- This process is dynamic and continuous
- It determines the changes of the organisation.
- It defines the strategy formulation, implementation, and evaluation activities should be performed on a continual basis, not just at the end of the year or semi annually.
- Strategic management process never really ends in real time.

- It involves many organisations conduct formal meeting semi annually to discuss and update the firm's vision/mission, opportunities/threats, strengths/ weakness, strategies, objectives, policies, and performance .
- For management process, good communication and feedback are needed to firm in order to ensure accountability in firm business.
- It is formal in larger and well established organisations refers to that participants responsibilities, authority, duties, and approach are specified.
- This model usually associated with the cost, comprehensiveness, accuracy and success of planning across all types and sizes of organisation.

LIMITATION OF THE STRATEGIC COMPONENTS MODEL

Limitations are important to understand the strategic management components model. Major limitations are as follows:

- The model is holistic
- The model is analytical
- The model is nonpolitical

Holistic

- The strategic management process involves strategy formulation, implementation and control. It is unrealistic because of potential tendency to minimize difficulties of the implementation of the strategy. In the following cases:
- Manager face greater risk, if planning may be inflexible.
- Holistic approach is too difficult to development of strategies. It appears in superior of the organisation,

Analytic

Strategic management model generally explains the logical or analytical process in many businesses actually use in their strategic activities. However, it does not describe the procedure and practice or routines necessary carry out each process.

Non-Political

It is the third limitation of the strategic management model. The strategic management largely devoid of subjective assessments, biased interpretations, human errors, self serving voting by individual managers, intuitive decision making, favoritism and other forms of political activity.

2.12 VISION, MISSION AND OBJECTIVES

The Vision

According to Board of Studies of the Institute of Chartered Accountants of India

A strategic vision is a road map of a company's future - providing specifics about technology and customer focus, the geographic an product markets to be pursued, the capabilities it plans to develop, and the kind of company that management is trying to create. We shall discuss the vision of Cadbury.

Case - 2.4: Cadbury's Vision

Cadbury's world-wide vision is "Working together to create brands that people love." Cadbury has successfully done this for over 200 years. This success has been built upon understanding the needs of our consumers, customers and colleagues and by operating to a clearly defined set of values.

But around us, the world changes. We want to recognise this as well as ensure the continuation of our own heritage.

Our strategy is to:

Create robust and sustainable regional positions in our core categories of confectionery and beverages through organic growth, acquisition and disposal.

We will achieve this by managing for value. Our managing for value process incorporates:

- setting stretching financial objectives
- adopting value-based management for major strategic and operational decisions and business systems
- creating an outstanding leadership capability within our management
- sharpening our company culture to reflect accountability, aggressiveness and adaptability
- aligning our management rewards structure with the interests of our shareowners.

In India, Cadbury India has defined its vision as "Life full of Cadbury, Cadbury full of life"

This means:

- Broadening our consumer appeal and extending our reach to newer markets
- Sustained growth of our market share through aggressive product development
- Striving for international quality in our products and processes
- Focussing on cost competitiveness, productivity and innovative utilization of assets
- Energising and developing our people

Questions

1. Explain the vision of Cadbury India limited

Source: cadbaryindialimited

How can you lead if you do not know where are you going?

George Newman, the Conference Board

Management's job is not see the company as it is .... but as it can become.

John W Teets, CEO, Greyhound Corporation

Elements of a Strategy Vision

Important strategy vision elements are as outlined:

- The mission statement defines one of the roles the organisation that special identify the business interest and path for growth and development.

- Strategy vision defines the organisations strategies path, technologies, customer groups and competitive scenario and the activities it performs in terms of well.
- Nature of technology, productivity, innovative is an important to define an organisation business.
- Mission and vision statements are crisply to be defined by organisation.
- Organisation should prepare future for its survival, growth and profitability.
- Vision and mission statement prepared and responsible by chief executive of the organisation.
- Vision and mission statements are clearly direction of the organisation future.

Development of Strategic Vision

Strategic management process is effective when strategy making begins with a vision of the organisation or company that needs to head vision. It is a noteworthy exercise in terms of thinking carefully about their objectives, goals and policies how to successfully. It involves selecting the market areas in which to participate, putting the organisation on strategic path and attempted to commit to follow that path i.e. strategic vision.

- The entrepreneurial challenge in developing a strategic vision is to think creatively about how to prepare a company for the future about products, services and technology.
- It involves forming a strategic vision is an exercise in intelligent entrepreneurship.
- It focuses on need to change direction not in order to survive apart from in order to maintain their success.
- Well articulated strategic visions develop enthusiasm for the course management has charted and engages members of the organisation.
- It clearly and crisply illuminates the direction in that organisation is headed.

Mission

Organisation/company mission statement is the basic issue point of the strategic management. Organisation/ company mission will guide future execution policies and objectives. It sets the policies and objectives which are formulated for execution of policies and objectives of business organisation. The mission statement contains the business philosophy of strategic decision makers, a definition of the organisation/ company's business, a statement of the major goals of the organisation/company. The organisation/company mission explains the product, market, and technological areas of the business.

According to Board of Studies of the Institute of Chartered Accountants of India

A company's mission statement is typically focused on its presents business scope – "who we are and what we do", mission statements broadly describe an organisation present capabilities, customer focus, activities and business makeup.

Mission According to Thomson Watson, Jr., former chairman of IBM

"The basic philosophy, spirit, and drive of an organisational have far more to do with its relative achievements than technological or economic resources, organisational structure, innovation and timing. It also expresses the core values and beliefs of the firm".

2.13 THE NEED FOR EXPLICIT MISSION OF ORGANISATION

Defining organisation mission is time consuming, tedious and not required by any external body like experts. The organisation mission including few specific directives, which are broadly outlined or implied objectives and strategies traits, it is statement of attitude, outlook and orientation of the organisation rather than of details and measurable targets in the business.

King and Cleland designed the organisation mission as listed below:

- To ensure unanimity of purpose within the organisation
- To provide a basis for motivating the use of the organisation's resource.
- To develop a basis for motivating the use organisation's resources.
- To establish a general tone or organisational climate, for instance, to suggest business like operation,
- To serve as a focal point for those who can identify with the organisations purpose and direction, land to deter those who cannot from participating further in the organisation's activities.
- To facilitates the transaction of objectives and goals into a work structure involving the assignment of tasks to responsible elements within the organisations,
- To specify organisational purposes and the translation of these purposes into goals in such a way that cost, time, and performance parameters can be assessed and controlled.

Fundamental Elements of Mission

Fundamental elements are as follows:

- A general belief that the product or service which can provide benefits at least equal to its price.
- A general belief that the product or service which can satisfy a customer needs.
- Using of the technology for production which will provide a product or service at a quality and cost competitive to customer.
- Hard work and the better interaction of the organisation employees that help for survival, growth and profitable also to the organisation.
- Business philosophy of the management will also create in a favorable public image and will provide financial and psychological rewards from those willing to invest their labor, money and helping organisation towards success
- The organisation's promoters self –concept in the business that can be communicated to and adopted by employees and stockholders.

Components of Mission Statement

They are three components of a mission statement, they are as listed below:

- Specification of the basic product or service of the organisation.
- Primary market for the goods and service of the organisation.
- Principal technology has adopted for production or distribution of goods and service of the organisation.

What is our mission? And what business are we in?

Peter Drucker and Theodore Levitt are discussed the what is our mission and what business are we in?. It emphasis on business planning and it clearly clarify the corporate mission and define accurately the business in the firm that can be engaged operation in. They are raising some questions as listed below:

- What is company Mission?
- What is company ultimate purpose?
- What do company want become?
- What kind of growth do companies seek?
- Do you understand company business correctly and define it accurately in its macro connotation?
- Do you know company customers?
- What human need you intend to serve through company offer?
- What brings us to this particular business?
- What would be the nature of company business in the future?
- In what business would company like to be in, in the future?

The corporate mission is an expression of the growth, survival, of the firm. It is a grand design about the company's future. It is relating with common purpose that relating to the entire firm.

2.14 DEFINING ORGANISATION MISSION

Defining organisation mission as listed below:

- Identification
- Understanding
- Reconciliation and priorities
- Co-ordination with other elements

Identification

Identification refers to identification of core business environment functions like internal factors and external factors of the organisation. Every business organisation faces a slightly different set of claimants, who vary numbers, size, influence, and importance. These are defining in organisation in terms of mission, strategic executives and mangers must identify all claimant groups and weight their realties to implement and get to success.

Understanding

Understanding refers to an organisation has understand of their employees and outsiders like suppliers, distributors, competitors, customers, general public for creation of good relationship to accomplishment of goals and objectives of the organisation. Strategic decision makers should understand the core demands of each group. Then strategic mangers will to make decisions and able to appreciate their concerns and initiates which are clearly defined in actions.

Reconciliation and priorities

Reconciliation and priorities refers to the concerns of various claimants that can be created conflict, for instance; the priorities for claims of government, creditors and stockholders. Therefore, these cases claims must be reconciled; to achieve unified approach by strategic managers have must define a mission that resolves the competing conflicting and contradictory claims. Objectives and strategies are clearly focused to be mission statements of the organisation which must display a single-minded to achieve though multidimensional approach to business aims.

Co-ordination with other elements

Co-ordination refers to core elements of the strategy makers, strategy makers can be Co-ordinated among the people who have served their best service to the organisation. Co-ordination helps to strategy makers for formulation of strategy, implementation, Controlling, monitoring and evaluating of the organisation superior goals. Organisation strategy basic requirement is that the co-ordination among the functional department's human resource of the organisation. Strategy makers must concentration and interaction of external people of the organisation.

Understanding Mission and Purpose

Strategist should understand the mission and purpose of the organisation. Mission is a statement which clearly defines the role of the organisation and its responsibility towards the society. Organisation have some purpose, that is useful for strives in business. Purpose is anything which an organisation strives for. It is business policy; both terms are either used jointly or individual. Mission specifically refers to the needs of the society apart from the purpose relates to what the organisation strives to achieve in order to fulfill its mission to the society.

Objectives and Goals

- Objectives should define clearly the organisation's relationship with its environment.
- Objectives should facilitate towards the accomplishment of mission and vision.
- It should provide the basis for strategic decision making.
- It should be provided standards for performance appraisal.
- It can be understandable.
- It can be concrete and specific.
- It can be related to a time frame.

- It can be measurable and controllable.
- It should be challenging in nature.
- Different type's objectives correlated with each other.
- It can be set within constraints.

Case 2.5: Objectives of IOCL

Objectives

To serve the national interests in the oil and related sectors in accordance and consistent with government policies.

To ensure and maintain continuous and smooth supplies of petroleum products by way of crude refining, transportation and marketing activities and to provide appropriate assistance to the consumer to conserve and use petroleum products efficiently.

To earn a reasonable rate of interest on investment.

To work towards the achievement of self-sufficiency in the field of oil refining by setting up adequate capacity and to build up expertise in laying of crude and petroleum product pipelines.

To create a strong research and development base in the field of oil refining and stimulate the development of new product formulations with a view to minimise/eliminate their imports and to have next generation products.

To maximise utilisation of the existing facilities in order to improve efficiency and increase productivity.

To optimise utilisation of its refining capacity and maximise distillate yield from refining of crude to minimise foreign exchange outgo.

To minimise fuel consumption in refineries and stock losses in marketing operations to effect energy conservation.

To further enhance distribution network for providing assured service to customers throughout the country through expansion of reseller network as per marketing plan/Government approval.

To avail of all viable opportunities, both national and global, arising out of the liberalisation policies being pursued by the Government of India.

To achieve higher growth through integration, mergers, acquisitions and diversification by harnessing new business opportunities like petrochemicals, power, lube business, consultancy abroad and exploration & production.

Obligations

Towards customers and dealers: To provide prompt, courteous and efficient service and quality products at fair and reasonable prices.

Towards suppliers: To ensure prompt dealings with integrity, impartiality and courtesy and promote ancillary industries.

Towards employeesDevelop their capability and advancement through appropriate training and career planning.

Expeditious redressal of grievances: Fair dealings with recognised representatives of employees in pursuance of healthy trade union practice and sound personnel policies.

Towards community: To develop techno-economically viable and environment-friendly products for the benefit of the people.

To encourage progressive indigenous manufacture of products and materials so as to substitute imports.

To ensure safety in operations and highest standards of environment protection in its manufacturing plants and townships by taking suitable and effective measures.

Towards Defence Services: To maintain adequate supplies to Defence Services during normal and emergency situations as per their requirement at different locations.

Financial Objectives: To ensure adequate return on the capital employed and maintain a reasonable annual Dividend on its equity capital.

To ensure maximum economy in expenditure.

To manage and operate the facilities in an efficient manner so as to generate adequate internal resources to meet revenue cost and requirements for project investment, without budgetary support.

To develop long-term corporate plans to provide for adequate growth of the activities of the Corporation.

To endeavour to reduce the cost of production of petroleum products by means of systematic cost control measures.

To endeavour to complete all planned projects within the stipulated time and cost estimates

Questions

1. Explain the objectives of iocl

Source: IOCL

2.15 STRATEGIC LEVELS IN ORGANISATION

There are three levels in strategic management. They are as outlined:

- Corporate Level Strategic Management
- Business Level Strategic Management
- Functional Level Strategic Management

Role of Mangers at Various Levels

In most sophisticated organisations, one can find two types of managers.

- General Manager
- Functional Manager

General Manager: General Manager is individual who bears the responsibility for the overall performance of the organisation. He has the responsible of the survival, growth and development of the organisation. He has guide and monitoring the performance of the organisation with effective utilization of scarce and available resource.

Functional Manager: Functional Manager is an individual who bear responsibility for specific business functions like human resource development, purchasing, production, customer service, sales, finance and accounting, research and development. In this case authority and responsibilities confined each functional manager. Strategic managers oversee and manage the overall activities with in the organisation. This responsibility has puts unique position of the strategic manger in the organisation which being able to direct the organisation in a strategic sense.

A typical multi-business company has three levels of management as listed below:

- The corporate level
- The business level
- Functional level

General managers are found at the first two of these levels, but their strategic roles are different which depending on their sphere of responsibility. Functional managers too have a strategic role, though of a different kind, now we shall look at each of the three levels and strategic roles assigned to managers within them.

Exhibit 2.3: In Focus Managerial Style

Managerial functioning involves taking decisions, which reflect in styles in the realm of human behavioural styles. The more a manager understands these behavioural styles, higher is the facilitation in the exercise of decision-making.

According to the author, managerial competence is increased when other possibilities for behaviour are made available to managers, and has worked on 10 competencies for managers using the Enneagram framework.

The 10 competencies are: leadership, strategy-building abilities, decision-making skills, change management skills, delegation skills, communication skills, negotiation, influencing ability and use of power, conflict management skills and teamwork.

As per the experience of the author, the outcome from the Enneagram was more effective than the MBTI (Myers Briggs Type Indicator), although the MBTI is easier to administer and interpret.

According to the Enneagram, one passion dominates the behaviour of each individual. It is based on the person's passions or vice. Because the focus is on negative passions, it offers a way to transform a person.

The types are perfectionist, helper, achiever, artist, observer, trouble-shooter, optimist, boss and the mediator.

The author goes on to discuss the nine flaws and the strengths:

Ones: When ones are optimistic and enthusiastic about future, they approach persons and situations without suspicion. They focus on the bright side of life. Perfectionist attitude and the TQM managerial style becomes strength for them.

Twos: When Twos strive to express themselves as very empathetic persons, they become altruistic and their customer service style becomes strength.

Threes: When threes take on a greater loyalty to their whole group then their achievement orientation and MBO style becomes their strength.

Fours: When fours make an effort to counteract disorder and error in the pursuit of perfection they become hard working and are able to overcome their moodiness, and their innovative style becomes strength for them.

Fives: When fives take pride in being strong persons, they gravitate naturally to power and when they become involved with other persons, their strategic management becomes strength.

Sixes: When sixes are seldom upset by inner conflicts, they make excellent reconcilers. When they overcome their worries, their bureaucratic style is an advantage and they are participative managers.

Sevens: When sevens become more observant and empathetic, and accept pain, failures and hard work, their optimistic style becomes an asset for them.

Eights: When eights seek out people who need their help, their autocratic style becomes strength.

Nines: When nines set objectives for themselves and others take on the image of being efficient persons, then their participative style becomes an asset for them.

The author states that an understanding of Enneagram type helps one to understand managerial style and other managers' styles. This identification is also a source of comfort because it shows that one is not alone in this particular managerial style.

The book is full of analytical descriptions and illustrations of managerial styles and is written in an understandable and formal style.

However, according to the reviewer, whether it is MBTI or Enneagram, the questionnaire administering method of determining managerial styles has a lot of limitations.

On the contrary, an ideal way to develop managers should be to make them understand the various styles (analytically), appreciate them in their own merits and finally, try to develop in them skills/ability of adopting the appropriate style, depending on the particular or contextual need, rather than prescribing ideal percentile patterns, which may result as products of immaturity.

Source: The Hindu, dated 2002/07/08

Corporate Level

The corporate level of strategic management consists of the chief executive officers/ president/chairman, the board of directors, senior executives, corporate staff and administrative officers. They are the responsible for the apex for decision making within the organisation. The CEO is the main general manager at this level. His or her strategic role is to overlook the development of the strategic issues for decisions in the organisation. Typically, this role involves defining the mission and goals of the organisation, it determining organisation business it should be in allocating resource among the different organisation functions and providing leadership for the rest of the organisation.

Business Level

In multi–business organisation, the business level consists of the business and corporate managers and their support staff. In a single industry company, the business and corporate levels are very important and equal. Business level is self-contained and has its own functional departments like as finance, production, purchase, marketing and human resource departments.

The main strategic managers at the business level are the heads of the functional departments. Their strategic role is to translate general statements, mission and vision of the business decision strategies for organisation. Business level managers are concerned with strategies which are specific to a particular business.

Functional Level

Functional managers bear responsibility for the specific business functions like human resource development, manufacturing, production, marketing, accounting and finance, research, and development departments' functions. Functional level strategies are playing significant role in strategic decisions and buildup their own responsibility to develop functional strategies in manufacturing, marketing, R&D, and so on. This help to fulfill the strategic objectives that set by business and corporate level general managers. It is important for general managers to listen and develop to strategies at competitive environment of business. An equal responsibility of the managers at the functional level involves strategy implementation in terms of the execution of corporate and business level decisions.

CHARACTERISTIC OF STRATEGIC MANAGEMENT DECISIONS AT DIFFERENT LEVELS

Characteristic of Strategic Management Decisions at Corporate Level

- Corporate level decisions tend to be value oriented, conceptual, and less concrete than those at the business or function level of strategy formulation and implementation.
- Corporate level decisions are also characterized by greater risk, cost and profit potential, as well as by longer time planning and greater needs for flexibility.
- These characteristics are logical consequences of the more far-reaching futuristic, innovative and pervasive nature of corporate–level activity.
- Instance of corporate level decisions include the level of choice of business, dividend policies, source of long term financing and priorities for growth.

Characteristic of Strategic Management Decisions at Functional Level

- Functional level decisions principally involve action–oriented operational issues.
- These decisions are made periodically and lead directly implementation of some part of the overall strategy formulated at the corporate and business levels
- Functional level decisions are relating short range and involve low risk and modest costs because they are dependent an available resources.
- Functional decisions usually determined actions requiring minimal organisation wide co-operations.

- Functional level decisions are usually concrete and quantifiable; they receive critical attention even though their comparative profit potential is low.
- Functional level decisions include generic versus brand name labelling, basic versus applied R&D, high versus low inventory levels, general versus specific purpose production equipment, and close versus loose supervision.

Characteristic of Strategic Management Decisions at Business Level

- Bridging corporate and functional level decisions are those made at the business level
- Business level decisions are less costly risky, and potentially profitable than corporate level decisions, but they are more costly, risky, and potentially profitable than functional level decisions.
- Business level decisions involve plant location, marketing segmentation and geographic coverage and distribution channels.

BENEFITS OF STRATEGIC MANAGEMENT

- The strategic management approach emphasizes interaction by managers at all levels of the organisation at hierarchy in planning and implementation.
- Strategies formulation activities should enhance the problem prevention capabilities of the organisation. As a result of encouraging and rewarding subordinates attention to planning considerations, executives are aided in monitoring and forecasting responsibilities by workers who are alerted to needs of strategic planning.
- Every strategic plans are attached the employee motivation and morale should improve in terms of employees better productivity and reward relationship.
- Gaps and overlaps in activities among diverse individuals and groups should be reduced as participation in strategy formulation.
- Resistance to change should be reduced. The required participation helps eliminate the uncertainty associated with the change, which is at the root of most resistance.

RISKS OF STRATEGIC MANAGEMENT

- Strategic management is relatively recognized that the strategic management process is costly in terms of time invested by the chief executive of the organisation
- If the formulators of strategy are not intimately involved in implementation, individual responsibility for input to the decision process and subsequent conclusions can be avoid.
- Strategies must be trained to anticipate, minimize or constructively respond when participating subordinated become disappointed over unattained expectations.

CHAPTER **3**

Strategic Analysis

Contents

- Strategic Analysis
- Issues to consider for strategic analysis
- Situational Analysis
- The methods of industry and competitive analysis
- Strategic groups
- Swot analysis
- Swot analysis of Indian dairy industry

Learning Objectives

- know the importance of strategic analysis in the formulation of strategy
- Learn competitive analysis methods in business organization
- Describe the SWOT and TOWS analysis
- Understand different methods used in portfolio analysis

"Analysis is the critical starting point of strategic thinking"

Kenichi Ohmae

"If you're not faster than your competitor, you're in a tenuous position, and if you're only half as fast, you're terminal"

George Salk

"The idea is to concentrate our strength against our competitor's relative weakness"

Bruce Henderson

3.1 INTRODUCTION

In this chapter, we shall discuss about the strategic analysis and its tools, major issues consider for strategic analysis, situational analysis, the methods of industry and competitive analysis, the concept of strategic groups, swot analysis and portfolio analysis. Strategic management process includes a set of managerial decisions and actions which determined the long-term planning and effective performance of superior objectives and goals of the organization. It involves important aspects like setting the organization mission, company or organization profile, external environment, operating industry, multinational analysis, developing objectives, development of strategic analysis and choice and implementing the strategies, to accomplishment of the long term objectives and short-term objectives and finally control, monitor, guide and evaluation of organization objectives.

3.2 STRATEGIC ANALYSIS

SWOT is the heart of Strategic Analysis. SWOT analysis is the process of carefully inspecting the business and its environment through the various dimensions like Strengths, Weaknesses, Opportunities, and Threats. Strengths are referred to the company's core competencies, and it includes proprietary technology, skills, resources, market position, patents, and others. These are analyzing the strength of businesses' position and understanding the important external factors that may influence that to company's position.

Strategy formulation is not a task in which strategic managers can be getting by opinions, good instincts, and creative thinking from the strategic managers in the company. Strategic analysis solidly based on the company's internal and external environment situation.

- Industry and competitive conditions
- A company's core competitive capabilities, resources, internal strengths and weakness and market situations of the company.

These are the most important situational considerations in strategic analysis. The process of company's strategic analysis will be assisted by the pest analysis, scenario analysis, five forces analysis, market segmentation, and directional policy matrix, competitor analysis, critical successes factor analysis, swot analysis, strategic choice, and strategy implementation. These strategic analysis tools are discussed below:

- ***PEST Analysis:*** *It is* a technique for understanding the "environment" factors like political, economic, social and Technology in which a business operates
- ***Scenario Planning***: it is a technique that builds various plausible views of possible futures for a business
- ***Five Forces Analysis***: it is a technique for identifying the forces which affect the level of competition in an industry level and business level.
- ***Market Segmentation:*** It is a technique which seeks to identify similarities and differences between groups of customers or users of company's products and services.
- ***Directional Policy Matrix***: it is a technique which summarizes the competitive strength of a businesses operations in specific markets and specific nature of business in different markets.
- ***Competitor Analysis***: It is a wide range of techniques and analysis that seeks to summarise a businesses' overall competitive position in business level and industry level.
- ***Critical Success Factor Analysis***: it is a technique to identify those areas in which a business must outperform the competition in order to succeed in the market and business.
- ***SWOT Analysis***: it is a useful summary technique for summarizing the key issues arising from an assessment of a businesses "internal" position and "external" environmental influences to company.
- **Strategic Choice:** This process involves understanding the nature of stakeholder expectations along with identifying strategic options, and then evaluating and selecting strategic options in the business.
- **Strategy Implementation:** it is often the hardest part in strategic analysis. When a strategy has been analyzed and selected, this task is ready to translate it into organizational action.

3.3 ISSUES TO CONSIDER FOR STRATEGIC ANALYSIS

Strategy evolves over a period of time

- Different forces which are driven and constrain in company and that must be balanced in strategic decisions will be made by strategic managers in company.
- It is to be considering the possible implications of routine decisions in company environment.
- It is results of a series of small decisions are taken over an extended period of time in organization.

- An organization manager effort to increase the growth momentum which happens apart from the changing strategy in an business environment.

Balance

- The process of strategy formulation is often explained as one of the matching the internal core potential of the company with the utilization of opportunities.
- Strategic analysis is to involve a workable balance between diverse and conflicting considerations in organization.
- A strategic manager in organization has responsible to make decisions that are balancing the opportunities, influences, threats and constraints.
- Pressures in organization are driving towards a particular choice like entering a new market.
- The major constraints existed in organizations like existence of big competitor in the market.
- Strategic constraints will be producing and impact on organization in terms of changes in nature, degree, magnitude and its importance in organization.
- These mentioned issues are some extent to manage by strategic managers in company. Apart from the several issues are beyond the control of a manager in organization.

Exhibit 3.1: Balance

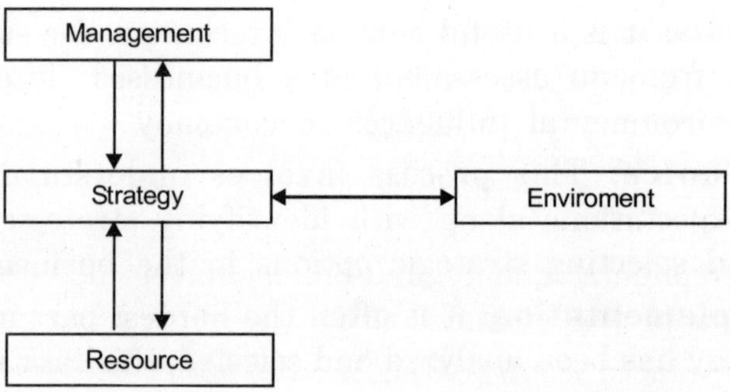

Risk

- Maintaining balance is very important to organization.
- The complexities and intermingling of variables in the environment which reduces the strategic balances in the organization. It will be major risk to strategic managers.
- Risk is uncertain and the business is to no exception.
- Risks are competitive markets, liberalization, globalizations , booms , recessions, technological advancement and inter company relationships are affecting business and pose risk at varying degree which depends on nature of problems.

- Strategic analysis is to identify potential imbalances or risks and assess their consequences.

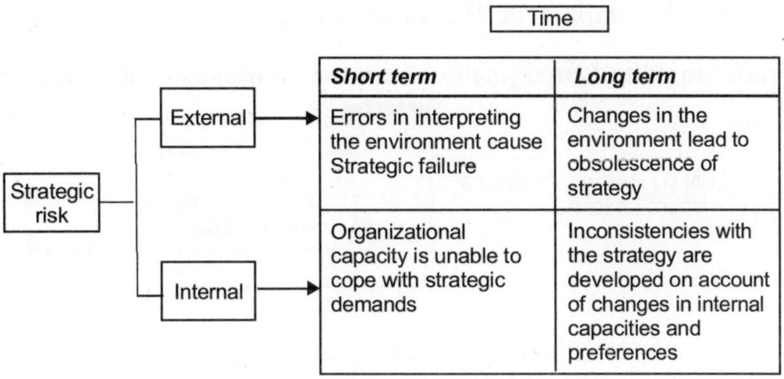

- External risks are inconsistencies between strategies and forces in the environment.
- Internal risks occur on account of forces either within the environment or are directly interacting with the organization on the programme basis (routine basis).

3.4 SITUATIONAL ANALYSIS

- Situational analysis is to influence to internal and external environment of the organization or company or business enterprises.
- Internal environment analysis of the strength and weakness of the firm.
- External environment analysis of the opportunities and threats of the firm.
- Macro environmental factors like demographic, economic, social values and life styles, governmental and regulation, technological factors. These things already discussed in the business environment chapter.
- The company's macro environment includes all the relevant factors and influences to firm within outside boundaries of the organization.
- Situational analysis is the analysis of the internal and external environment factors for making the decisions of the company towards its direction, objectives, strategy and its business model.
- Its watchful eye to see what is happening in the outside forces of the firm and make proper assessment of the opportunities and threats of the organization.
- Strategic managers are ready to scan external environment of the company and they must watch potential important environment forces and assess their impact and it influence to business , and will be adaptation in form of proper direction this purpose strategy is needed in business.

- Development of appropriate and suitable business strategy which based from the forces such as macro environment that will be shaped and impact immediately industry and competitive environment. These are almost certainly pertaining to the impact of the enterprise.

Figure 3.1: From Thinking Strategically about the Company's Situation to Choosing a Strategy

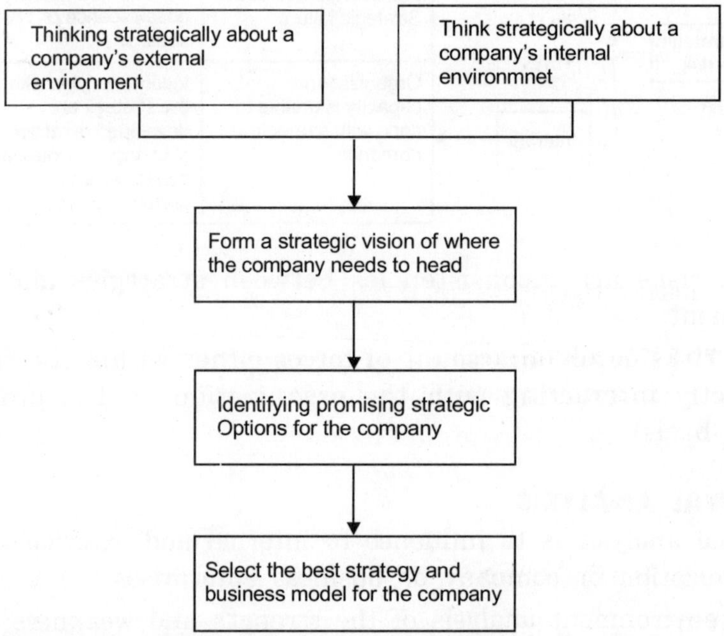

Figure 3.1 clearly outlined from think strategically about the company's situation to choosing a strategy:

- Before development of marketing strategy, it is very important to conduct some form analyses which are helpful to development of marketing strategy in the company.
- It should be essential part of business plan and should be reviewed over time in this way ensure its current situation in business.

  Many tasks are helpful to conduct an analysis of raw introduction of strategy and provide a checklist of the most important factors to take into account for development of marketing strategies in enterprise as listed below:

Product Situation

- Strategic consultant should know the current products and services which are offered by the company.

- Strategic manager should know the core products and subsidiary/ supporting / secondary products and services available in the market.
- Strategist observes that company's products and services that are meet the core clients' needs in market.

Competitive Situation

- Who are main competitors and what are the main competitive products and services in market?
- What are competitive advantages of competitors?
- What is the competitive level in industry?

Distribution Situation

- What are channels available for distribution of products and services?
- How are you getting your product to market?
- Do you need to go through different distributors or other intermediaries?

Opportunity and Issue Analysis

- What are current opportunities to company?
- What are future opportunities to company?
- What are the current threats to company?
- What are the futures challenges to company?
- How to faces challenges in company?

Framework of Strategic Analysis

- Framework of strategic analysis is the starting point of strategic management.
- Industries widely differ in terms of economic characteristics, competitive situations, and future profits prospects.
- Economic characters vary in industries according to factors like overall size and market growth rate.
- Pace of the technological change in industries.
- The geographical boundaries of market extended to worldwide.
- Increases the buyer and sellers of the similar products and differentiated,
- Economies scales helps to industries to face cutthroat competition in industry.
- Different types of distribution channels which accessed and used by buyers and industries.
- Industries competition focuses on the best competitive prices for the products and services which are available very competitive price to customers.

Figure 3.2: Framework of Strategic Analysis

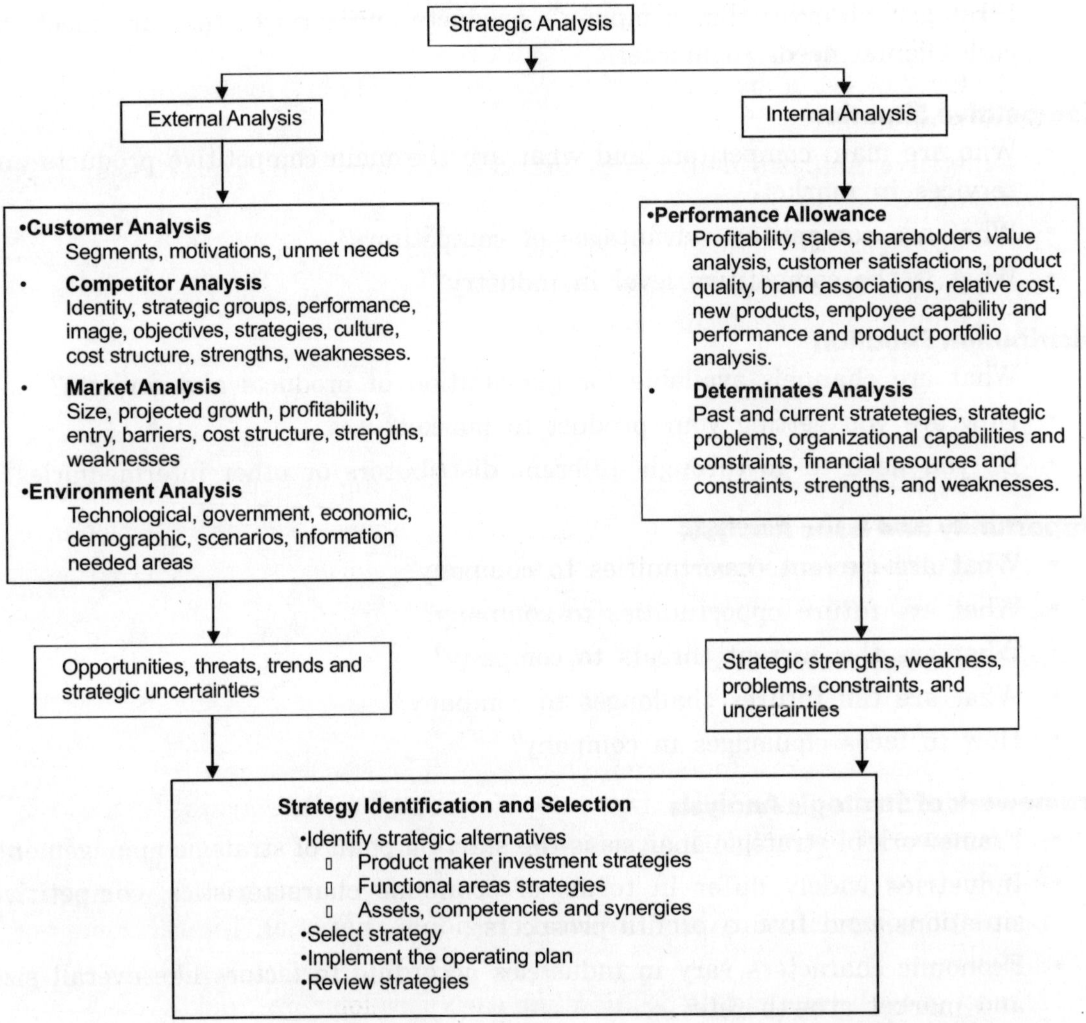

- Industries offer new product features and new performance to customers.
- Strategy frameworks help to create brand reputation in the market.
- It creates challenges and smoothly and cooperation with company and its supplies and customers.
- Competitive situation innovation of new products and services in different market in the world.

3.5 THE METHODS OF INDUSTRY AND COMPETITIVE ANALYSIS

Industry analysis begins with a definition of products and markets, skills and competitors contained within the industry, followed by industry structural analysis, and concluded with the identification of the key success factors for the industry. The methods of industry and competitive analysis are listed below:

- Industry and competitive analysis will be done using a set of concepts, and techniques.
- Industry can set a fix and a clear key traits industry identifying different drivers of industry.
- Competitive analysis determines market positions and strategies of rival companies.
- Key success of the industry is its profit outlook.
- Industry and its competitive analysis provides a route for thinking strategically about industries overall situation and drawing conclusions which are relating about whether industry represents an attractive investment for company funds.
- It is examining a company's business in the context of internal and external environment.
- Industry and competitive analysis aims at developing insight in several issues.
- It is to know the intensity of competition, to analyze the degree of change.

Analyzing of these issues have build and understanding of a enterprise environment and form industry and competitive analysis issues are outlined:

Dominant Economic Features of the Industry

Industry is significantly different from their basic character and structure. Industry and competitive analysis have overview of the industry's and its firm's dominant economic features. Industry is "a group of firms whose products have same and similar attributes such that they compete for the same buyers". Dominant economic features of the industry as listed below:

- Market size
- Scope of competitive rivalry in local, regional, national, international, or global.
- Market growth rate and its position like early development, rapid growth, and takeoff, early maturity, saturation, and stagnation, decline in business life.
- Number of rivals and their relatives' sizes in market.
- What are the small and dominant companies?
- Number of buyers and their relative sizes and know the extent industry rivals have integrated in terms of backward or forward or both.
- To know the types of distribution channels used to access customers in the market.
- To know the pace of technological changes in terms of production process innovation and new product introductions.

- To know the products and services of rival firms are highly differentiated, weakly differentiated or essentially identical.
- To know the companies economies of scale in terms of purchasing, manufacturing, transportation, marketing and advertising.
- To know the key industry participants are clustered in a particular location. For instances, lock industry in Aligarh, Sarees and diamonds in Surat, Information technology in Bangalore, Hyderbad, Noida, similarly, there is also concentration of business in different countries on account of geographical and other reasons.
- To know the high rates of capacity utilization are crucial to achieving low cost production efficiency.
- Capital requirement of the company and easy of entry and exit in market.
- To know the industry profitability is above or below par value of the share.

Nature and Strength of Competition

- Industry and competitive analysis investigation into industry's competitive process. It discovers the main sources of competitive pressure and analyzes the how they are strong in each competitive force in industry.
- This step is essential and basic requirement of the managers for formulation of successful strategy, Strategic manager cannot create a successful strategy without in depth understanding of the industry's competitive character.
- Competitive pressures in various industries are not same.
- Competitive process works in similarly enough to use a common analytical framework in gauging the nature and intensity of competitive forces.
- Competitive analysis is the powerful tool for systematically diagnosing the principle competitive pressures in a market and assessing competitive strengths how is strong and how is important,
- Competitive analysis is easy to understand and apply to firm's environment.

Triggers of Change

Industry economic features and competitive structure explains about its fundamental character which are relating with changing ways of environment factors. Industry is ready to adjust changes in its activities. Changes will be occurred in internally or externally. Industry economy and competitive forces are ready to face constraints from changes which either relevant to business or not relevant force of the business. Industries character and trends and new development in market will be gradually produce changes. These are important and enough to require strategic response from participating firms in market. Popular hypothesis enable to industries and its life cycle going through changes and it explains the reasons for changing of life cycle. Industry life cycle strongly key changes of the growth rate of industry and business enterprise. When changing the industry and business activities that time ready to face serious and constraints problems to enterprise.

The Concept of Driving Force

- The concept of driving force is the important to judge what growth stage an industry is.
- It is identifying the more analytical value which are relating to the specific factors that are causing fundamental industry and competitive adjustment analysis.
- Industry and competitive conditions are changed due to pressure, motion of create incentives.
- The most dominant and important forces in enterprise is called as driving force.
- It is the biggest influence on different kinds of changes will be taken place in the industry's structure and competitive environment.

Analyzing driving forces has involved two steps:

Identifying what are the driving forces in industry.

Assessment and what are impact of the driving forces in industry.

The most common driving force

Many and powerful events will be affected an industry, apart from industry powerfully enough to quality as driving forces. Some of driving forces are unique and specific to a particular industry situation. Therefore, many driving forces are changing nature, these are falling into general category that affecting different industries simultaneously. Important and most common driving forces are outlined:

- The internet and new e-commerce opportunities and threats it breeds in the industry.
- Increasing globalization and liberalization.
- Changes in the long term industry growth rate of firms.
- Product innovation in firms.
- Market innovation in industry.
- Entry or exit of major firms in markets.
- Technology transfer
- Effective changes in terms of cost and efficiency.

Identifying the companies that are in the strongest/weakest position

The next step is to examining the industry's competitive structure of firm, it is to study the market positions of rival firms in market. Strategic grouping technique is one of the important and dominant techniques that revealing the competitive positions of firms. Strategic grouping techniques are one of the useful analytical tools for comparing the market positions of each firm separately or forming a group of firms. It is very difficult to assess and examine to each firm competitors and competitive positions in market.

3.6 STRATEGIC GROUPS

The Concept of Strategic Groups

Generally, an industry often differ from each other with respect to several factors like distributions channels used, market segment served, product quality, technological leadership, customer service, pricing policy, advertising policy, and promotions, within most industries. It is possible to observe groups of organization in which each member follows the same basic strategy as other organizations in the group but strategy is different from one that followed by companies in other groups. A strategic group principally consists of those rival firms with similar competitive approaches and positions in the market. These groups of organizations are known as strategic groups.

Normally, a limited number of groups capture the essence of the strategic difference between companies with an industry.

Implications of Strategic Groups

The concept of strategic groups has a number of implications for industry analysis and the identification of opportunities and threats are as outlined.

- Organization immediate competitors are those in its strategic groups. Since all the organizations in a strategic groups are pursuing similar strategies, consumer tend to view the products of such organization as being direct substitute for each other thus major threat to a company also can come from within its own strategic groups.
- Different strategic groups can have a different standing with respect to each of Porter's five competitive forces. It means, that, the risk of new entry by potential competitors, the degree of rivalry among organizations within a group, the bargaining power of suppliers, and the competitive force of substitute products can all vary in intensity among different strategic groups within the same industry.
- Identify the competitive characteristics that differentiate firms in the industry. It is typical variables like price , quality range in the form of high, medium, and low; geographic coverage in the form of local, regional, national and global; degree of vertical integration like none, partial , full; product line breadth in terms of wide and narrow ; use of distribution channels in form of one , some and all; and degree of services offered like no – frills , limited , full.
- Assigns similar services and products firms that fall in about the same strategy space to the same strategic group.
- For this purpose plot the firms on a two variable map and it using pairs in different characteristics.

- Draw circles around each strategic group in this way make the circles that proportional to the size of the groups. These groups have respective share of total industry sales revenues.

The above mentioned procedures for constructing a strategic group map and deciding that firms belong in which strategic group have straightforward.

Likely Strategic Moves of Rivals

- Firm always watching what are doing their competitors in market. Unless if firm is neglected their competitors. It impact on firm businesses, profit, and growth rate and end up its competitive battle in market.
- A company cannot expect to competitor result without proper monitoring their actions, understanding their strategies and future anticipating moves.
- Company watches their competitor just like as spy.
- Company watch competitors latest strategies, moves , forces, growth, development, alliances, joint venture, technology innovations, strategic alliances with partners, core competencies , core resources , core strengths and weakness of their competitors.

3.7 KEY FACTORS FOR COMPETITIVE SUCCESS

Industries Key Success Factors are those factors that most affect industry and its members are able to prosper their market place:

- Particularly relating with strategy elements, product attributes core resources, competencies, competitive capabilities, and business outcomes that associated between profit and loss.
- Competitive success factors are very important all kinds of business enterprises.
- Competitive success factors will shape the company will be financially strong and competitively successful in local, national and international market.

Industries Key Success Factors

The primary purpose of industry analysis is to identify the requirements and trends that determine the **key success factors** for the business. The key determinant success factor in the industry as listed below:

- Customer requirements,
- Competitive factors that must be met,
- Regulations/industry standards in the business,
- The resource requirements to implement competitive strategy, and other
- Technical requirements to build a competitive position.
- It may be used to identify the internal strengths and weaknesses of the organization.

- It can be scrutinizing industry competitors, as well as customer needs, vertical industry structures, channels of distribution costs barriers to entry, availability of substitutes, and supplier.
- A strategist seeks to determine whether organization's current internal capabilities represent strengths or weakness in the new competitive factors.

Apparel Industries Key Success Factors

Apparel industries key success factors are appealing designs and color combinations which create only on buyer interest and low cost manufacturing efficiency to permit attractive retail pricing and ample to improve margins of profit.

Tin and Aluminum Cans

Tin and aluminum cans key success factors are the cost of shipping empty cans is substantial, and another factor is plant located close to end use customers so that plant's output can be marketed within economical shipping distances to regional market share is far more crucial than national share.

Determining the Industry's Key Success Factors

- To know the prevailing and anticipation competitive condition.
- To give top priority for analytical consideration.
- Strategic managers understand the industry situation and less than competitive successes.
- Strategic managers pay attention to the kinds of resources and its competitive valuable.
- Give training to strategic managers for improvement of competitive skills.
- Acquired the stronger market position.
- Efforts better than rivals for gaining competitive advantage that is one of golden opportunity of the firms.
- Industry's key success factors are cornerstone for the company's strategy and trying to gain sustainable competitive advantage.

Prospectus and Financial Attractiveness of Industry

The final step of industry and competitive analysis is to use outcome of the analysis have drawn conclusions about the relative attractiveness or unattractiveness of the industry. The analysis is to be either short or long term that depends on industry circumstances. Strategist have responsible person to assess the industry outlook carefully, deciding about present industry and competitive conditions in company in this way attractive business opportunity for the growth, development, survival, earning of profits that can be gloomy prospect. Important prospectus and financial attractiveness of industry as listed below:

- The industry's growth potential rate.

- Industry's profitable is favorable or unfavorable that affected by the prevailing driving forces of the company.
- Currently rivalry permits to company earn adequate profitability and competitive forces will become very stronger compare to weak.
- The company's competitive position in the industry and its position are likely to grow in terms of stronger or weaker.
- The companies potential to convert into weak competitive position into strong competitive position in this way achieve the mission and vision of the company.
- Companies able to buildup counteract policy to unattractive situation convert into attractive situation in company.
- Reduce the degree of risk and make certainty in futures company business.
- The severity of constraints which confronting the industry as a whole.
- Company continued participation in business activities and it is very important and able to cope and use resources successfully for the business interest.

A general concept that relating with industry: If an industry's overall profit prospects are above average, the industry can be considered attractive: if its profit prospects are below average, which time it is unattractive. Therefore, strategist make mistake to evaluate the industries as being attractive or unattractive to all type industry participants and all potential entrants. The term attractiveness is relative and not absolute. Industry environments is unattractive to weak competitors may be attractive to strong competitors in market.

Assessment of industry enhance to fundamental attractiveness that is relating with current industry participants who are employed strategies for calculated to strengthen in long term competitive position of business, expansion of business in terms of sales, investment, additional facilities and modern equipment which are needed in the industry.

In the case, the industry and competitive situation is judged as unattractive, this time more successful industry participants may be chosen cautiously to invest, look for different ways to protect their long term competitiveness and profitability of the business. If company is strong that time company is ready to acquire small firms and diversified their business activities and convert into successful business venture. In the case weak companies, these are considered to be unattractive industry. These are merging with a rival to strengthen the market share and profitability or alternatively looking for outside industry for attractive diversification and its new opportunities properly utilized by weak industries.

3.8 SWOT ANALYSIS

SWOT is the heart of Strategic Analysis. SWOT analysis is the process of carefully inspecting the business and its environment through the various dimensions of Strengths, Weaknesses, Opportunities, and Threats. SWOT" is an acronym which represents "Strengths", "Weaknesses", "Opportunities", and "Threats".

Strengths

Strengths are the companies' core competencies, and include proprietary technology, skills, resources, market position, patents, and others. Strengths are an inherent capability of the organization. And it can be used to gain strategic advantage over its competitors in business.

Weaknesses

Weaknesses are conditions within the company that can lead to poor performance, and can include obsolete equipment, heavy debt burden, poor product or market image, weak management, and others. A weakness is an inherent limitation or problems of the organization. And it creates strategic disadvantages to business enterprise.

Opportunities

Opportunities are outside conditions or circumstances that the company could turn to its advantage, and could include a specialty niche skill or technology that suddenly realizes a growth in broad market interest. An opportunity is a favorable condition in the organization's environment. And it enables to be strengthening its position in business.

Threats

Threats are current or future conditions in the outside environment that may harm the company, and might include population shifts, purchasing preferences, new technologies, or an increase in competition. A treat is unfavourable condition in the organization's environment that causes a risk for, or damage to the organization's position in market.

Swot analysis is to identify the strategies that will create a firm specific business model that will the best support, it fit, or match a firm's resources and capabilities to the demands of the environment in which enterprise operates. Strategic managers compare and find the gap the various alternative possible strategies against each other with respect to enterprise ability to accomplish major goals and superior profitability of the firm's. Strategic manager identify the set of strategies that will be created and sustain a competitive advantage in the form of functional level, business level, global, corporate level, operational strategy.

Functional Level Strategy

It directed towards to the effectiveness of operations within company in terms of manufacturing, marketing, material management, product development and customer services.

Corporate level Strategy

It is concerned with the overall purpose and scope of the business to meet its stakeholder expectations. This is a crucial level since it is heavily influenced by investors in the business and acts to guide strategic decision-making throughout the business. Corporate strategy is often stated explicitly in a "mission statement" of company. It focuses on maximization of the long term profitability of company. It enhances to increase the market share and business development process in market.

Business level Strategy

It is concerned more with how a business competes successfully in a particular market. It concerns strategic decisions about choice of products, meeting needs of customers, gaining advantage over competitors, exploiting or creating new opportunities etc.

Operational Strategy

It is concerned with how each part of the business is organized to deliver the corporate and business-unit level strategic direction. Operational strategy therefore focuses on issues of resources, processes, people etc.

Global Strategy

It is addressing how to expand business operations outside the home country to grow and prosper in a world where competitive advantage is determined at a global level.

The organization performance in the market place is significantly influenced by the three dominant factors are listed below:

- The organization correct market position
- The nature of environment opportunities and threats
- The organizations resource capability to capitalize the opportunities and its ability to protect against the threat.

Significance of SWOT Analysis

Major significance of SWOT analysis as outlined:

It provides a logical Framework:

- It provides logical framework for systematic and sound approachable issues having and bearing on the business situation.
- It helps to generation of alternative strategies and the choice of a strategy.
- Different managerial perceptions that relating about organizational strengths and weaknesses and the environment opportunities and threats that lead to differences are approaches to specific strategies and finally determine the choice of strategy. It takes place through an interactive process in dynamic backdrop in business.

It presents a comparative account

- It presents the information about both external and internal environment in a structured form.

- It possible to compare external opportunities and threats along with internal strengths and weaknesses.
- It helps strategist to form suitable strategy that matching to internal and external environment factors of company.
- The pattern of strengths, weakness, opportunity and threats are comparing with from one to another.

It guides the strategist in strategy identification

- Strategist can be faced problems when the organization cannot match in the SWOT pattern.
- Organization must have certain opportunities along with the specific threats, it is equally true that , the organization may have powerful strengths coupled with major weaknesses in the light of the critical success factors.
- SWOT analysis is guided to strategist to think about the organization overall position that helps strategist to identify the major purpose of the strategy under focus in business.

SWOT analysis helps to strategic managers to craft a business model. It will allow to company to gain competitive advantages from its industries. Competitive advantage leads to be increased profitability, and maximizes a company's chances of survival in the fast changing, global competitive environment that characteristics are existed most of industries today. Changing of environment, a company constantly develops a marketing information system to track relevant trends and developments. These can be categorized as opportunity and a threat.

Figure 3.3:SWOT Analysis: What to Look for in Sizing Up a Company's Strengths, Weakness, Opportunities, and Threats

Potential Resources Strengths and competitive capabilities	Potential Resources Weaknesses and Competitive Deficiencies
A	B
Potential Company Opportunities	Potential External Threats to Company's Well-Being
C	D

Part – A: Potential Resources Strengths and competitive capabilities

- A powerful strategy which is supported by competitively valuable skills and experience in key areas in firm.
- A strong financial condition which helpful to grow the business.
- Brand reputation and company image.

- A widely recognized market leader in market and an attractive customer base to firm.
- Ability to take advantage of economies scale in production of goods and services.
- Advanced and superior skills in technology.
- Cost advantages of firm.
- Strong and advertising network of firm.
- New product innovation skills of firm.
- Ability to proven skills in improving product quality process.
- Sophisticated use of e – technologies and relating communication processes.
- Superior skills in supply chain management of firm.
- A reputation of good customer services of firm.
- Better product quality relative to their competitor.
- Wide geographic coverage and strong global distribution capability of firm.
- Strategic alliances , joint ventures with other firms that provide to access valuable technology , competences, core distribution channels, products and services and attractive geographic markets.

Part – B: Potential Resources Weaknesses and Competitive Deficiencies

- No clear strategic decisions in business.
- Obsolete facilities of firm
- Weak financial position and heavy burdened too much debt of firm.
- Firm's unit cost higher than competitor price.
- Missing the core competences.
- Deficiencies in terms of skills, intellectual property capital relative leading rivals in market.
- No cost control measure of firm.
- Plagued with internal operation problems of firm.
- Falling behind rivals in putting e- commerce capability and strengths of firm.
- To narrow a product line relative to rivals of firm.
- Short on financial resources to fund which promising strategic initiative of firm.
- Not attracting new customers as rapidly as rivals in market.
- Leaving of experienced, trained and skilled employees from the firm.
- Inadequate distribution channels of firm.

Part - C: Potential Company Opportunities

- Expansion of business activities in this way getting of additional customer base to firm.
- Expansion of product segments
- Expanding the firm's product line and meet the requirement the broader range of customer needs in market.
- Effective utilization of existing skills and technologies for how to enter new market with new product and services.
- Using the internet and e- commerce network communications and technologies to dramatically cut costs in this way pursue new sales growth opportunities.
- Integration of backward and forward diversification of business.
- Falling trade barriers in attractive foreign markets of firm's.
- Firm's able to market share from rival firms in the market.
- Firm able to grow rapidly in form of rising demand from customers in different countries.
- Acquisitions of rival industries in market with technological expertise of firm's.
- Strategic alliances and joint venture of firms that expand the firm's market share, customer base and its competitive capabilities and core competences.
- Firms are opening to exploit emerging market due to new technologies.
- Firms enhance their brand image and company reputation.

Part – D: Potential External Threats to Company's Well – Being

- Likely entry of potential new customers in market.
- Loss of sales to substitute products in markets.
- Mounting competition from new internet start up companies pursuing e – commerce strategies in their business.
- Increasing the intensity of firm's competition in market.
- Technological changes impact for product demand reduced from customers.
- Slowdown in market growth of firm's.
- Adverse impact of foreign exchange rates and trade policies of foreign governments which affected to firm's business operation.
- New Government regulatory requirements.
- Growing bargaining powers of customers and vendors in market.
- Adverse demographic changes which threaten to curtain demand for the firm's products and services.
- Major vulnerability to industry driving forces.

Swot Analysis of Indian Dairy Industry

Strengths:	*Weaknesses:*
• **Demand profile:** Absolutely optimistic.	• **Perishability:** Pasteurization has overcome this weakness partially. UHT gives milk long life. Surely, many new processes will follow to improve milk quality and extend its shelf life.
• **Margins:** Quite reasonable, even on packed liquid milk.	• **Lack of control over yield:** Theoretically, there is little control over milk yield. However, increased awareness of developments like embryo transplant, artificial insemination and properly managed animal husbandry practices, coupled with higher income to rural milk producers should automatically lead to improvement in milk yields.
• **Flexibility of product mix:** Tremendous. With balancing equipment, you can keep on adding to your product line.	• **Logistics of procurement:** Woes of bad roads and inadequate transportation facility make milk procurement problematic. But with the overall economic improvement in India, these problems would also get solved.
• **Availability of raw material:** Abundant. Presently, more than 80 per cent of milk produced is flowing into the unorganized sector, which requires proper channelization.	• **Problematic distribution:** Yes, all is not well with distribution. But then if ice creams can be sold virtually at every nook and corner, why can't we sell other dairy products too? Moreover, it is only a matter of time before we see the emergence of a cold chain linking the producer to the refrigerator at the consumer's home!
• **Technical manpower:** Professionally-trained, technical human resource pool, built over last 30 years.	• **Competition:** With so many newcomers entering this industry, competition is becoming tougher day by day. But then competition has to be faced as a ground reality. The **market** is large enough for many to carve out their niche.

Opportunities:	*Threats:*
"Failure is never final, and success never ending". Dr Kurien bears out this statement perfectly. He entered the industry when there were only threats. He met failure head-on, and now he clearly is an example of 'never ending success'! If dairy entrepreneurs are looking for **opportunities** in India, the following areas must be tapped:**Value**	**Milk vendors, the un-organized sector:** Today milk vendors are occupying the pride of place in the industry. Organized dissemination of information about the harm that they are doing to producers and consumers should see a steady decline in their importance.The study of this **SWOT** analysis shows that the 'strengths' and

3.7 TOWS MATRIX ANALYSIS

Heinz Weihrich developed a matrix called TOWS matrix by comparing strengths and weaknesses of organization with that of market opportunities and threats. The Threats, Opportunities, Weaknesses and Strengths (TOWS) Matrix is an

addition: There is a phenomenal scope for innovations in product development, packaging and presentation. Given below are potential areas of value addition: Steps should be taken to introduce value-added products like *shrikhand,* ice creams, *paneer, khoa,* flavored milk, dairy sweets, etc. This will lead to a greater presence and flexibility in the market place along with opportunities in the field of brand building. Addition of cultured products like yoghurt and cheese lend further strength - both in terms of utilization of resources and presence in the market place. A lateral view opens up opportunities in milk proteins through casein, caseinates and other dietary proteins, further opening up **export opportunities.** Yet another aspect can be the addition of infant foods, geriatric foods and nutritionals. **Export potential:** Efforts to exploit export potential are already on. Amul is exporting to Bangladesh, Sri Lanka, Nigeria, and the Middle East. Following the new GATT treaty, opportunities will increase tremendously for the export of agri-products in general and dairy products in particular. Questions1. Explain the swot analysis of Indian diary. 'opportunities' far outweigh 'weaknesses' and 'threats'. Strengths and opportunities are fundamental and weaknesses and threats are transitory. Any investment idea can do well only when you have three essential ingredients: entrepreneurship (the ability to take risks), innovative approach (in product lines and marketing) and values (of quality/ethics).The Indian dairy industry, following its delicensing, has been attracting a large number of entrepreneurs. Their success in dairying depends on factors such as an efficient yet economical procurement network, hygienic and cost-effective processing facilities and innovativeness in the market place. All that needs to be done is: to innovate, convert products into commercially exploitable ideas. All the time keep reminding yourself: Benjamin Franklin discovered electricity, but it was the man who invented the meter that really made the money!

Source: http://www.indiadairy.com/ind_swot.html#Weaknesses

important matching tool that helps managers develop four types of strategies: SO Strategies, WO Strategies, ST Strategies, and WT Strategies. TOWS Matrix can be applied to the development of tactics necessary to implement the strategies, and to more specific actions supportive of tactics. It has been criticized that after conducting the SWOT analysis mangers frequently fail to come to terms with the strategic choices that the outcomes demand. TOWS inputs are recognized and integrates them more fully into the strategic planning process. The matrix is listed in figure 3.4

Figure 3.4: The TOWS Matrix

Internal and External Factors	Organizational strengths	Organizational weaknesses
	Strategic options	
Environmental opportunities (and risks)	SO: Strengths can be used to capitalize or build upon existing or emerging opportunities	WO: the strategies developed need to overcome organizational weaknesses if existing or emerging opportunities are to be exploited
Environmental threats	ST: Strengths in the organization can be used to minimize existing or emerging threats	WT: the strategies pursued must minimize or overcome weaknesses and as far as possible ,cope with threats existing or emerging threats

3.10 PORTFOLIO ANALYSES

Portfolio analysis is one of the magnificent analyses in order to current business portfolio; the company must conduct portfolio analysis to identify and evaluates the various businesses which make up the company. Top management views their product lines and business units are relating with the portfolio analysis. It involves series of investments in different products in different companies and expects return from their investments. A business portfolio is a collection of businesses and products which make up the company. The best business portfolio is the one that appropriate to the company's strengths and weaknesses to opportunities in the business environment.

- The term portfolio analysis can be defined as "set of techniques that help to strategist in taking strategic decisions with regard to individual products or businesses in a firm's portfolio".
- It is primarily used for competitive analysis and corporate strategic planning in multi business firms in market.
- It can be used in less diversified firms, these consists of main business and other minor complementary interests.

Advantage of Portfolio Analysis

Significant advantages of portfolio analysis are outlined:

- It is multi product approach.
- It involves investment in multi business firms.
- Investment can be channellised to different firms in market.
- It helps investor to minimize risk and maximize return from their investment in different companies.
- It analysis and design the current business portfolio and decide which business should receive more, less or no investment in business.

There are three important concepts relating of portfolio analysis are outlined below:

- Strategic business units
- Product life cycle
- BCG group share matrix

3.11 STRATEGIC BUSINESS UNITS

Some organizations encounter difficulty in controlling their divisional operations as the diversity, size, and number of these units continues to increase. And corporate management may encounter difficulty in evaluating and controlling it's numerous, often multi industry divisions. Under these conditions, it may be come necessary to add another layer of management to improve strategy implementation, promotion synergy, and gain greater control over the diverse business interests. It can be achieved by grouping various divisions' in terms of common strategic elements. These groups commonly called strategic business units (SBUs)

- Strategic business unit begin to identifying key businesses also termed as strategic business unit.
- SBU is a unit of the company. It has a separate mission and objectives.
- It can be planned independently of its mission, vision and objectives from other company businesses.
- The SBU can be a division of a company, it has a product line within a division or even a single product or brand.
- SBUs are common in organizations; these units are located in multiple countries with independent manufacturing and marketing setups.

Characteristics of SBUs

- Single business or collection of related businesses which can be planned for separately in different division in across global.
- It has consists of competitors in market.
- Division strategic manager is responsible person for strategic planning and profit of the company.

Advantages of SBUs Organizational Structure

Exhibit 3.2: Advantages of SBUs Organizational Structure

- It improves coordination between divisions with similar strategic concerns and product/ market environment.
- It tightens the strategic management and control of large, diverse business enterprises.
- It facilitates distinct and in depth business planning at the corporate and business levels.
- It Channels accountability to distinct business unit.

Disadvantages of Strategic Business Unit Organizational Structure

Exhibit 3.3: Disadvantages of Strategic Business Unit Organizational Structure

- It places another layer of management between the divisions and corporate management.
- Its dysfunctional competition for corporate resource may increase.
- The role of the group vice president can be difficult to define.
- It is difficulty in defining the degree of autonomy for the group vice presidents and division managers.

Experience Curve

- Experience curve is one of the important concepts.
- It is used for applying a portfolio approach.
- The concept is similar to a learning curve.
- It explains the efficiency increase and thereby gained workers through repetitive productive work.
- Experience curve is based on the commonly observed trend that costs decline as a firm accumulative experience in the form of a cumulative volume of production.
- It is implication that larger firms in an industry would tend to have lower unit costs as compared to those for smaller companies, thereby gaining competitive cost advantage in emerging markets.
- Experience curve results from a variety of factors like learning effects, economies of scale, product redesign, and technological improvements in production.
- It is applicable to various areas in strategic management. For instance, experience curve is considered a barrier for new firms contemplating entry in an industry and it used to buildup market share and discourages competition.

3.12 STAGES IN PRODUCT/MARKET EVOLUTION OR PRODUCT LIFE CYCLE

Product life cycle is the second factor to ascertainment of strengths and weakness of organization. Stages in product life cycle are essential from the point of view of successful of the organization. As a result, strategist can use changing patterns associated with different stages in product lifecycle/market evolution as a framework for identifying and evaluating the organization's strengths and weakness. It is another important concept in strategic choice. This is useful concept for guiding strategic choice.

Figure 3.5: Product Life Cycle

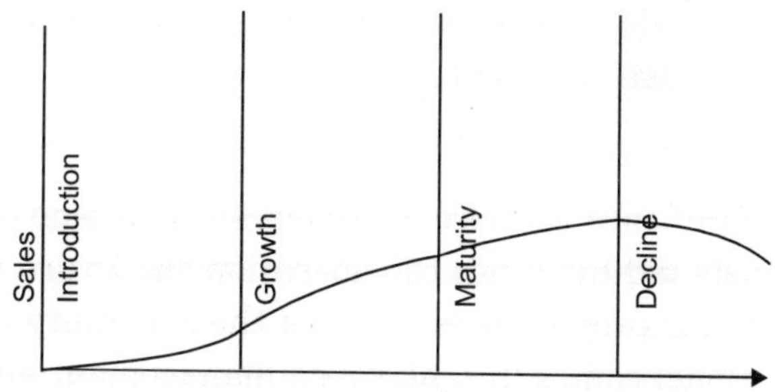

Figure 3.5 indicates the product life cycle .There is four major stages of product life cycle / market evolution. PLC is an S – shaped curve which exhibits the relationship of sales with respect of time for a product that passes through the successive stages.

They are as below:

- Introduction stage is slow sales growth
- Growth stage is rapid market acceptance
- Maturity stage is slow down in growth rate and
- Decline/Saturation stage is sharp downward drift.

And typical changes in functional capabilities often associated with business success at each stage of the development of product /market cycle.

Advantage of Product life Cycle

- It can be used to diagnose a portfolio of products or business in order to establish the stage at which each of them exists in business.
- Strengths are needed in the growth stage because of rapid growth brings competitor into the market. This stage involves with brand recognition, product or market differentiation and the financial resources to support both heavy marketing expenses and affect the price competition and effective cash flow can be key strengths at this stage.
- As the product/market moves through a "shakeout" phases and into the maturity stage, this stage market growth continues but at a decreasing rate the number of market segments begins to expand, while technological change in product.
- Particular attention is to be paid on the businesses which are in the declining stage.

While the products markets move toward a saturation decline stage, this stage strengths and weakness center on cost advantages, superior supplier or customer relationships and financial control. Product expansion is suitable for introduction and growth stages. Mature businesses stages use as source of cash investment in other businesses which needed resources. Harvesting, retrenchment strategies may be adopted for declining stage of businesses.

3.13 BCG MATRIX

Portfolio analysis is a significant exercise for corporate strategic planning. Investment and financial decisions should take into consideration the entire portfolio of the firm. It presents a framework for proper assessment of the capability of various operations of company. The BCG model comes into play as a management analytical tool. BCG is the acronym for Boston Consulting Group—a general management consulting firm highly respected in business strategy consulting.

During the 1960s, a number of management consulting companies developed a serious of conceptual techniques whose stated purpose was to help the top officers of diversified better management their portfolio of business. These techniques are known as portfolio planning techniques. Portfolio matrix first time developed by the Boston Consulting group which is named after them as BCG matrix. it can be used to classify product portfolio in four business types based on four graphic labels including Stars, Cash Cows, Question Marks and Dogs; it can be used to determine what priorities should be given in the product portfolio of a company; to classify an organization's product portfolio according to their cash usage and generation; and offers management available strategies to tackle various product lines.

Mission of BCG

BCG aims to help the world's best organizations make decisive improvements in their direction and performance by sparking breakthrough business ideas.

We see the essence of our work as a virtuous circle of insight, impact, and trust.

We continually strive to generate deep **insight** into what drives value creation and competitive advantage in our clients' businesses and the economy as a whole.

We work collaboratively with clients to convert insight into strategy that will have a substantial positive **impact** on performance.

Consistently delivering impact earns the **trust** that is the foundation of lasting relationships. These relationships serve as a platform for still deeper insight and more significant impact.

BCG seeks to stimulate continuous growth and success for our clients and, by doing so, to forge lifelong bonds with them.

The main objective of the Boston Consulting Group (BCG) technique is to help senior manager will identify the cash flow requirements of the different business in their portfolio. The BCG Growth – Share Matrix is based on two dimensional share matrixes. In the matrix:

- The vertical axis represents relative market growth rate and provides a measure of market attractiveness.
- The horizontal axis represents relative market share and serves as a measure of company strength in the market.

Using the matrix, organization can identify four different types of products or SBUs as follows:

Figure 3.6: BCG Growth – Share Matrix

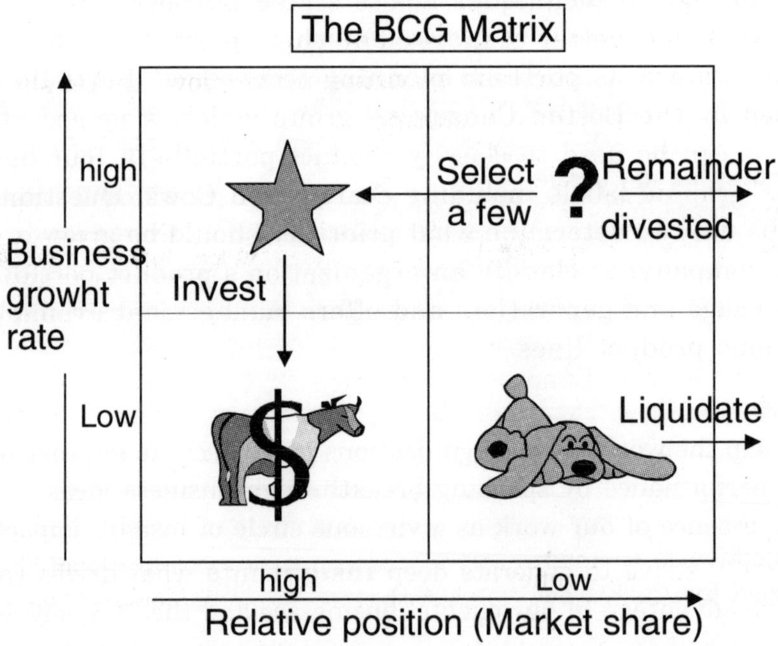

Stars

- Stars are leaders in high growth markets. Stars are products or SBUs that are growing rapidly.
- They tend to/should generate large amounts of cash (investment) but also use a lot of cash because of growth market conditions.
- They represent best opportunities for expansion.

Cash Cows

- These products are said to have high profitability
- These require low investment
- They are market leaders in a low-growth market
- They are established, successful, and need less investment to maintain their market share.

Question Marks

- Question Marks have not achieved a dominant market position.
- And hence do not generate much cash.
- They tend to use a lot of cash because of growth market conditions.

Dogs

- Dogs often have little future.
- And are big cash drainers on the company.
- They generate very little cash by virtue of their low market share in a highly low growth market.

Available Strategies to Pursue

There are four strategies available to pursue:

Build

- The product or SBU's market share needs to be increased to strengthen its position.
- Short-term earnings and profits are deliberately forfeited because it is hoped that the long-term gains will be higher than this.
- This strategy is suited to Question Marks if they are to become stars.

Hold

- The objective is to maintain the current share position and this strategy is often used for Cash Cows so that they continue to generate large amounts of cash.

Harvest

- Here management tries to increase short-term cash flows as far as possible (e.g. price increase, cutting costs) even at the expense of the products or SBU's longer-term future.
- It is a strategy suited to weak Cash Cows or Cash Cows that are in a market with a limited future.
- Harvesting is also used for Question Marks where there is no possibility of turning them into Stars, and for Dogs.

Divest

- The objective of this strategy is to rid the organization of the products or SBUs that are a drain on profits and to utilize these resources elsewhere in the business where they will be of greater benefit.
- This strategy is typically used for Question Marks that will not become Stars and for Dogs.

Limitations of the BCG Matrix

- It is clearly defining a market is very difficult task as a result, accurately measuring share and growth rate can be a problem. This creates the potential manipulation or distortion.

- Dividing the matrix into four cells is based on a high /low classification scheme.
- It does not recognize the markets with average growth rates or the business with average market share.
- The relationship between market share and profitability underlying BCG matrix.
- The BCG matrix is not particularly helpful in comparing relative investments opportunities across different business units in the corporate portfolio.
- Strategic evaluation of a set of business requires examination of more than relative market shares and market growth.

Ansoff's Product - Market Growth Matrix

The Ansoff's product growth matrix is a useful tool which helps businesses decide their product and market growth strategy. This matrix, developed by H. Igor Ansoff, is a handy tool for thinking about how its growth depends upon it markets in new or existing products in a both new and existing markets. Companies always looking for good future, companies are identifying the growth opportunities for the future for their product and market. It should be noted that this is an environment led process which sees the company's market situation as a leading feature. It may not be suitable in a situation of a contracting market.

The matrix shows the major choices that available to company, faces in its mission for growth and opportunities in future. Company can be targeted to new or existing markets with new or existing products. The results-in the boxes, these boxes are suggested routes for the company's growth strategy.

Figure 3.7: Ansoff's Matrix

	Existing products	New products
Present market	Market pentration	Product development
New market	Market development	Diversification

Market Penetration

- A market penetration strategy refers to growth strategy when the company will aim to sell its existing products within its existing markets that it already serves but in greater numbers.

- This will entail a greater effort in sales and marketing to achieve higher product sales, in this way achieve the greater market share.
- This can be achieved through improving the products quality and/ or by productivity gains leading to cost reductions.
- It might require greater spending on advertising or personal selling.
- Over competition in a mature market that requires an aggressive promotional campaign which supported by a pricing strategy that designed to make the market unattractive for competitors in market.
- It is also done by increasing the customer base for their products and services.

Product Development

- A product development strategy entails developing new products for sale in existing markets.
- It aims introducing new products into existing markets.
- This strategy for company growth by offering modified or new products to current markets.
- It requires the new development of new competencies and requires the business to develop modified products that can be appealed to existing markets.

Market Development

- Market development refers to growth strategy which occurs when a company attempts to sell its existing products into new markets.
- It is a strategy for company its growth by identifying and developing new markets for current company products and services.
- This strategy achieved through new geographically market, new product dimensions or packaging, new distribution channels or different pricing policies to attract different customers or create new market segments.

Diversification

- Diversification refers to growth strategy that to occur when a company decides to sell newly developed products within a new market.
- It is strategy by starting up or acquiring businesses outside the company's current products and markets.
- It involves risk due to introducing new products into new market.
- Generally, the business is moving into markets in which it has little or some time no experience.
- There are a wide range of possibilities for achieving this strategy but they fall into two main group are related and unrelated diversification.

Related diversification involves developing new products to sell in new markets but within the same industry or broad area as before.

Unrelated diversification occurs when a company decides to enter a new business area as well as developing new products and finding new customers.

3.14 ADL MATRIX

It is a combination of the two aforementioned dimensions that helps us to use ADL for marketing decision-making. Now let's consider options in more detail. Competitive position has five main categories as shown below:

	Stage in Industry maturity			
Competitive position	Embryonic	Growth	Mature	Ageing
Dominant	Fast grow build barriers /Act offensively	Fast grow/Attend cost leadership/ Renew defend position/Act offensively	Defend position/ Attend cost leadership/Renew fast grow/Act offensively	Defend position/ Renew Focus/ Consider withdrawl
Strong	Differentiate fast grow	Differentiate lower cost/Attack small firms	Lower cost focus/ Differentiate grow with industry	Find niche/Hold niche harvest
Favourable	Differentiate focus grow	Focus differentiate defend	Focus differentiate harvest/Find niche/ Hold niche turn-around grow with industry/Hit smaller firms	Harvest turnaround
Teanable	Growth with industry/Focus	Hold niche turn-around/Focus grow with industry withdraw	Turnaround hold niche/Retrench	Divest retrench
Weak	Find niche/catch up grow with industry	Turnaround retrench niche or withdraw	Withdraw/Divest	Withdraw

Dominant

- This is particularly extraordinary position.
- Often this is associate with some form of monopoly position or customer lock-in e.g. Microsoft Windows being the dominant global operating system.

Strong

- Here companies have a lot of freedom since position in an industry is comparatively powerful e.g. Apple's iPod products.

Favourable

- Companies with a favourable position tend to have competitive strengths in segments of a fragmented market place.

- No single global player controls all segments.
- Here product strengths and geographical advantages come into play.

Tenable

- Companies may face erosion by stronger competitors that have a favourable, strong or competitive position.
- It is difficult for them to compete since they do not have a sustainable competitive advantage.

Weak

- The performance of firms in this category is generally unsatisfactory although the opportunity for improvement do exist in market.
- Of course there are opportunities to change and improve, and therefore to take an organization to a more favourable, strong or even dominant position.

3.15 THE GENERAL ELECTRIC MODEL™

The general Electric Model developed by GE with assistance of the Mckinsey consulting and Company. It is similar to the BCG growth share matrix. So that, there are differences are outlined below:

- Market attractiveness replaces market growth, it one of the dimensions of industry attractiveness It includes a broader range of factors rather than just the market rate.
- Competitive strengths replaces market share, it is one of the dimension by which the competitive position of each strategic business units is assessed.

Figure 3.8: GE Matrix Grid

Market Attrativeness	Business Position: High	Medium	Low
High	Invest	invest	Protect
Medium	Invest	Protect	Harvest
Low	Protect	Harvest	Divest

This figure 3.8 indicates the GE Matrix Grid. Each of the above mentioned two factors is related according to criteria such as outlined below:

Figure 3.9: Criteria for rating Business Position and Market Attractiveness

Evaluating the ability to compete: Business Position	Evaluating the Market Attractiveness
Size	Size
Growth	Growth
Share by segment	Customer satisfaction levels
Customer loyalty	Competition: quality, types
Margins	Effectiveness, commitment
Distribution	Price levels
Technology skills	Profitability
Patents	Technology
Marketing	Government regulations
Flexibility	Sensitivity to economic trends
Organization	

The criteria used to rate market attractiveness and business position assigned different ways because some criteria are more important than others. The each SBU is rated with respect to all criteria, finally, overall rating for both factors are calculated for SBU . Based on these ratings, each sbu is labeled as high, medium or low with respect to a market attractiveness and business position.

Every organization has to make decisions about how to use its limited resources most effectively that's where this planning models can help determining which sbu should be stimulated for growth , which one maintained in their present market position and which one eliminated.

Case 3.1: Comparison with competitors growth in software industry
With the wave of consolidation sweeping the software industry and small and medium sized software vendors needing scale to survive, Netkraft's sell-out was anticipated. When queried earlier, both company executives and its VC partners had brushed aside any such happening, saying that there was space for small and medium sized companies to survive in the current highly competiitive market place. "Medium sized software vendors, who have recently succumbed to the merger wave, include Kshema Technologies, which was acquired by MphasiS , and iVega which merged with the Kolkata-based TCG Software of the Chatterjee Group. Adea Solutions, which has a development centre in Hyderabad, has emerged as a global player with a comprehensive portfolio of services including solutions development and delivery in domains like consulting, retail, finance and healthcare. The firm, which has a widespread global presence, employs around 1,500 people. Adea chief executive Abid H Abedi was awarded the Ernst & Young Entrepreneur of the Year award in 2003. Abedi had earlier stated that, with the expansion of the company's labs in Dallas and Hyderabad, its delivery capabilities are bound to be substantially effective in this competitive marketplace. Netkraft, which has managed to overcome its financial crisis and earn profits, is said to have made around $8 million last fiscal and is

expected to touch the $10 million revenue figure this fiscal. The company started operations in 1998 and presently earns around 50 per cent of its revenues from the retail vertical. It recently joined the growing band of Level 5 CMMI certified companies. BANGALORE: US-based Adea Solutions, a global provider of business process and technology consulting services, has pipped a few international software firms to acquire Bangalore-based Netkraft.

Netkraft, which focusses on retail, healthcare and banking and finance solutions, is currently owned by private equity firm Actis, US technology fund Jumpstart and employees. Sources said that Ernst & Young was the advisor for Adea on this deal.

The deal size could not be confirmed. While Actis holds around 45 per cent, Jumpstart owns around 20 per cent of Netkraft with the employees holding the balance.

Netkraft had been in the news when its original promoters, Prashanth Prakash and Atul Jalan, left the company, though they still have a stake in the company, a year ago.

Sources added that a Texas-based software multinational firm too was keen to acquire the company. When contacted by The Economic Times , Anand Sudarshan, CEO of Netkraft, declined to comment

Questions

1. Discuss the comparison with competitors growth in software industry

Source: Times news net work, June 10,2004

CHAPTER 4

Strategic Planning

Contents

- Corporate strategy
- Nature, scope and concerns of corporate strategy
- What does corporate strategy ensure in firm's businesses
- Dealing with strategic uncertainty
- Implications of strategic uncertainty
- The stages of corporate strategy formulation–implementation process
- Strategic alternatives
- Michael porter's generic strategies
- Cost leadership strategies
- Differentiation strategy
- Focus strategy
- Generic strategies comparative skills and resource requirement
- Best cost provider strategy
- Distinctive features of the generic competitive strategies
- Grand strategies/Directional strategies
- Characteristics and scope of various grand strategies
- Expansion strategy
- Retrenchment/Divestment strategy
- Combination strategy

- Diversification
- Retrenchment, divestment and liquidation strategy
- Turnaround strategy
- Issues for successful turnaround strategies

Learning Objectives

- Learning the corporate strategy, nature, scope and concerns of corporate strategy
- Understand the stages of corporate strategy formulation–implementation process
- Know the Michael porter's generic strategies
- To know the generic strategies comparative skills and resource requirement

4.1 CORPORATE STRATEGY

- Corporate strategy is the design framework of the firm growth and development.
- Its main objectives is growth of the company in a particular direction, extent, pace and timing.
- Corporate strategy involves the objectives design, implementation, control of objectives of firm which are helpful to growth of company's.
- It determines the company's mission, vision and longterm development and growth of firms.
- Corporate policy depends on its corporate strategy management that will be made by strategist of company.

Nature, Scope and Concerns of Corporate Strategy

Corporate strategy is basically concerned with the choice of businesses, products and markets of the company's. Nature, scope and concerns of corporate strategy as outlined below:

- It can be involved and viewed with objectives which are designed framework of strategy in the firm.
- Strategy designed framework is leading to be that filling the firm's strategic planning gap.
- Actually, it is concerned with the different choice of the firm's products and markets. It generally involves the changes/additions/deletions in the firm's existing product market postures in businesses. It serves the customers needs and requirements and meets and serves the business requirement.
- It able to ensure that the right fit to businesses and how to achieve between the firm's and its business environment.
- It helps and focuses to buildup the relevant competitive advantages for the firm's in market.

- Both corporate objectives and corporate strategy bring together and describe the firm's business concepts in a systamatic manner.

What does Corporate Strategy Ensure in Firm's Businesses

- Corporate strategy first time ensure that the firm's business growth and correct alignment of the firm's and its environment.
- It ready to serves and ensure that the design strategy which for filling the strategic gaps in business.
- It helps and serves to buildup the firm's relevant competitive advantages,
- It primary strategy ensure that the masterminding and working out the right opportunity which fit between the firm and its external environment.
- Corporate strategy purposefully firm's weakness converts into strengths and threats converts into opportunities in this way ensure to firm's businesses.
- It ensures that responding the environment is part and parcel of a firm's existence in market.
- It ensure to arise a major question which is good and how to methodical to response to firm's.
- Corporate strategy is the opposite of adhoc responses to the changes in the environment in competition, consumer tastes, technology and other variables in firms.
- It definitely involves the amounts is to long-term, well thought out and prepared responses to the various forces in the business environment.

Strategy is Partly Proactive and Partly Reactive

The company strength's strategy is typically a blend in the following circumstances:

(1) Proactive actions on the part of managers and responsibility to improve the company's market position and financial performance.

(2) It is needed reactions to unanticipated developments and fresh market conditions in firm's businesses.

The biggest portion of firm's current strategy flows from previously initiated actions like experiences, resources, strengths, and competitive capabilities alongwith business approaches. These are working well enough to merit continuation and newly launched managerial initiatives to strengthen the overall position and performance in terms of growth rate and market share of firms. These things are involved in management game plans. It is deliberate and proactive. It is standing the product of firm's product and services management analysis and strategic thinking that determine about the company's situation analysis and its conclusion about how to position the company in the market place and how to tackle the task of compositing for buyer patronage.

Figure 4.1: A Company's Actual Strategy Is Partly Planned and Partly Reactive

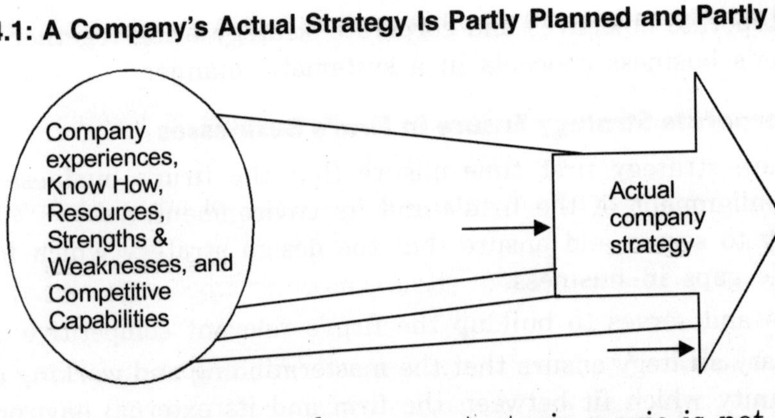

This figure clearly indicates the every strategic movie is not the result of proactive plotting and deliberate management design. Things are happened in firm which cannot be fully anticipated or planned in firms. When the market and competitive conditions of firm will take either unexpected turn or some aspect of a company's strategy hits stone wall. Some kind of strategic reaction or adjustment is required to companies. Therefore, a portion of company's strategy is always developed the project. It is coming as a reasoned response to unforeseen developments in form of fresh strategic maneuvers on the part of rival firms in market. These are shifting customer requirements and expectations to new technologies and market opportunities which are suitable to be changing political or economic climate or other unpredictable or unanticipated happenings in the surrounding environment. But apart from adapting strategy which have to changes in the market. And also a need to adapt strategy in terms of new learning emerges. It is pieces of the strategies which are working well in firm and which aren't and as management hits upon new ideas for improving the strategy. Crafting a strategy involves stitching together either a proactive or intended strategy and then adapting first one piece and then another as circumstances that surrounding the company's situation change or better options to emerge as a reactive/adaptive strategy.

Dealing with Strategic Uncertainty

- Strategic uncertainty is representation of the future uncertain trend or event which has unpredictable in real business.
- Information gathering and additional analysis in firm's will not able to reduce the uncertainty.
- Scenario analysis is basically acceptable uncertainty in business. Scenario can be used driven description of two or more future scenarios.

- Each uncertain require suitable strategy to make into certainty in firm's business.
- Strategic uncertainty is the strategic implications of strategic managers.
- It is key construct in strategy formulation.
- External analysis will be emerged with so many of strategic uncertainties to company's.
- Uncertainties can be managed; these can be grouped into logical clusters or themes.
- Strategic uncertainty is useful and assesses the importance of each cluster in order to set problems with regard to relevant and appropriate information gathering and analysis.
- Suitable strategic decisions help to strategist to gathering information, analysis of uncertainties in businesses.
- In changing conditions of uncertainty, strategist can form a suitable strategy for changing context of uncertainty of business.

Implications of Strategic Uncertainty

- Each strategic uncertainty involves potential trends or event which can be impact on present, proposed and even potential strategic business units of company's.
- Impact of strategic uncertainty will be depended on the strategic business unit to a firm.
- Some of strategic business units in firm which more important to compare to other units in strategic business units.
- Established strategic business units may be indicated in terms of associated of sales, profits and costs of products and services.
- Sales, profits and cost of products and services may not reflect the true value to a firm.
- Information needed areas are affected several strategic business units of company's.
- Strategic uncertainty implications are to be relevant to impact on strategic uncer-tainty.

4.2 THE STAGES OF CORPORATE STRATEGY FORMULATION–IMPLEMENTATION PROCESS

Craft and executing strategy are the heart and soul of managing a business enterprise. Crafting and executing a company formulation's strategy has involved the five stages of managerial process as outlined below:

Figure 4:2: The stages of Corporate Strategy Formulation – Implementation Process

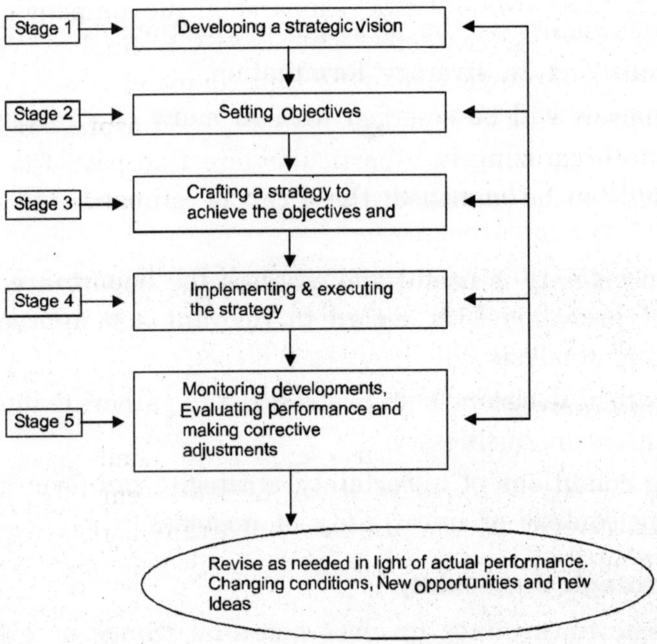

Figure 4.2 indicates the stages of corporate strategy formulation implementation process are listed below:

(1) Developing a strategy vision as concerned with company's future products and services which based on customer–market-technology.

(2) Setting objectives and using them as yardstick for measurement the company's performance and progress relating with present and future.

(3) Crafting a strategy to achieve the desired outcomes and move the company alongwith the strategic discipline which management has charted.

(4) Implementation and executing the selected strategy efficiently and effectively discharge in company.

(5) Monitoring, developments and initiating corrective adjustments towards the company's long term direction, objectives. Strategy or execution in light of the company's actual performance.

Stage 1: Developing a Strategic Vision

- Strategic vision is the future of the company's products, services, market, customer and technology. These are focused to improve its current market position and its future prospect.
- It must be determine the proper directional path the company and should take changes in the company's product and services.

- Strategic manager in company carefully draw and reasoned to make conclusions about how to try to modify the company's business and market position in business.
- Top management's views and conclusions about the company's attribute towards the products, services, customer, market and technology, these are focusing and constitute a strategic vision for the company.
- A strategic vision defines management aims and aspirations for the business and points an organizing in a particular direction path towards the strategic path for identifying the current trends and estimation of the future trends towards the company's business.
- Well and clear defined strategic vision ready to communicates management's aspirations to stake holders and it helps to guide and encourage energies of company personnel in a common direction.

Mission and Strategic Intents

- Strategic managers should be clearly know about their role and responsibilities to company, these are expressed in terms of statement of mission.
- Mission and strategic intents are very important both external stake holders and others managers in the company's.
- Mission statements clearly defined and it should be accomplish by strategic mangers in firms.
- Mission statements intents is not concerned with the details of strategic business unit competitive strategy or the directions and methods the businesses, it will be taken to achieve completive position rather, the concern of firm's overall directional strategic decision.

Strategic managers of a subsidiary will be responsible for changing and developing a strategy to business. While defining of strategy should be clear and it fit into the firm's subsidiary business and entire group.

Hamel and Prahalad have highlighted the importance of clear strategic intent can go much further in business and activities are listed below:

- It can be provided to motivation and galvanise alongwith enthusiasm throughout the organisation
- It is providing what they call a sense of density and discovery in business.
- When the absence of these, there is risk of different parts of the organisation in terms of different levels of management, all members of the organisation, it should be pulling in different directions in firm's activities.

Decisions is major part of the overall mission in a major corporation, it will exercise constraints elsewhere in business activities. The corporation aspire to earn short-term profits or long-term growth; it focus on selected countries corporation ready to make investment particularly in internal innovation use and develop the new products, or the acquisition of the other businesses. For this purpose, to develop strategic choice with regard to strategic matter explicit and it can helps to make strategic decisions.

Stage 2: Setting Objectives

Setting objectives play a magnificent role for development and designing of the company mission and vision. Basically, they represent the quantum of growth in this way seeks and achieve in the given timeframe. It also endows the companies features, products, services, and its characteristics that ensures the projected the growth. Objectives are setting the process, and also tackling the environment and deciding to appropriate objectives in business.

- The objectives provide the basis for major decisions of the firm and also said the organisational performance to be realised at each level at each level.
- The main purpose of the setting objectives is to convert the strategic vision into specific performance targets such as results and outcomes of the management in company.
- Setting objectives are yardsticks for tracking the company's progress and performance.
- Setting objectives is the specific tool for truly stretching an organisation to reach its full potential core capabilities.
- Company objectives should be improved the financial positions, economic positions and business positions.
- Company objectives are to be more intentional and focused on actions.

The balanced Scorecard Approach

- It is a combination of strategic and financial objectives of the company.
- It measuring the company performance for this purpose, it is require for setting both type of financial and strategic objectives and tracking their achievement.
- Strategic manager take more care and design the strategic objectives than on achieving financial objectives in business.

A NEED FOR LONG TERM AND SHORT TERM OBJECTIVES

A company can set and formulate financial and strategic objectives. These objectives are based on the both short-term and long term performance relating to business. Short term or annual objectives focuses too and attention to delivering immediate performance improvement in current year. Long term objectives focus on long term prosperity of firms or companies.

Long term objectives

Short run profit maximization is rarely based on the best approach to achieving sustained corporate growth and profitability of the firm. It is recognised by the strategic managers of the firm. Therefore, to achieve long term prosperity purpose strategic managers designed long term objectives. Long term objectives of the firm or company or organisation as listed below:

- Profitability
- Productivity
- Competitive position
- Employees development
- Employee relationships
- Public responsibility
- Technological leadership

Profitability

Profitability is an important functional area of the long-term objectives of the firm. The ability of any business to operate in the long run depends on attaining on acceptable level of profits. Strategically managed firms characteristically have a profit objective usually expressed in return on equity.

Productivity

Productivity is essential need for each strategist in the corporation. Strategic managers try to improve the productivity of their systems. Companies that can improve the input –output relationship normally increase profitability. Productivity objectives are some times stated in terms of desired decreases in most. This is an equally effective way to increase profitability.

Competitive position

Competitive position can increases profitability and productivity of the company. Companies or firms or organisation's competitive position reduces the cost of production of the output. The corporate success depends on the firm's competitive position. It is strongly dominated in the market.

Employee development

It refers to experienced employees are the asset of the organisation. For long-term purposes, the company's employees need training for further course of action that effectively and efficiently managed to produce productivity in the competitive position. Therefore, it is one of the major long-term objectives of the organisation.

Employee relationships

All companies actively seek good employee committed relations with organisational environment. Strategic manger should know the employee needs and expectations. Strategic managers take a decision to welfare programme for the employees of the companies. It is only can improved of the employee's relationship in the organisation.

Technological leadership

Technological leadership gives clear picture of the organisation goals and objectives for the long term changes in the business scenario; many companies state their objectives in terms of their technological leadership to meet technical requirement of the company.

Public responsibility

Business recognises their social responsibilities towards customer and society. Public responsibility is buildup long-term images in the society through providing social work to public, in this way a company discharge their responsibility towards public.

QUALITIES OF LONG TERM OBJECTIVES

Acceptable

Acceptable measures in companies are likely acceptable by the strategic managers to pursue objectives. Quality objectives are consistent with perceptions and preference of the company mission and vision. Even if certain long term objectives are frequently designed which are to be acceptable due to major interest groups which belong to external to the company.

Flexible

Long-term objectives should be modifiable in the event of the extraordinary changes due to environmental forecasts. At the same time, flexibility is usually increased at the expenses of specific events of the firms. Like wise, employee confidence may be tempered; therefore, adjustment of a flexible objective may affect their job in company.

Measurable

Objectives must clearly and precisely measurable in business. It clearly state what will be achieved and with what time frame. Objectives should measurable because of misunderstanding of long-term objectives of the company.

Motivating

Research studies indicate the people are most productive when objectives are set at a motivating level. This is the major problem to individuals and groups. Therefore, they are different in their perceptions of high enough. One valuable recommendation to strategic managers is to develop multiple objectives to motivating to individual and specific groups in the company.

Figure 4.3: Qualities of Long term Objectives

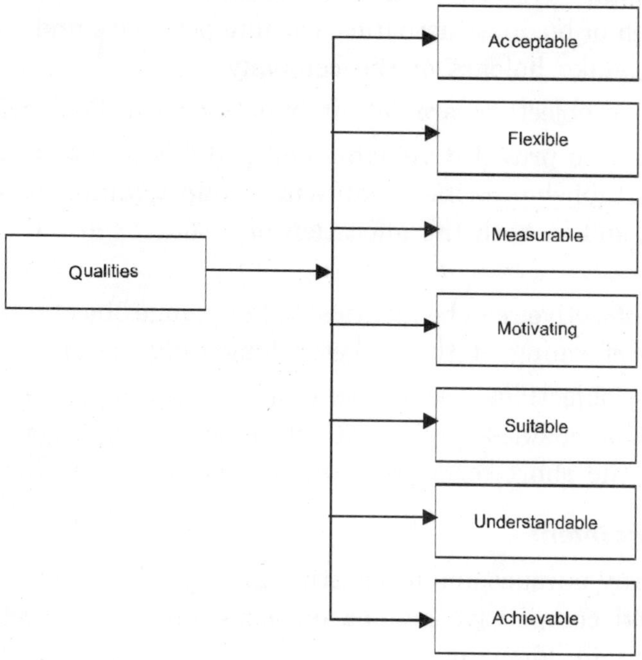

Figure 4.3 indicates the qualities of long term objectives of the company.

Suitable

Long-term objectives are suitable to the broad aims of the organisation or company. It is clearly expressed in the statement of company mission. Each objective should be a step toward attainment of overall goals.

Understandable

Strategic mangers clearly understand at all levels in organisation for accomplishment of objectives. They are should be understand major criteria for monitoring and evaluating of the organisational mission.

Achievable

It is the last long term quality objectives of the organisation. Achievable strategies always focus on mission and vision of the organisation or company. It is very difficult task to strategist to face complex external difficulties in the business. Strategist designs a suitable strategy for implementation for the achievement of the goals and objectives of the company or firms or organisation.

- In totally objectives should be quantitative, measurable, realistic, understandable, challenging, hierarchical, obtainable and concurrent among organisational units in business.

- Each objective can be associated with a time line in company. Objectives generally stated in terms of growth of assets, sales volume, market share, diversification of business activities, earning per share and social responsibility towards the stake holders of the company.
- Clearly defined objectives are definitely brought excellent benefits to company.
- Objectives can be provided valuable and suitable direction, allow synergy, aid evaluation, establish priorities, reduce uncertainty, minimize conflicts, stimulate exertion and aid in both the allocation of resources and the design of jobs in a company.
- Short range objectives can be identical to long range objectives if an organisation is already performing at the targeted long range level.
- Short range objectives are relating to the current year business trends, development of business policy with in a year. Long term objectives will not be affecting the short term goals and objectives of the firm's.

Concept of strategic intent

- When company pursues ambitious strategic objectives and concentrates its full resources and competitive actions on achieving that objectives i.e. strategic intent exhibit in company.
- Company objectives sometimes play other role like signaling unmistakable strategic intent to make quantum gains in competing against key rivals and establish itself as a clear cut winner in the market place and enhance core competency and resources in company.
- It can be dominant in company with in the industry in terms of unseating the existing industry leader, delivering the best customer service of any company and turning a new technology into products and services which capable of changing the way people work and live in company.
- Ambitious companies strategic intent to be invariable due to proportion to their immediate capabilities and market positions.

The need for objectives at all organisational levels

- Objectives are to be formulated by the top level management in all organisation.
- Setting of objectives needs to be broken down into performance targets for each separate business, product line, functional department and individual work unit in company.
- Company performance can't reach full potential without clearly defined objectives in each area of organisation. It contributes directly to the desired companywide customs and results.

- Strategic and financial objectives are setting to performance targets for each organisation unit which support rather than conflict with or without negotiable the achievement of company.

Stage 3: Crafting a Strategy to Achieve the Objectives and Vision

Crafting a strategy to achieve the objectives and vision is the third stages corporate strategic process in strategic management.

- A company's strategy is at full power only when it's processed from the corporate level to the business level and then from the business level to the functional level and operating levels in firms.
- Middle level and frontline managers cannot do good strategy making without understanding the company's long-term direction and higher level strategies apart from the vision and mission of the company.
- Strategy makers in a company are belong to same team and involved in many different pieces of the overall strategy crafted at various organisational levels that need to be in sync and united.
- Achieving the unity is the basic tools in strategy making and it is partly a function of communicating the company's basic strategy, this themes effectively across the whole organisation and establishing clear strategic principles and guidelines for lower level strategy that helpful in making strategy at lower level in company.
- Cohesive strategy making down through the hierarchy becomes easier to achieve when company strategy is distilled into pithy , easy to grasp terminology that can be used to drive consistent strategic action throughout the company.
- The greater number of company's strategic personal who are knowing , understanding and make to the company's basic direction and looking for strategy, it is the smaller the risk that people and organisation units will go off in conflicting strategic directions towards crafting strategy and achieve the mission and vision of the company.
- Many strategic people are given a strategy making role when strategic decision making is pushed down to frontline levels.
- Good communication of strategic themes and guiding principles of among themes members, thus it serves a valuable strategy unifying the company's vision and mission purpose.
- A company's strategic plan lays out its future direction, performance targets and strategy.
- Development of a strategic vision, setting objectives, and crafting a strategy are basic direction setting tasks of a company.

- In this stage involves to map out the company's direction that based on its short-term and long range performance targets and competitive moves and internal action approached, these can be used in achieving the targeted business results.
- Crafting strategy constitute a strategic plan for coping with industry and competitive conditions, it is the expected actions of the industry's key players, challenges and issues that stand as obstacles to the company's success.

Figure 4.4: Structuring Strategic Decisions

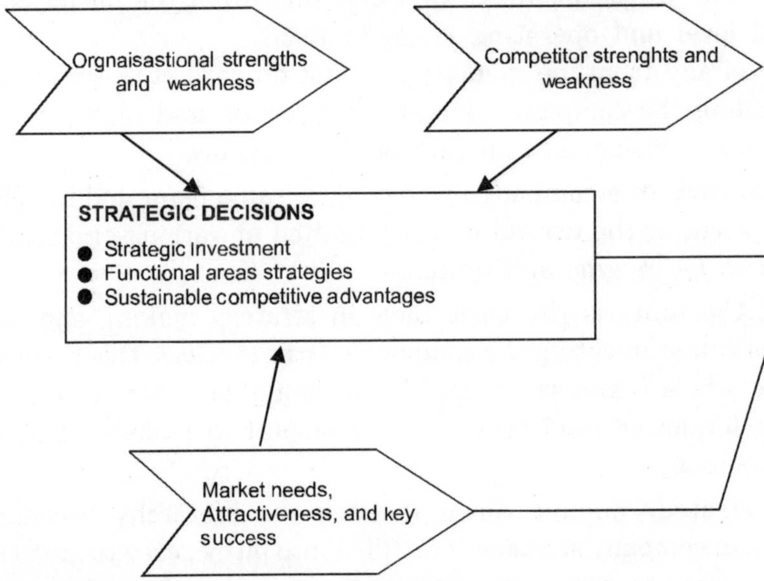

Figure 4.4 exhibit the strategic structuring decisions are based inputs from a variety of assessments are relevant. Strategic decisions based on three types of assessments are outlined below:

- First stage is concerned organisational strengths and weaknesses.
- Second stage is concerned evaluates the competitor strengths, weaknesses and strategies.
- Third stage is concerned assesses the competitive context in the form of the customers and their needs, the market, and the market environment.

Stage 4: Implementing and Executing the Strategy

Managing strategy, implementation and execution of strategy is on operation oriented. It involves activity which aimed at shaping the performance of core business activities in a company. It is supportive manner in a company. These things are easily and the most demanding to firms and it can be time consuming part of the strategy management and implementation process in firms. Strategic manager take special initiative for convert strategic plans into actions and results and able to cope and direct organisational change , in this way motivate people , build and strengthen company competences and competitive capabilities , create a strategy which work in better climate and either meet or beat standard performance targets in a company.

Managing strategy, implementation and execution of strategy process includes the following principal aspects:

- Trained and skilled staffing in the organisation that consciously building and strengthening strategy supportive competences and competitive capabilities and organizing the work effort in this achieve strategy.
- Development of budget that guide to company how to efficient utilization of ample resources into those activities critical to strategic success.
- It ensures that policies, objectives and operating procedures facilities rather than impede effective execution.
- A company can be using the best known practices to perform core business activities and pushing for continuous improvement.
- Installation information or software and operating systems which ensures to company personnel to better to use and carry out their strategic roles day in and day out.
- Motivating is the special tool to top level management of company, it is useful to motivate their employees and to pursue the target objectively energetically.
- Providing incentives and rewards to employees who have done excellent achievement performance, objectives which is the output of good strategy execution.
- Crafting culture of company and its work climate conducive to successful strategy implementation and execution.
- Exerting and internal leadership that needed to drive for implementation forward and try to keep to improving strategy execution in business. Organisation has responsible to take appropriate decisions on the basis of strengths, weakness of the firms.

Good strategy execution involves creating strong which is "fits" between strategy and organisational capabilities and executed by the skilled top level management in enterprise, it is based between strategy and the reward structure. And also it is between strategy and internal operating systems, and between strategy and the organisational climate and culture in a company.

Stage 5: Monitoring Developments, Evaluating and Making Corrective Adjustments

- Monitoring developments, evaluating and making corrective adjustments are one of the magnificent and significant stages in strategic management.

- A company's strategy formulation, implementation and monitoring developments, evaluating and making corrective adjustments are never final; it is continuous process for dramatic changes in terms of improvement.
- An effective managing strategy is ongoing process; it is not now and then task of company.
- It involves be evaluating the company's process, assessing the impact of new external developments and making corrective adjustments which are relating of company's vision, objectives, policies and execution of strategy into different methods in companies.
- This stage decides whether to continue or change the company's mission and vision and objectives.
- Company's strategist always give directions relating with strategy which seem well to be matched industry and competitive and performance targets are being met in this way strategist may decide to stay the course.
- Well defined, planned and fine tuning strategic plan and continuing with on going efforts to improve strategy execution are sufficient in a company.
- Company can be developing appropriateness strategies and its directions which are cope and overcome encounters disruptive changes in its external environment.
- Poor strategy monitoring impact to company's business and reduce its operation efficiency in terms of profit, sales and customer base. For avoiding the poor strategy monitoring, a company must to take corrective action when evaluation of strategy and try to avoid to poor monitoring, poor execution.
- External and internal conditions of company, a strategist reformulate a suitable strategy, to make proper objectives, mission, vision and policy and appropriate direction towards the growth and development of company's performance in terms of competitive advantages and core competence.
- A company ready and expected to modify, changes its strategic vision, direction, objectives, and strategy over time in business.
- Proficient strategy execution provides on opportunity to firms for learning of new things, changes from internal and external environment.
- Well defined strategy execution and well assessment of company performance which is needed for improving company's normal and desirable results.
- Strategy execution is continuously searching the dramatic changes for improvement in this way making corrective adjustments whenever and wherever a company is required.

4.3 STRATEGIC ALTERNATIVES

Strategic alternatives are provided a magnificent role in planning perspective. Strategic alternatives always develop alternatives for strategy formulation, implementation and control of short term and long term planning perspective in companies.

Michael Porter's Generic Strategies

According to Michael Porter's, a choosing strategy in organisations which gains competitive advantage, it is choosing from three generic competitive approaches. They are as listed below:

- Cost leadership/low cost
- Differentiation
- Focus

These strategies are known as generic because of all business or industries can pursue them regardless of whether they are manufacturing, service or not -for – profit organisations. Each of the generic strategies results from a company making consistent choices on product, market and distinctive competencies.

The product/market distinctive-competing choices and generic competitive strategies at business level industries are listed below:

- Cost leadership
- Differentiation
- Focus

And its choices as listed below:

- Product differentiation
- Market segmentation
- Distinctive competency

Michael Porter's calls these strategies as generic strategies. Cost leadership strategy emphasizes to be producing standardized products at a very low per unit cost for consumers who are price sensitive. Differentiation strategy aims to be producing products and services which are considered unique in industry wide and directed towards to consumers who are relatively price insensitive.

- Michael Porter's imply different organisational arrangements and make careful and proper control procedures and designed to be appropriate incentive systems for human resources in enterprise.
- In the case of the larger firms with greater accessibility of resources which typically compete on a cost leadership or differentiation basis.
- In the case of the small firms often compete on a focus basis in business.

Porter gives stresses to need for strategists to perform cost benefit analyses to evaluate the sharing opportunities which are existed among company's and potential strategic business units. When sharing activities and resources that enhances competitive advantage by lowering costs or raising differentiation in company's. In additionally, prompting sharing, Porter stresses the need for company's to transfer skills and expertise among existed autonomous business units effectively in order to gain competitive advantage. These are depending upon the type of industry, size of firm and nature of competition, various strategies can yield major advantages in the form of cost leadership, differentiation, and focus.

Figure 4:5: Michael Porter's Generic Strategy

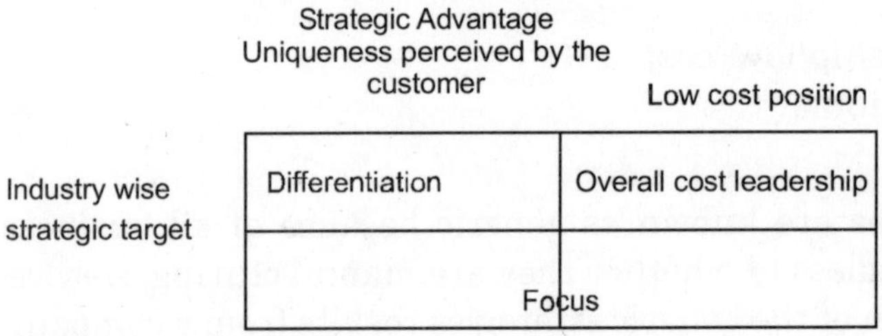

4.4 COST LEADERSHIP STRATEGIES

A company's goal in pursuing a cost leadership or low cost strategy is to out perform competitors by doing everything. It can to pursue goods or service at a cost lower than their competitors. Cost leadership strategy is required strategies choice of product and service into different market segmentation and its competitors. It pursued in conjunction with differentiation. Cost leadership strategies are gain to forward, backward and horizontal integration strategies. A successful cost leadership strategy usually utilization of the entire firm's in the form of higher efficiency, low overhead , limited perks to human resources, minimize the waste, intensive screening of budget and its tools like income and expenditure, effective using the wide span control, rewards linked to cost containment, and broad employee participation in cost control efforts in firm's in this reduce cost of the product and services.

Exhibit - 4.1: Advantage of Cost Leadership Strategy
There are two advantages occurs from cost leadership strategy. They are as mentioned below: • Cost leadership strategy refers to lower costs of product and service offered by the company, the cost leader is able to charge a lower price than its competitors. The cost leader makes a higher profit than its competitors because of its lowers costs of products and service. • If industry rivalry increases and companies start to compete on price, the cost leader will be able to withstand competition start to compete on price; the cost leader will be able to withstand completion better than other companies because of its lower costs. For both reasons, cost leaders are likely to earn above–average profits.

Exhibit – 4.2: Disadvantages of Cost Leadership Strategy

Important disadvantages of cost leadership strategy are outlined:

- The principal dangers of the cost –leadership approach risk in competitors ability to find ways of producing at lower cost and beat the cost leader.
- Competitor's ability to easily imitate the cost leader's method is another threat to the cost leadership strategy.
- The cost leadership strategy carries a risk that the cost leader, the single-minded desire to reduce costs, may lose right to changes in customer tastes.

Strategic Choices

The company cost leader strategy is choosing a low level of product differentiation. Differentiation is expensive for company; if the company expands resources to make its product unique then its costs rise. The cost leader aims for a level of differentiation not marketing inferior to that of the differentiator (a company competes by spending resources on product development) but a level obtainable at low cost.

The cost leader also normally ignores the different market segments and positions. Its product is to appeal to the average customer. The main reason is that the cost leader makes it choice by developing a line of products and tailored to the needs of different market segments. It is an expensive proposition. A cost leader normally engages to only a limited amount of market segmentation. Customer happy when the company normally charges a lower price than its competitors attracts customers to its products and service.

In developing distinctive competencies, the overriding goal of the cost leader must be to develop competencies. It enables to increase its efficiency and lower its costs compared with its competitors. The development of distinctive competencies in manufacturing and material management is central to achieving this goal. Companies is pursuing a low cost strategy may attempt to ride down the experience therefore; they can lower their manufacturing costs. Achieving a low cost position may also require that the company develop skills in flexible manufacturing and adopt develop skills in flexible manufacturing and adopt efficient materials -management techniques.

4.5 DIFFERENTIATION STRATEGY

Differentiation strategy refers to the differentiated company's ability to satisfy a customer needs. A differentiation strategy should be pursued only after a careful study of buyer's needs and preference to determine the feasibility of incorporating one or more unique product features. It helps to company to charge a premium price; a price considerable above the industry average. Company ability to increase by charging premium prices (rather than by reducing costs of the output) allows the differentiator to outperform its competitors and gain above average profits. The premium price is usually substantially above the price charged by the cost leader, and customers pay it therefore, they believe the product-differentiated qualities to be worth the difference. Successful differentiation provides greater product flexibility , greater compatibility, lower costs, improved services, less maintenance , greater convenience or more features in this strategy.

Exhibit 4.3: Advantages of Differentiation Strategy
Advantages of differentiation strategy as outlined : • The company's unit price must be higher than that of the average company and its unit cost must be equivalent to that of the average company. • The company's unit must be lower than that of the average company and its units price must be equivalent to that of the average company. • The company must have both a lower unit and a higher unit price than the average company.

Exhibit 4.4: Disadvantages of Differentiation Strategy
Major disadvantages of differentiation strategy are listed below: • Developing the distinctive competency needed to provide a differentiation advantage is often expensive to company. • A differential cost usually has higher costs than the cost leader. • The main problems with the differentiation strategy center on the company's long-term ability to maintain its perceived uniqueness in customers' eye in market. • A differentiation strategy is the ease to competitors can imitate a differentiator's product and the difficulty of maintaining a premium price.

Strategic Choice of Differentiation strategy

The differentiate strategy chooses a high level of product differentiation to gain a competitive advantage. Differentiation can be achieved with quality, innovation and responsive a product appeal to customers' psychological desires can become a source of differentiation. A company pursues a differentiation strategy strives to differentiate itself along as many dimensions as possible. The less it resembles its rival, the more it is protected from competition, and the wider is its market appeal.

A differentiator chooses to market segment. Company offers a product to design for each market differentiator, but a company chooses to serve just niches where it has a specific differentiation advantage.

A differentiated company concentrates on the organisational function that provides the source of its differentiation advantage. Differentiation based on the innovation and technological competency depends on R&D function. A differentiator does not want to increase costs unnecessarily.

4.6 FOCUS STRATEGY

Focus strategy is the third generic competitive strategy and one of the foundations of business level strategy. Focus strategy is directed towards serving the need of a limited customer group or segment. A focus strategy is the focused company concentrates on serving a particular market niche that may be defined geographically, by type of customer, or by segment of the product line. A successful focus strategy depends on an industry segments like customer, product line, geographical segment.

Once company has chosen its market segment, a company may pursue a focus strategy through either a differentiation or a low cost approach. A focused company is a specialized differentiator or cost leader. Because of their small size, few focus firms are able to pursue cost leadership and differentiation simultaneously. If a firm uses a low cost approach , it competes against the cost leader in the market segment where it has no cost advantage with focus strategy , a company concentrates on small volume custom products , where it has a cost and leaves the large volume standardized market to the cost leader.

If a focuser pursues a differentiation approach, then all the means of differentiation that are open to the differentiators are available to the focused company. The point is that the focused company competes with the differentiator in only one or in just a few segments. Focused companies are likely to develop differentiated product qualities successfully because of their knowledge of a small customer set or knowledge of a region. Further more, concentration on a small range of products. Some times allows a focuser to develop innovations faster than a large differentiation. A focused company concentrates on building market share in one market segment and, if successful, may begin to serve more and more market segments.

Exhibit 4.5: Advantages of Focus Strategy

An important advantage of focus strategy as listed below:

- Focus strategy is protected from competitors to the extent therefore; it can provide a product or service.
- Focus strategy gives the focuser power over its buyer therefore; they cannot get the something from anyone also.
- It permits a company stay close to its customers and to respond to their changing needs.
- It can be developed superior skills in customer responsiveness, its based unit's ability to serve the needs of regional customer.

These are advantages are focused to efficiency, quality, innovation and customer responsiveness of the company.

Exhibit-4.6: Disadvantages of Focus Strategy

An important and major disadvantages of focus strategy are listed below:

- Key focuser failure due to powerful suppliers of goods and service.
- Therefore, the competitor is strong control of market segmentation.
- A large differentiator sometimes is not experience to focus strategy due to the difficulty of managing a large number of market segments.
- A focuser produces at a small volume, its production costs often exceed. Higher cost can also reduces profitability and even loss of the business, so that this factor has one of important disadvantages of focus strategy.
- The focuser's in niche can suddenly disappear because of technological changes in customer tastes.
- Focuser is not concentrated of efficiency, quality, innovation and customer responsiveness

It impact is to failure of focus strategy in company.

Strategic Choices of Focus Strategy

The specific product/market/distinctive competency choice is made by a focused company. Differentiation can be high or low because the company can pursue a low-cost or differentiation approach. As for customer groups, a focused company chooses specific niches in which to compete, rather than going for whole market, like the cost leader. A focuser may pursue any distinctive competency because it can pursue any kind of differentiation or low cost advantage.

A focused strategy company can take to develop a competitive advantage explain why there so many small companies in relation to large ones. A focused company has enormous opportunity to develop its own niche and compete against low cost and differentiated enterprises, which tend to be larger. A focus strategy provides an opportunity for an entrepreneur to find and then exploit a gap in the market by developing an innovative product that customers cannot do without.

Generic Strategies Comparative Skills and Resource Requirement

Generic strategies comparative skills and resource requirement are presented below:

Generic Strategy	Commonly Required skills and Resources	Common organisational Requirement
Overall Cost Leadership	• Sustained capital investment and easily to access capital. • Process business reengineering skills • Intensive supervisions of labor in firm's	• Tight cost control in firms. • It required frequent and detailed/control reports. • It structured organisation responsibilities.

Contd....

	• Low cost distribution system. • Products designed for ease in manufacture.	• Incentives based on meeting strict quantitative targets
Differentiation	• Strong marketing abilities in firms business • Product engineering in business • Creative flair in firms. • Strong capability in basic research in firms. • Corporate reputation for quality or technological leadership. • Long tradition in the industry or unique combinations of skills drawn from other business. • Strong co-operation from channels in business.	• Strong coordination among function like in R&D, product development, and marketing • Subjective measurement and incentives instead of quantitative measures. • Amenities to attract highly skilled labour, scientists or creative people in business.
Focus	• It is the combination of the above policies directed towards particular strategic target.	• It is the combination of the above policies directed towards the particular strategic targets.

Best Cost Provider Strategy

Best cost provider strategy is the new model. It is the further development of three generic strategies. The five competitive generic strategies are coming under the best cost provider strategy model. This model is being pursued competitive advantage in business.

Figure 4.6: The Five Competitive Generic Strategies

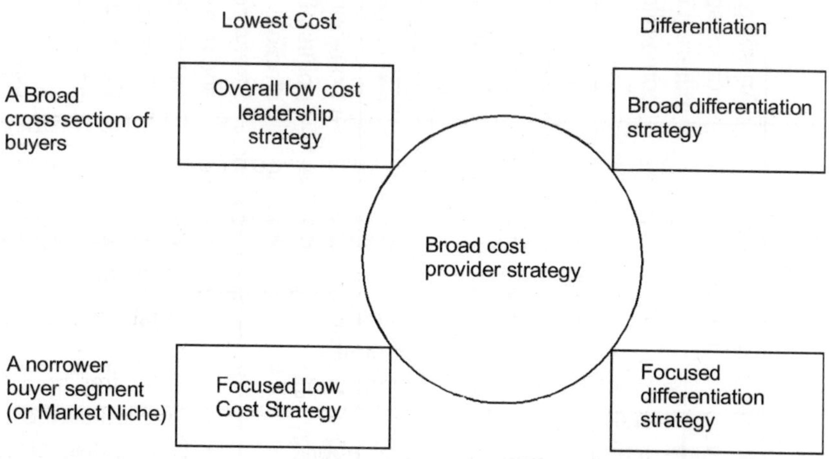

Figure 4.6 Indicates the five generic competitive strategies as outlined:

- Overall low cost leadership strategy
- Broad Differentiation strategy

Type of feature	Low cost provider	Broad differentiation	Best cost provider	Focused low cost and focused differentiation
• Strategic targets	A broad section of the market	A broad section of the market.	Value conscious buyer	A narrow market niche where buyer needs and preferences are distinctively different from the rest of the market.
Basics of competitive advantage	Lower costs than competitors	An ability to offer buyers something different from competitors.	More value for the money	Lower cost in serving the niche (focused low cost) or special attributes that appeal to the tastes or requiremtnts of niche members(focused differentiation)
Market emphasis	Try to make a virtue out of product features that lead to low cost	Build in whatever features buyers are willing to pay for, Charge a premium price to cover the extra costs of diff-erentiating features.	Either underprice rival brands with comparable features or match the price of rivals and provide better features to build a reputation for delivering the best value	Communicate how the focuser's product attributes and capabilities aim at catering to niche member tastes and or specialized requirements
Sustaining the strategy	• Offer economical prices/ good value • Aim at contributing to a sustainable cost advantage the key is to manage costs down, year after, in every area of the business.	• Communicate the points of difference in credible ways • Stress constant impr-and use innovation ovement to stay ahead of initiative competitors. • Concentrate on a few differentiating features. tout them to create a reputation and brand image.	Develop unique expertise in simultaneously mana-ging costs down and upscaling features and attributes	Remain totally dedicated to serving the niche better than other competitors ; don't blunt the firm's image and efforts by entering other segments or adding other product categories to widen market appeal.

Contd....

Type of feature	Low cost provider	Board Differentiation	Best cost provider	Focused low cost and focused Differentiation
Product line	A good basic product with few frills (acceptable quality and limited selection)	Many product variations, wide, selection, strong emphasis on differentiating features	Good to excellent attributes several to many upscale features.	Features and attributes that appeal to the tastes and or special needs of the target segment.
Product emphasis	A continuous search for cost reduction without sacrificing acceptable quality and essential features	Creation of value of buyer ; strive for product superiority.	Incorporation of upscale features and attributes at low cost.	Tailor made for the tastes and requirements of niche members.

- Focused Low – Cost Strategy
- Broad cost Provider Strategy
- Focused Differentiation Strategy

Distinctive Features of the Generic Competitive Strategies

Distinctive features of the generic competitive strategies are presented in table:

Grand Strategies / Directional Strategies

A firm's uses various strategy alternatives for achieving its growth, survival objectives. Grand strategies are also called as master or business strategies that are intended to provide basic direction for strategic actions. Grand strategies aim is the long term sustainable development and growth of the organisation.

Grand strategies indicate how long range objective will be achieved. Thus, grand strategy can be defined as a comprehensive general approach that guides major actions.

Grand strategies serve as the basis for achieving major long term objectives of a single business; concentration market, market development, product development, innovation, horizontal integration, vertical integration, joint venture, concentration diversification, conglomerate diversification, retrenchment, turnaround, divestiture and liquidation. Grand strategies are usually combined all strategies of the organisation or company arena.

Figure 4.7: Grand strategies Structures in enterprises

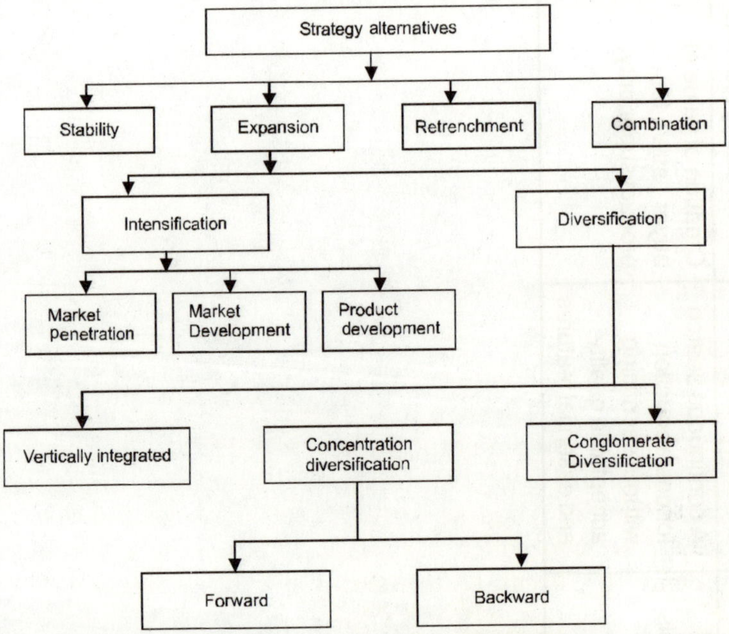

A grand strategy is principally consisting of stability strategies, expansion strategies, retrenchment strategies and combination strategies. These strategies are known as grand strategies or master strategies or direction strategies.

Features of Grand Strategies

The basic features of grand strategies are presented in the table:

Strategy	Basic Feature
Stability	• Stability strategy refers to the maintaining status quo of the existing business operation. • Stability strategy aims at slow growth rate. • It can be maintained the existing level of efforts in business. • It is satisfied with incremental growth in of its functional performance in terms of its customer groups, customer functions.
Expansion	• An organisation desired to expand extents its business network widening the scope of its customer groups, customer functions and state of the art technologies. • Intensive expansion is a fundamental approach to safeguard and develop the organisations product market and thereby increased the volume of scales, profit, market share and total business network very rapidly. • It can be entering new businesses that are unrelated to existing businesses.
Retrenchment	• An organisation decides to reduce its business operation by reducing the scope of customer groups or customer functions or alternative technologies with view to have better control for better performance, retrenchment strategies are accepted. • It can be drops the business as such through sell out or liquidation.
Combination	• Combination strategy refers to the combination of the stability, expansion and retrenchment strategy in different levels of the organisation

4.7 CHARACTERISTICS AND SCOPE OF VARIOUS GRAND STRATEGIES

Stability Strategy

Stability strategy refers to the maintaining status quo of the existing business operation. Stability strategy aims at slow growth rate. It is followed as a matter of principle when an organisation attempts incremental growth of its functional performance in terms of its customer groups, customer functions, and alternative technologies, whether in combination or individually. Thus when organisation decides to serve the same target customer groups with same products service and follows the same objective to maintain the stable business status, it can be termed as stability strategy.

Characteristics of stability strategy

- A firm opting for stability strategy maintains with the same business, same product–marked posture and functions, maintaining same level of effort as at status quo of the existing business.

- It aims to enhance functional efficiencies in on achievement way, it is achieved through better deployment and utilization of resource.
- It involves the assessment of the firm which is maintaining status quo in terms of desired income and profits.
- It can be helped to business to incremental improvements in functional efficiencies.
- Generally, this strategy will be quite modest in business growth objectives; it is applicable only firms which modest growth objective will vote for this strategy.
- This strategy is a safety oriented and status quo oriented strategy.
- It does not require much fresh investments.
- It is fairly frequently employed strategy in business.
- Firm's which are followed this strategy, these firm's are definitely expect benefits from concentrating its resource and attention towards the existing business/ products and markets.
- And also rewards are limited in firms.
- Stability strategy does not permit the firm's renewal process for bringing in fresh investments and new products and markets for the firm.

Expansion Strategy

When an organisation desired to expand extents its business network widening the scope of its customer groups, customer functions and state of the art technologies, we have the making of an expansion strategy. Expansion or growth strategy is principally adopted when an organisation enhance its level of objectives with high target. Intensive expansion is a fundamental approach to safeguard and develop the organisations product market and thereby increased the volume of scales, profit, market share and total business network very rapidly.

Characteristics of expansion strategy

- Expansion strategy is just opposite to stability strategy.
- Expansion strategies are those strategies which are high rewarded in firms and also risk is too high in business.
- It is flexible and most frequently employed generic strategy.
- It is the true growth strategy; the firm's aims to expansion business activities in this way to meets its growth objectives in firms.
- It involves the redefinition of the business activities of company.
- It requires fresh investments and it involves the process of renewal of the firm in this way introducing new business/products/markets are facilitated only by expansion strategy.

- It is highly versatile strategy; it offers several permutations and combinations for growth. For this purpose, the firm's opting for the expansion strategy can generate many alternatives within the strategy by altering its propositions regarding in terms of products, markets, functions and pick the one that suits it most.
- It has fold two major routes; intensification and diversification.
- Intensification and diversification is the tool of growth strategies; it pursues difference it's actually growth in business.
- Firm's intensification strategy pursues growth by working its current business operation in businesses.
- Intensification can be encompasses with the three alternative routes as outlined;
  (a) Market penetration strategy
  (b) Market development strategy
  (c) Product development strategy
- Diversification strategy refers to expansion of business into new business that are outside the current businesses and markets.
- An important type's diversification as listed below:
  - Related diversification
  - Unrelated diversification
  - Internal diversification
  - External diversification
  - Horizontal diversification
  - Vertical diversification
  - Active diversification
  - Passive diversification
  - Concentric diversification
- Vertically integrated diversification involves that firm's are going into new businesses which are related to current ones.
- Vertical integration further classified into two broad components such as forward integration and backward integration.
- The firm's remain vertically within the given product process sequence; it is intermediaries in the chain become new businesses.
- Concentration diversification refers to introducing new products which are connected to the firm's existing process or technology. There fore, the new products are not vertically linked to the existing ones. They are not considered as intermediates.

- They serve new functions in new markets and it is spinned off from the firm's existing facilities.
- Conglomerate diversification refers to a new business is added to firm's portfolio. It is unrelated diversification and it disconnected from the existing business operation of firm's in the form of process/technology/function. In this strategy, there is no connection between the existing business and new business.

Retrenchment/Divestment Strategy

When an organisation decides to reduce its business operation by reducing the scope of customer groups or customer functions or alternative technologies with view to have better control for better performance, retrenchment strategies are accepted. In retrenchment strategy, unattractive and unwanted areas of business are sequenced gradually. It is a not matter of failure of business planning, rather well planned exercise to get rid of unprofitable parts of business which will help the organisation concentrate its total attention to the most profitable and promising areas of business only.

Characteristics of retrenchment/divestment strategy

- It involves retrenchment of some of the activities in a given business of the firm or sells out of some of the business assets.
- It is one of the corporate strategies to reduce its operation by reducing the scope of customer groups and customer functions.
- It involves the redefinition of the businesses operation.
- Compulsions in this strategy are different and vary in business operation.
- Retrenchment is necessary in the following firm's conditions:
  - When business unprofitable
  - When high competition from the competitor
  - When industry is over capacity
  - When failure of strategy

Combination Strategy

In changing business environment, an organisation may also find it beneficial to adopt a unique combination of stability, expansion and retrenchment indifferent levels related areas of business which depending on the business environment. In other words, combination strategy refers to the combination of the stability, expansion and retrenchment strategy in different levels of the organisation

Major Reasons for Organisations Adopting Different Grand Strategies

A firm's is adopted stability strategy in the following conditions:

- It is less risk, it involves less change and people feel comfortable with things which are happen in firms.

- The business environment relative stable condition.
- Expansion of business is threaten to firm's.
- Firm's consolidation required through stabilizing after a period of rapid expansion of business operation.

A firm's adopted expansion strategy in the following conditions:

- It imperative when environment demands increase the pace of activity in firm's operations.
- It is the results of expansion business operation in firms; chief executive is the responsible person for firm's growth.
- Increase the size of business operation which is control over the market vis – a – vis competitors.
- It is advantage to firm's in this way enhancing the scale of operations.

Firm's adopted retrenchment strategy in the following conditions:

- When the management no longer wishes to remain in business both partly or wholly due to continuous losses and unviability.
- When business environment can be faced threaten to firm's operations.
- It can be ensure to be reallocation of resources form unprofitable to profitable business.

Firm's combination Strategy is adopted in the following conditions:

- An organisation is large and ready to faces complex environment in business operations.
- An organisations is consisting of different businesses, each of which comes under the different industry that requiring a different response.

Product Market Expansion Greed

Expansion or growth strategy can either be via intensification or diversification. Product market expansion greed developed by Igor Ansoff gave framework as presented that explained the intensification options available to a firm.

Table 4.1 : Product Market Expansion Greed

I. Growth in existing product markets. Increased market share. Increased product usage. Increase the frequency. Increase the quantity used Find new application for current users.	II. Product development. Add product features, product refinement. Develope a new generation product. Develope new product for the same market
III. Market development expand geographically. Target new segments.	IV. Diversification involving new products and new markets related/unrelated

Market Penetration

Market penetration strategy is one the most important expansion strategy on the current business. The firms direct its core resources to the profitable growth of a single product. It is in a single market and with a single technology.

Market Development

Market development is consisting of marketing present's products and services which offered by company, company is required to be adding different channels of distribution or by changing the content of advertising or promotional media.

Product development

It involves substantial modification of existing products and services or creation of new, but these are related items that can be marketed to current customers through established channels.

4.8 DIVERSIFICATION

Diversification refers to company is diverting the business focus from the existing traditional areas to new promising areas. Since technology is changing day-by-day, 'customer' demands are changing accordingly. Company introduced new and substitute products and service available in the market to meet the customer's expectations and to draw their attention. These are changing attitudes of the customers, the company has been opening more and more new areas of promising business. Diversification may involve internal or external, related or unrelated, horizontal or vertical, active or passive dimensions. The change of business focus may be either in terms of customer function, customer group and new alternative technologies.

Types of Diversification

Types of Diversification

An important type's diversification as listed below:

Related diversification
Unrelated diversification
Internal diversification
External diversification
Horizontal diversification
Vertical diversification
Active diversification
Passive diversification
Concentric diversification
Conglomerate diversification

Related diversification

Related diversification is diversification into new business activity that is linked to company's existing business activity normally these activities are commonality between one or more components of each activity's of existing business activity of value chain. Normally these linkages are based on manufacturing marketing or technological commodities.

Related diversification options for manufacturer in business as outlined:

- Exchange or share assets or competencies, thereby exploiting the following:
  - Brand name of company
  - Marketing skills of company
  - Sales and distribution capacity
  - Manufacturing skills
  - R&D and new product capability
- Economies of scale for company's products and services.

Unrelated diversification

Unrelated diversification is diversification into a new business area that has no obvious connection with any of the companies existing areas.

Unrelated diversification options for a manufacturer as outlined:

- Manage and allocate cash flow in company
- Obtain high rate of investment in company
- Obtain to bargain price
- Refocus a firm
- Reduce risk by operating in multiple product markets
- Tax benefits
- Obtain liquid assets in company
- Vertical integration of company
- Defend against a takeover in firms.

Internal diversification

Diversification business activities with in the company such is known as internal diversification. It means that a company ready to introduce new products with the same geographical areas.

External diversification

External diversification involves to diversification of the business activities like manufacturing, products, marketing, technological changes diversified with the other companies to save to be operating cost of the goods and service.

Horizontal diversification

Horizontal diversification is undertaken in order to increase market share by expansion of same product lines with more varieties to serve customers in different areas, of different types and affluence levels. Horizontal diversification may be taken up to expand business geographically in new territories by taking up an increase market share and improve business volume.

Vertical diversification

Vertical diversification means diversification into a new production line to produce items required as inputs for other main products of the same company. Vertically integration refers to company diversify its business into a number of different business areas. Diversification into a new production line to produce goods and service required as inputs for other main products of the same company. For instance a company diversifies its business into number of different business areas like banking and finance services, energy and utility, health care and insurance, manufacturing retail, telecom. It may be undertaken by a company with the purpose of either maintaining continuous flow of products and service to customer. Vertical Integration Company offer numerous products and service for satisfying customers. A company is opening its own sales and marketing division and showrooms for selling product and service to customer instead of selling through agents and distributors. It can be controlled over the input supply and output distribution also.

Vertical integration further classified into two broad categories. They are listed below:

Backward or Upstream integration

Forward or Downstream integration

Upstream or back ward integration

Back integration or upstream refers to company is diversifying the business operation towards some of the raw materials or input supply. Backward integration involves moving into intermediate manufacturing and raw material production.

Downstream or forward integration

Forward integration or downstream refers to company is diversifying business operations for marketing sales distribution of products and services and taking up these activities to bring the organisation closer to the ultimate customer.

Figure 4.8: Stages in the Raw material to Consumer Production Chain

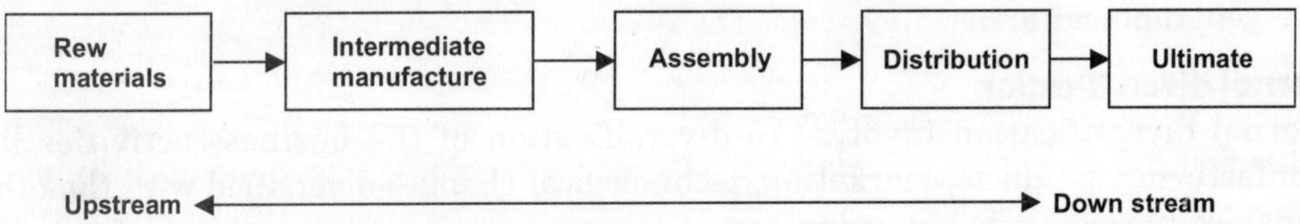

Figure 4.8 highlights the stages in the raw material to customer production chain. It indicates the four steps are listed below:

Intermediate manufacture

Assembly

Distribution

Ultimate customer

Backward integration involves moving into intermediate manufacturing and raw material production. Forward integration involves movement into distribution. At each stage in chain, value is added to the product. It means that a company at that stage takes the product produced in the previous stage, transforms it in some way and then sells the output at a higher price to a company at the next stage in the chain. The difference between the price paid for inputs and the price at which the product is sold is a measure of the value added at that stage.

Figure 4.9: The Raw material to Consumer Production Chain in the Personal Computer industry

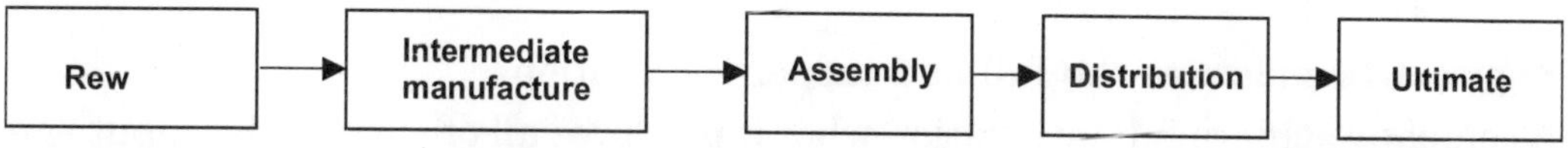

Examples	Examples	Examples	Examples
Dow Chemicals	Intel	Apple	Bizmart
Union Carbide	Motorola	Compaq	Computer world

As an example of the value added concept, consider the production chain in the personal computer industry. This figure indicates that the computer industry. Raw materials companies include the manufactures of specialty ceramics, chemicals, and metal such as Dow Chemicals and Union Carbide. These companies sell their output to the manufacturers of intermediate products the intermediate manufacturers include companies like. Intel and Motorola, transform the ceramics, chemicals and metal they purchase into computer components such as micro processors, memory chips, and disk drives. In doing so they add value to the new materials, they purchase. These components are then sold to assembly companies like Apple and Compaq, which take these components and transform, them into personal computers i.e., add value to the components they purchase many of the completed personal computers world, which in turn sell them to final customers. The distribution also value added to the product by making it accessible to customers, and by providing service and support thus value is added by companies at each stage in the raw materials to consumer chain.

Viewed this way, vertical integration involves a choice about which value added stages of raw material to consumer chain to compete in.

Figure 4.10: Full and Taper Integration

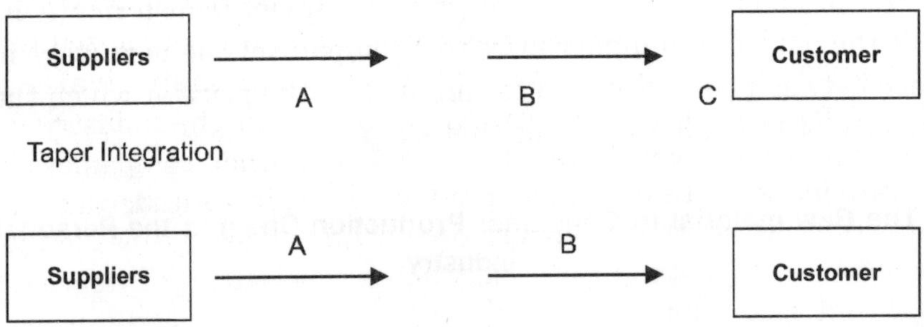

Figure 4.10 indicates the full and tapper integration.

A company achieve full integration what it produces all of a particular input needed for it's possess or when it disposes of all of its input through its own operations.

Taper integration occurs when a company buys from independent suppliers in addition to company -owned suppliers or when it disposes of its output through independent outlets in addition to company owned outlets.

Creating Value through vertical integration

A company pursuing vertical integration is normally motivated by a desire to strengthen the competitive position of its original or core business. There are four vital arguments for pursuing a vertical integration strategy. They are as listed below:

- Enables the company to build barriers to new competition
- Facilitates investments in efficiency–enhancing specialized assets.
- Protects product quality
- Results in improved scheduling

Enables the company to build barriers to new competition

Company's vertical integrating backward to gain control over the source of inputs and distribution channels. Company can build effective distribution channels for distribution of products and service. Company build barrier to new entry into its industry to extent to apply to this strategy effectively to avoid competition. Therefore, thereby enabling the company to charge a higher price and make greater profits.

Facilitating investments in specialized assets

A specialised asset is an asset that is designed to perform a specific task and whose value is significantly reduced in its next best use. A specialised asset may be a piece of equipment or skills. The skills acquired by the companies or individuals through training and experience. Companies and individuals invest in specialized asset because these assets allow them to lower the costs of value creation and to better differentiate their product offering from that of competitors, thereby, facilitating premium pricing. These specialized assets use very specialized purposes. Companies always invest in specialised equipment because it enables it to lower its manufacturing costs and increase its quality. Secondly it invests in developing highly specialized technological knowledge because it develops better products than their rivals. Therefore, specialisation can be achieving a competitive advantage at the industry level.

A company may find it very difficult to persuade other companies' in adjacent stages in the raw material to consumer production chain to undertake investments in specialized assets. As result, companies or individuals are to realize the economic gains associated with investments. It may have to vertically integrate into such adjacent stages and make the investment itself.

Protecting Product Quality

Companies' main aim is protecting product quality. Vertical integration enables a company to become a differentiated player in its core business. If company is integration, therefore it can protect product quality without affect standard ness of the product quality.

Improved Scheduling

Strategic advantages arise from the easier planning, coordination and scheduling of adjacent processes. It made possible in vertically integrated organisations or companies can be particularly important in companies trying to relate the benefits of just in time inventory systems.

Disadvantages Of Vertical Integration

Cost disadvantages

Cost is the main factor of the company to gain a production cost advantages. Meanwhile vertical integration can raise costs, if a company becomes committed to purchasing inputs from company owned suppliers when low cost external sources of supply exist. Company owned might high operating costs compared with the independent suppliers.

Technological changes

Technological changes are other disadvantages of the vertical integration. When technology is changing fast and outdated its plants and equipment. Therefore, it is also major disadvantages of the company.

Demand uncertainty

It can also be extremely risky in unstable or unpredicted demand condition. In this case, it is very difficult to achieve their activities in company.

Others

Vertical integration poses problems of balancing capacity at each stage in the value chain.

Integrating forward or backward often calls for radically different skills and business capabilities.

Backward vertical integration into the production of parts and components can reduce a company's strength.

Concentric diversification

Concentric diversification is to concentrate the direction of business for expansion and diversification is to concentrate the direction in the same and attendant product lines. Concentric diversification may take the form of marketing related or technology related diversification.

Active diversification is the long-term expansion of the business activities. Passive diversification is the short term and negative impact to continuous of long term contracts with partners.

- The concentration diversification, the business is linked to the company existing business through its process, technology and marketing.
- The new product is only connected in a loop like manner at one or more points in the company's existing process or technology or product chain.

Conglomerate Diversification

- It refers to the new businesses or products are disjointed from the existing businesses or products in every way;
- It is a totally unrelated diversification.
- In process or technology or function, these are no connection between the new products and the existing ones.
- It is no common thread at all with the company's present position.

Creating Value through Diversification

Most companies first consider diversification when they are generating financial resources, therefore, it is excess to maintain to competitive advantage in their original or core business. The diversified company can generate value in three main routes. They are listed below:

- Acquiring and restructuring
- Transferring competencies
- Economies of scope

Acquiring and Restructuring

Acquiring and restructuring involved by acquiring and restructuring poorly run enterprises. A restructuring strategy rests on the presumption that an efficiently managed company can create value by acquiring inefficient and poorly managed enterprises and improving their efficiency. This approach can be considered diversification because the acquired company does not have to be in the same industry as the acquiring company for the strategy to work. Improvements in the efficiency of an acquired company can come from a number of sources. They are listed below:

The acquiring company usually replaces the top management team of the acquired company with more aggressive top management team.

The new top management team is encouraged to sell off any unproductive assets like executive's jets and elaborate corporate head quarters and to reduce staffing levels.

The new top management team is also encouraged to intervene in the running of the acquired business to seek out routes of improving the unit's efficiency, quality, innovativeness, and customer responsiveness.

To motivate the new top management team and other employees of the acquired unit to undertake such actions, increases in their pay may be linked to industries in the performance of the acquired unit.

The acquiring company often establishes performance goals for the acquired company.

Case 4.1: Reliance to acquire German firm Trevira for Rs 440 crore

RELIANCE Industries Ltd on Thursday announced it would acquire German polyester producer, Trevira GmbH, for 80 million euros (roughly Rs 440 crore). The acquisition will make RIL the world's largest polyester fibre and yarn producer. Trevira, former division of multinational Hoechst, which operates polyester plants in Germany, Belgium and Denmark, will add 1.3 lakh tonnes to RIL's existing polyester capacity. This will take RIL's polyester capacity, combined with its expansion plans in India, to 1.8 million tonnes - the largest in the world. "This European acquisition will transfer the entire intellectual property portfolio of Hoechst to India," Mr. Mukesh Ambani, RIL's Chairman and Managing Director, told reporters, on the sidelines of RIL's annual general meeting, here today. This is the second overseas acquisition of RIL after it acquired the US-based Flag Telecom last year. According to RIL, Trevira is a highly specialised polyester producer with several valuable patents and technologies and strong R&D. The company has been adding polyester capacity through major acquisitions since 2002 when it acquired IPCL followed by the acquisition of the NOCIL petrochemicals division earlier this year. Over the next three years, RIL intends to hike its total petrochemical capacity to 15 million tonnes from the present 12.4 million tonnes. Responding to queries, Mr. Ambani said Reliance Industries' plans to retail transport fuels have been delayed. However, the company will be adding 300 to 400 new retail outlets every quarter, starting from the second quarter this fiscal. "We are in the 75-outlets zone at the moment," Mr. Ambani told reporters. He said the company would put up its planned 5,800 retail outlets over the coming three to five years. Of these, five to 10 per cent would be set up in the rural areas. The company will also focus on setting up highway outlets. RIL stock today closed at Rs 422.80, up Rs 11.75 on BSE today. Around 56 lakh shares changed hands

Questions

1. Explain the grand strategies of Reliance industries limited

Source: Reliance industries limited.

Transferring Competencies

Companies diversification strategy on transferring competencies seek out new business related their existing business by one or more value creation functions, for instance, manufacturing, marketing, materials management and R&D. They want to create value by drawing on the distinctive skills in one or more of their existing value creation function in order to improve the competitive position of the new business. It can improve the efficiency of their existing business.

Economies of Scope

It arises when two or more business units share resources like;

- Manufacturing facilities
- Distribution channels
- Advertising
- R&D costs
- Each business unit utilised their capacity better and reduced to operating cost.

4.9 RETRENCHMENT, DIVESTMENT AND LIQUIDATION STRATEGY

When an organisation decides to reduce its business operation by reducing the scope of customer groups or customer functions or alternative technologies with view to have better control for better performance, retrenchment strategies are accepted. In retrenchment strategy, unattractive and unwanted areas of business are sequenced gradually. It is a not matter of failure of business planning, rather well planned exercise to get rid of unprofitable parts of business which will help the organisation concentrate its total attention to the most profitable and promising areas of business only.

- These things are done through an attempt to find out the problem areas and diagnose the causes of firm's problems.
- Once identified the problems, firms will be taken next steps to solve the problems.
- This result is to search different type's retrenchment strategies in businesses.
- For retrenchment process, a firm will be selected and adopted at turnaround strategy.
- And also adapt to divestment strategy to reduce functional activities in firms.
- If none of these actions cannot be worked, that time a firm can be chosen to abandon the activities totally in terms of liquidation strategy.

4.10 TURNAROUND STRATEGY

Many companies restructure their operations divesting themselves of their diversified activities, because they wish to focus more their core business area. An integral part of restructuring, therefore, it is the development of strategy for turning around the company's core or remaining business areas.

In this section, we shall review in some detail the various steps to be taken by companies for turnaround troubled business areas. We shall first look at the causes of corporate decline and then discuss the main elements of successful turnaround strategies.

- Retrenchment can be done either internally or externally in firm. Internal retrenchment which takes into place that is emphasis to laid on improving its internal efficiency which is known as a turnaround strategy.

There are certain conditions or indicators are the main reasons for turnaround is needed to firm's have to survival, growth, development and increased profitability. The major danger signs in industry are listed below:

- Persistent negative cash flow in business
- Negative profits in business
- Declining market shares of firm's
- Deterioration in physical facilities in business.
- Over manning, high turnover of employees and low morale of human resource in firm's.
- Uncompetitive products and services in industry.
- Mismanagement is the main reason in firm.

4.11 THE CAUSES OF CORPORATE DECLINE

The seven causes are an important of the corporate decline. Figure 4.11 indicates the seven causes are impact of the corporate declines. They are listed below:

- Poor management
- Over expansion
- Inadequate financial controls
- High costs
- New competition
- Unforeseen demand shifts
- Organisational inertia

Figure 4.11: Major Causes of Corporate Decline

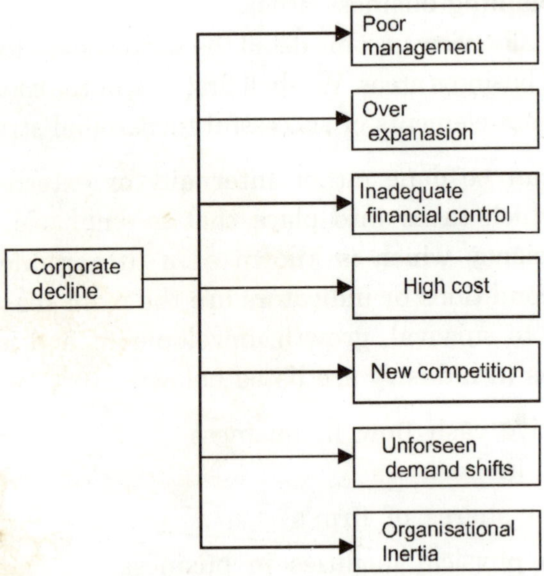

Poor Management

Poor management involves a multitude of sins; it is ringing from sheer incompetence to neglect of core businesses and an insufficient number of good mangers. Therefore, these things are not necessarily a bad thing. Research study shown that in the presence of a dominant and autocratic chief executive with a passion for empire building strategies characterises involved for many failing companies.

Over Expansion

Rapid expansion and extensive diversification, these diversifications tend to be poorly conceived and ads little value to a company much diversification its result is loss of control and inability to cope with recessionary conditions. Moreover, companies expand rapidly their business involve large amounts of debt financing. Adverse economic conditions can limit a company's ability to meet its debt requirements and can their precipitate a financial crisis.

Inadequate financial controls

It is the common trend of the business. Financial manger is a failure to assign profit responsibility for the financial consequences of their actions, it can encourage to mid level mangers to employ excess staff and spend resource beyond what is necessary for maximum efficiency of the company.

High Costs

Inadequate financial control can lead to high costs. Its common cause like low labor productivity and management has failure to introduce new labor saving technologies and high rate of wages for employees. These are important factor for companies competing on costs in the global market and have a failure to realise economic of scale, therefore, it result impact on companies low market share.

New Competition

New competition is essential to companies for competition in the industrial world. A company ready to tackle competition from rivals. Because of new technology made huge cutthroat competition and increase in productivity at low cost of output. Many companies have failure because of unable to face threats of competitors. Therefore, new competition kills idle companies in the business world.

Unforeseen Demand Shifts

Environment threat like marketing, technology, political, social, legal, cultural environment can change open market opportunities for new products. Its consequence is the unforeseen demand shifts from old to new products. Therefore, customer has preference to buy new product at a low cost. When companies have failure to fulfillment of the above fact then have a failure in the business world.

Organisational Inertia

The emergence of powerful new competition and unforeseen shifts in demand might not be enough to cause corporate decline. Organisation is slow to respond to environmental changes.

Main Elements of Successful Turnaround Strategies

The main steps of turnaround strategies for successful of companies business. They are listed below:

- Changing leadership
- Redefining strategic focus
- Asset sales and closures
- Improving profitability
- Acquisitions

Figure 4.12 Main Elements of Successful Turnaround Strategies

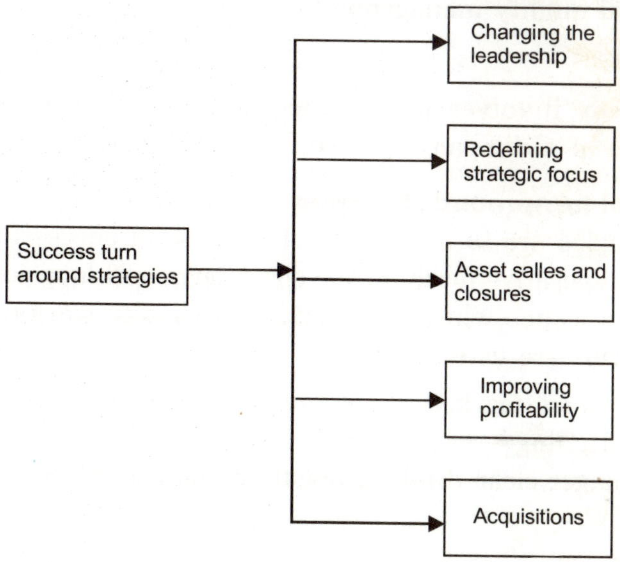

Changing the Leadership

Old leadership had failure, new leader is an essential element of retrenchment and turnaround situation to resolve crisis, to motivate lower level mangers, listen to views of others and delegate power when appropriate.

Redefining Strategic Focus

It refers to redefining company's strategy for restructuring of business. It is identifying the business in the portfolio which has the best for the company for long-term profit and growth prospectus and concentrating investment there.

Assets Sales and Closures

Having redefined its strategic focus, a company should divest as many unwanted assets as it can find buyer for and liquidate whatever remains. It is important not to confuse unwanted assets with in profitable assets.

Improving Profitability

Improving profitability involves number of steps to improve efficiency, quality, innovation and customer responsiveness. It involves in the following issues:

- Layoffs white and blue collar employee
- Investments in labor saving equipment

Assessment of profit, it is responsibility to individuals and subunits within the company, by a change of organisational structure if necessary.

- Tightening financial controls
- Cutting back on marginal products
- Reengineering business process to cut costs and boost productivity and

Introducing total quality management

Acquisitions

Turnaround strategy involves making acquisition primarily to strengthen the competitive position of a company's remaining core operations.

Issues for successful turnaround strategies

Turnarounds strategies are to be successful because of successful issues which are relating to firm's imperative focus on the short-term and long term financing needs as well as strategic issues which are suitable to make workable action plan for turnaround with firms are listed below:

- Analysis of product, market, production processes, competition and each market segment positioning.
- Strategic manager clear thinking about the market place and production logic.

- Proper implementation of plans by target setting, and get feedback and take right remedial action.

Contribution Elements for Turnaround in Firms

- Changes in top level management in business
- Initial credibility building actions in firm's
- Neutralizing external pressures
- Initial control
- Identifying quick pay off activities
- Quick cost reductions
- Revenue generations
- Asset liquidation for generating cash
- Mobilizations of the organisations
- Better internal co-ordination

4.12 DIVESTMENT/CUTBACK STRATEGY

It involves the sale and disposing off or shedding business units or product divisions or segments of business operations to reinvest the resources for other production and potential business purposes:

- Divestment is usually a part of revival, rehabilitation and restructuring plan attempted when a turnaround strategy becomes unsuccessful.
- The strategy in the case may be to sell off a part of business or products, or giving up the control over a subsidiary or a demerger so that the wholly owned subsidiaries may be floated off as independent organisation.
- Organisation may be choose to divest in two ways: a part of the organisation may choose to divest by way of serving its financial and managerial control and separating it as independent organisation for all purposes. Alternatively, an organisation may sell a unit outright for which marketing strategy should be proven.
- The basic objective underlying organisation unit may be hindrance on the total profitability and growth, particularly when opportunities of strategic alternative investment exist. So, divestment may be a sensible positive strategic decision and not due to helpless condition. Further there may be other types of strategies like business level strategy, functional level strategy, annual strategy, grand strategy, and corporate strategy.

Case 4.2: MFL off the disinvestment list: CMD
Madras Fertilisers Ltd had been taken out from disinvestment list by the centre, but its fortunes had taken a beating due to an anomaly in the Government's fertiliser pricing policy, chairman and Managing director Mr. Sukumar N. Oommen said today. "MFL was on the block for disinvestment. The new government at the Centre has now decided to put disinvestment on hold. I do believe that MFL will be retained in the public sector", Mr. Oommen said after announcing a tie-up with ING Vysya Life here. He said the fortunes of MFL were dictated by the fertiliser policy of the government. If you look at our performance, we have achieved 102 per cent efficiency in urea production. The productivity of employees are on par with the private sector, Mr. Oommen said. However, the Government had not been compensating the company for higher performance. Under the existing administered pricing mechanism in the fertiliser industry, MFL should be compensated in full for the cost of production, he said. During the year ended March 31, 2004, the company is expected to report a loss of Rs 60 crore. We would have made Rs 40 crore profit, if you remove the anomaly, he said. - PTI
Questions 1. Discuss the **MFL off the disinvestment strategy**

Source: Business Line, dated April 17,2004.

Reasons to Adopt Divestment Strategy in Firms

- A business had been acquired which proves that to be mismatched and cannot be integrated within the company.
- Persistent financial problems which creates the negative cash flows from a particular business operations in company which is to be needed for divestment of that business.
- Firm unable to cope to severity of competition from rival firms; it may cause to divest business operations.
- Technological up gradation is required, in this case, the firm able to survival but where it is possible for the firm to invest in it, a firm preferable option would be taken for divest business operations.
- A better alternative which may be available for investment that causing a firm to divest a part of its unprofitable businesses in firm's operations.

Liquidation Strategies

- Retrenchment strategy is considered the most and extreme and unattractive is liquidation strategy; it involves closing down a firm and selling its assets.
- It is considered as the last resort because which leads to serious consequences like loss of employment for workers and other employees, termination of opportunities where a firm can pursue any future activities and the stigma of failure.
- In India, many small firms like small scale units, proprietorship firms and partnership ventures are liquidated frequently but medium and large sized companies rarely liquidate in India.

- The company management, government, banks and financial institutions, trade unions, suppliers and creditors and other agencies are extremely reluctant to take decisions or ask or formulate suitable policy for liquidation.
- Selling assets for implementing a liquidation strategy, it will be difficult to sell and difficult to find buyers for assets of liquidation firm. In this case, the liquidation firm cannot be expected adequate compensation from the selling assets which as treated scrap by buyers.

Liquidation – the Strategy of Last Resort

Sometimes a business crisis is too far gone to salvage or is not worth salvaging given the resources it will take and its profit prospects. Closing a crisis-ridden business down and liquidating its assets is sometimes the best and wisest strategy of all strategic alternatives. Liquidation is the most unpleasant and painful because of the hardships of job eliminations and the effect of business closings in local communities. Therefore, in hopeless situations, an early liquidation effort usually serves owner-stock holder interests better than an inevitable bankruptcy.

End Game Strategies

End game strategy steers a middle course between pressuring the status quo and existing as soon as possible.

An end game strategy is a reasonable strategic option for a weak business in the following circumstances:

- When the industry's longtime prospects are in attractive.
- When rejuvenating the business would be too costly or at best marginally profitable.
- When the firm's market share is becomingly costly to maintain or defend.
- When reduced levels of competitive effort will not trigger an immediate rapid falloff in sales.
- When the enterprise can re deploy the freed resources in higher opportunity areas.
- When the business is not a crucial or core component of a diversified company's overall lineup business.
- When the business does not contribute other desired features to a company's business portfolio.

CHAPTER 5

Formulation of Functional Strategy

Contents

- Introduction
- Reasons for functional strategies are needed to firms
- Marketing strategy formulation
- Developing the marketing mix
- Marketing strategy techniques
- Financial strategy formulation
- Production strategy formulation
- Research and development strategies
- Human resource strategies formulation

Learning Objectives

- This chapter plans to discuss about the marketing strategy formulation and its issues, process, development of the marketing mix, marketing analysis, planning, marketing environment, marketing strategy techniques. Financial strategy formulation, source of funds, projected financial statements, managing and using funds, evaluating the worth of a business. Production strategy formulation involves the production system, operations planning and control. Logistics strategy, research and development, human resource strategies are formulation in company.

"As market windows open and close more quickly, it is important that R & D be tied more closely to corporate strategy".

William Spender

"Most of the time, strategists should not be formulating strategy at all; they should be getting on with implementing strategies they already have"

5.1 INTRODUCTION

- For effective strategy formulation, strategists have to provide valuable direction to functional managers regarding the plans and policies which are adopted by firms.
- Functional strategies are typically: marketing, financial, production and human resources.
- Functional strategies are based on the functional capability factors in firms.
- For each functional area, we have to find the main areas and then discuss the sub areas of each functional area. These are regarding the content of functional strategies, important factors and the importance in process of strategy formulation.
- Functional strategies are operated below the strategic business units or business level strategies for functional level strategy formulation.
- Functional level strategies consist of guidelines that are set at higher levels.
- Functional managers need guidance and directions from the business strategy in order to make decisions which are relating with the functional areas.
- Operational plans explain the functional managers what has to be done meanwhile policies are stated how the plans are to be implemented.

Reasons for Functional Strategies Are Needed to Firms

The development of functional strategies is formulated by the top-level management of the firm's. The functional level involves the execution of policy which made by the top level management. Strategic managers need to be segregated into viable functional plans and policies and avoid non viable functional plans and polices which are compatible with each other in business. In this way, strategic managers in functional areas have discharge their role relating with functions in business. Strategic managers have study on environmental factors which affected to and relevancy to firms. Organization strategies which are affected the choice of functional strategies. Finally, the actual process of choice is influenced by objectives as well as subjective factors in different functions. Major reasons for functional strategies are needed to firms are listed below:

- The strategic decisions are implemented by all parts of a firm's/ organization.
- There is a standard basis available for controlling activities in the different functional areas of the business.

- When plans are clearly lay down that time functional managers to take decisions in flexible and short time and what is to be done and executive policies provide the discretionary framework within which decisions are needed to be taken by functional managers in each functions of business.
- Routine and similar situations are happened in different functional areas that are handled in a consistent manner by the functional managers in business.
- Each functional manager in business should be taken into coordination to all functional managers; it must takes place in different functional areas in business.

5.2 MARKETING STRATEGY FORMULATION

Marketing strategy formulation is one of major task to business firms. Ordinary marketing strategy formulation is not risk factor to firms; it is not created valuable impact to firms. Therefore, the present scenario, marketing strategy formulation that is considered to be the activities which are related to identifying the needs of customers and taking such actions which are satisfying them and inform of some return consideration from business. In marketing, it is more important to do what is right to do and what is immediately profitable venture to business to firms.

Relationship to marketing and other functions in business can be understood by the following mentioned factors:

- Single marketing department cannot produce superior value for the customer. All company departments must work together to accomplish and satisfy customer needs and requirements.
- Each department is a link in the value chain of firms.
- A company value chain is only as strong as the weakest link to firms.
- Marketers are challenged to find ways to get all departments to think customers and search knowledge about customers.
- Marketing competitive advantage and value chain gains should be taken purpose keep well partnering will produce a value delivery network; it consists of suppliers, distributors and ultimately customers.

Figure 5.1: Value Delivery Network

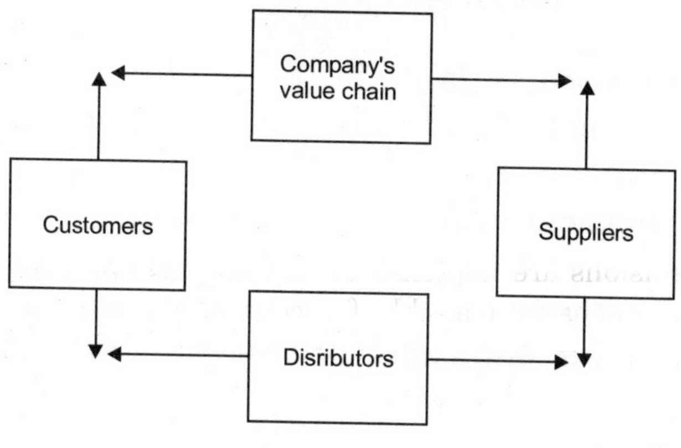

Marketing Issues

Marketing issues relate to policies in market analysis, business law, display, salesmanship and advertising etc, i.e. they are concerned with total process of marketing which covering both 'product mix' and 'market mix'. The product mix includes decisions regarding the type, quantity and quality of product design, contents shape, methods and techniques of production etc. Market mix covers the issues like price, place, promotion, channels of distribution, advertising policies, packaging and branding decisions, consumer psychology and behavior and pricing of the product etc.

Since the modern concept of market has treated as 'consumer as a king', every product is brought to satisfy customer needs. Hence its gamut is very fast. The policies in this field, therefore, deal with the following issues:

Organization's products / service; product life cycle and marketing strategy.

- Concentration of sales in few products or little customer segmentation.
- Ability to gathered information about the market.
- To know the market share or sub market share.
- Product/service mix and expansion potential: to know the life cycle of key products; to know the profit or loss of the product/service.
- To clearly know the channel of distribution; number, coverage, and control.
- To maintain effective sales organization: to find out knowledge about the customer needs.
- To improve product/service quality with image and reputation of brand name.
- Efficient and effective utilization of available resource for effective sales promotion and advertising.
- To aware of the pricing strategy and pricing flexibility.
- To effective monitoring and feedback of the marketing functions and expansion of product
- Effective implementation of after sales service and follow up.
- To keep standards, goodwill and brand loyalty.
- Spotting out of the present and potential markets, the size and nature of consumers.
- The degree of competition in the market and how best could it be met.
- The location of prospects and persuading them to purchase.
- To advertise online or not.
- Fixing price of product, offering rebated, discounts and other concessions.
- Compensating salesman adequately; and providing them with training and developmental opportunities.
- Selecting channels of distribution or employing representatives and agents.

- Dividing the total market into branch or dealer areas.
- Establishing advertising policies like:
  i. Setting up sales control policies.
  ii. And establishing sales volume and expense budgets.

Marketing Process

- In company, once the strategic plan has been defined the company's overall mission and objectives, marketing plays a role in carrying out these objectives.
- The marketing process is the process/stages of analyzing market opportunities, selecting target markets, development the market mix, and managing the marketing effort in business.
- Target customers are standing at the enterprise and make plan.
- Center of the marketing process in business.

Market is connecting customers

Today's market scenario is the competitive marketplace, companies must be customer oriented towards the products and services. Companies must win customers and win competitors and keep them by delivering greater value goods and services. Since companies have to failure to satisfy all customer requirements and needs in market. Companies must divide the total market on the basis segmentation and choose the best segments like market targeting and design strategies for profit oriented serving chosen segments and provide better services than their customers in market.

5.3 DEVELOPING THE MARKETING MIX

Marketing mix is the combination of 4 P's i.e. product, price, place and promotion. Company is decided to overall its competitive strategy. Firm's ready to begin planning the details of the marketing mix. The marketing mix is the set of controllable marketing variables in firm. Firms are using 4 P's and to produce valuable products and services and delivery to ultimate users of the product and services. The marketing mix is consisting of everything that the firm ready to do and influence the demands for products and services from the customers.

Product

- Product stands for the goods and service combination which offered by the company to the target market.
- Strategies are required for adding new products and removing the failure products from markets.
- Strategic decisions are relating with the branding, packaging, and other product features like guarantee and warranty.

Price

- Price refers to amount of money which is paid by customers for obtaining the product and services from company.
- Price strategies are pertaining to the location of the customers, price flexibility, related items within a product line and terms of sale.
- Pricing strategies are useful to company for entering into market especially with a new product that designed by the company.

Place

- Place refers to the company activities that make the product and services are available to target consumers.
- Strategist should be taken the responsibility for distribution of goods and services to ultimate customers. In many cases, the ownership is transferred from company to customers.
- Strategies applicable to middlemen like wholesalers, retails, must be designed by the company.

Promotion

- Promotion refers to the activities that communicate the merits of the product and persuade target consumers to buy it from the company.
- Strategies are needed to combine individual methods like advertising, personnel selling, and sales promotion into a coordinated campaign.
- Promotional strategies must be adjusted as a product move from an earlier stages form latest stage of its life.

Figure 5.2: The 4 P's and 4 C's of the Marketing

4 P's	4 C's
• Product	• Customer solution
• Price	• Customer cost
• Place	• Convenience
• Promotion	• Communication

For effective marketing program design purpose, it blends all the marketing mix elements into a coordinated program that in this way to achieve the company's marketing objectives by delivering value to consumers in business. The 4 P's seems to take the seller's view rather than the buyer's view and perhaps a better classification can be the 4 C's as outlined:

a. Product = Customer Solution
b. Price = Customer Cost
c. Place = Convenience
d. Promotion = Communication

Expanded Marketing Mix

Traditional mix is consisting of only 4 P's. Expanded marketing mix includes 4 P's plus people, physical evidence and process.

People

- People refers to all human actors who have play a part in delivery of the market that offering by company and thus influence the buyers perception, namely the firm's personnel and the customer in business.

Physical Evidence

- Physical evidence refers to the environment in which the market offering goods, it is delivered by the company and where the firm and customer interact.

Process

Process refers to the actual procedures, mechanisms and flow of activities by which the product or services is delivered to client/ customers.

Marketing Analysis

- Marketing analysis generally involves a complete analysis of the company situation.
- The company performs what it analyses regarding market
- Clearly identifying environmental opportunities and threats.
- Clearly analyzing company strengths and weaknesses to determine which opportunities the company can be pursued the best.
- Get feeding information and other outputs to each of the other marketing management functions in company.

Figure 5.3: Managing the Marketing Effort

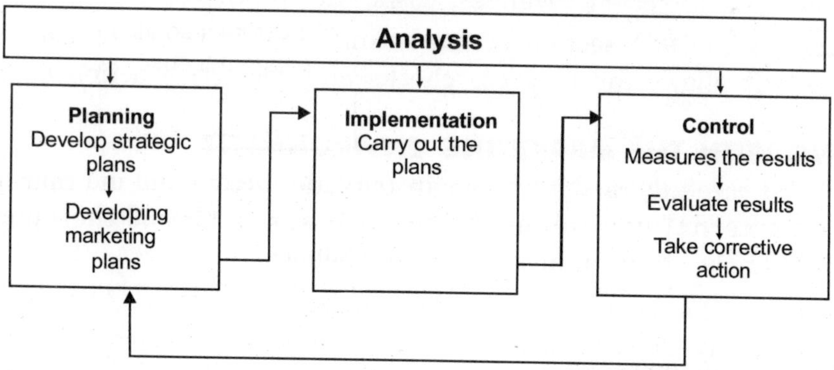

Marketing Planning

Generally marketing planning involves deciding on marketing strategies in company. It will help to the company which attains its overall strategic objectives. A detailed and well structured plan is needed for each business, product or brand. Particularly, a brand or product plan may contain different sections ; executive summary, current marketing situation, threats and opportunity analysis , objectives and issues , marketing strategies , action programs, budgets and controls.

- **Executive summary refers** to short summary of the main goals and recommendations to be presented in the marketing plan.
- **The current market situations refers** to the section of a marketing plan that explains the target market and the company's position in it, important sections are outlined:
  - A market description
  - A product review
  - Analysis of the competition
  - A section on distribution.
- **In the threats and opportunities section refers** to the managers forced to anticipate important developments that can have an impact on business either positive or negative to the firm.
- **Having studied the product's threats and opportunities refers** to the managers can set objectives and consider issues that will affect them. The objectives should clearly state as goals that the company would like to attain during the plan's term in business operation.
- **Marketing strategy refers** to the marketing logic by which the business unit hopes to achieve it marketing objectives. Strategies should be created for all marketing mix components in business operation.
- **The market budget refers** to the section of the marketing plan of company. It shows and projected revenues, costs, and profits of a firm.
- **Control** is the last section of marketing plan; it refers to used to monitor progress. It allows for progress checks and corrective action of a firm.

5.4 DEALING WITH THE MARKETING ENVIRONMENT

A company must carefully analyze its environmental factors and in order to avoid the threats from external environment and take advantage of the opportunities. Environmental areas to be analyzed as listed below:

- Environment forces are to close the company like ability to serve customers, other company departments, channel members, suppliers, competitors and publics.
- Environmental broader forces like demographic and economic forces, political and legal forces, technological and ecological forces and social and cultural forces.

5.5 MARKETING STRATEGY TECHNIQUES

Figure 5.4: Marketing Strategy Techniques

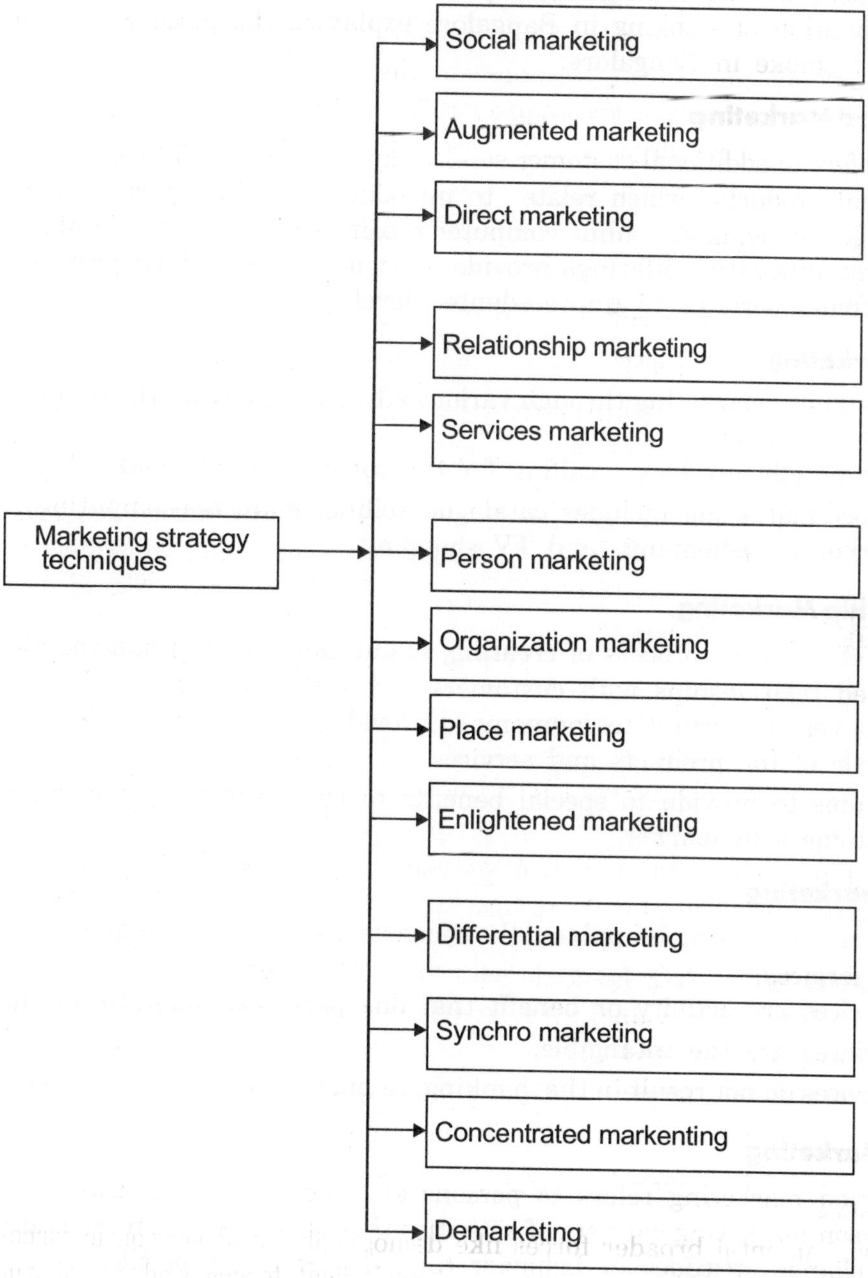

Social Marketing

- It refers to the design, implementation and control of programs. These are seeking to increase the acceptability in terms of a social ideas, cause or practice among a target group. For example the publicity campaign for prohibition of smoking in Bangalore explained the place where one can and can't smoke in Bangalore.

Augmented Marketing

- It refers to additional customer services and benefits built around the care and actual products which relate to introduction of high tech services such as movies on demand, online computer repair , services , secretarial services etc.,
- These innovative offerings provide a set of benefits which promise to elevate customer services to unprecedented levels.

Direct Marketing

- It refers to marketing through various advertising media which interact directly with customers.
- It generally involves calling for the consumers to make direct response.
- Direct marketing includes catalogue selling, mail, telecomputing , electronic marketing , shopping and TV shopping.

Relationship Marketing

- It refers to the process of creating, maintaining, and enhancing strong, value based relationships with customers and stake holders.
- It is very important to company to provide special services like services after a sale of the products and services.
- It aims to provide to special benefits to customers to get new and existing customers in market.

Service marketing

- Service marketing is applying the concepts, tools, and techniques for marketing to services.
- Services are activity or benefit that one party can offer to another.
- Services are the intangible.
- Services do not result in the, banking, savings, retailing, educational or utilities.

Person Marketing

- Person marketing refers to persons are marketing in market.
- Person marketing consists of activities that are undertaken to create, maintain or change attitudes or behavior towards particular people.
- Example, politicians, sports stars, film stars, professional i.e., market themselves to get votes, or to promote their careers and earn income.

Organizing Marketing

- It refers to activities which are undertaken to create, maintain, or change attitudes and behavior which relating with the target audience towards an organization.
- Organizing market practice by profit and nonprofit organizations.

Place Marketing

- It generally involves activities undertaken to create, maintain or change attitudes and behavior towards particular place.
- Tourism marketing is the best example for place marketing.

Enlightened Marketing

- It refers to marketing philosophy holding by the company that marketing should be support to the best long run performance of the marketing system.
- It consists of five principles are; customer oriented, marketing, innovative marketing, value marketing, senses of mission marketing and social marketing.

Differential marketing

- Differential marketing refers to market coverage strategy in which a company can decide to target several market segments and make designs for separate offer each segment in market.
- For instance, we shall take Hindustan Lever Limited has Lifebuoy, Lux and Rexona in popular segments and Liril and Pears in premium segments.

Synchromarkting

- It refers to the demand for the product which is irregular due to season, some parts of the day, or on hour basis, that can be causing idle capacity or over worked capacities.
- Synchromarketing can be used to find ways to after the same pattern of demand through flexible pricing, promotion, and other incentives.
- For instance, woolens or coolers; or hospitals underbooked on weekend or end of the week.

Concentrated marketing

- It refers to market coverage strategy in which a company goes after a large share of one or few sub markets.

Demarketing

- It refers to marketing strategies is to reduce demand temporarily or permanently.
- The aim is not to destroy demand, it only reduce demand or shift it.
- These things are happen when overfull demand.

- For example, buses are overloaded in the morning and evening, at the same time roads are busy for most of times. Zoological parks are over crowded on saturdays, sundays and holidays.
- It can be applied to regulate demand.

5.6 FINANCIAL STRATEGY FORMULATION

The financial management strategies are related to several finance and accounting functions in organization. Finance and accounting concepts are to be considered as central for strategy implementation. Financial information are; acquiring, needed capital, sources of fund, developing projected financial statements, budgets, management, usage of funds and evaluating the worth of business, ratio analysis, cash flow statement, maintain of books of accounts etc. strategist need to formulate financial strategies relating above mentioned issues in finance areas for implementation in organization.

Finance and Accounting Policies

Finance and accounting policies are outlined:

- Ability to raise short term and long-term capital: either debt or equity.
- To maintain good corporate level resource.
- To know the cost of capital relative to industry and competitors
- Tax consideration
- To build up effective relationship with owners, investors, financial institution and stock holders.
- To know the leverage position: capacity to utilization financial strategies, like lease or sale and lease back.
- To aware of the cost of entry and barriers of the entry.
- To know the price earning ratio
- Present working capital position of the organization.
- Effective cost control and ability to minimize cost of expenditure for production of goods and service.
- Financial size of the organization.
- Efficient and effective accounting system for cost, budget, and profit planning of the organization.
- To determine liquid position in the organization and determine the cash flow and fund flows and ratio analysis in organization.
- Account receivables and account payables, cost center, types of cost and standard and actual cost performance in organization.

Acquiring Capital to Implement Strategies / Sources of Funds

- Successful strategy implementation often requires and brings additional capital to business organization.
- Organization capital acquiring is based on the two important components such as equity and debt
- Capital structure is the combination of debt and equity, it is very vital to company for successful of business operations in this way maximize the benefits to company.
- Companies have enough debt in its capital structure to boost its return on investment by applying debt to products and projects earning more than the cost of the debt.
- In low earning periods, too much debt in capital structure components of an organization can endanger to stock holders return and jeopardize to organization survival.
- Fixed debt is very important to company to keep its financial status in constant manner and avoid to overpaying to debt holders due to pay fixed percentage of return to debt holder in business.
- If company is earning more profit, this company collects too much debt from public and reduces equity ratios in capital structure. It is more impact to business to maximize the benefits to business operations.
- Mergers, takeovers, acquisitions are the serious issues in today's scenario in acquiring capital.

Major Factors Regarding Financial Strategy

- Capital structure.
- Procurement of capital and working capital borrowings.
- Reserves and surplus as source of funds relating with lenders, banking and financial institutions.
- Source of funds is the important to implementation of the financial strategies in organization.
- Organizations having the different range of source of funds alternatives in the form that a company may rely on external borrowing and another company can be followed the internal policy of finance.

Projected Financial Statements/Budget

- Projected financial statement analysis is a central strategy implementation technique.
- It allows an enterprise to examine the expected results of various actions and approaches relating the finance and accounting.

- This analysis is used for estimation of future and impact of various implementation decisions in organization.
- Financial institutions request the projected financial statement when an organization seeks capital from the financial institutions.
- For this, an enterprise should prepare ratio analysis, fund flow statement and financial statements which are computed projected financial ratios under various strategy implementation scenarios.
- Financial statements and ratio have been providing the insight feasibility of company or enterprise for past years and current years for various strategy implementation approaches.

Projected Financial Budget

- Financial budget is the statement of income and expenditure for the particular period.
- It is document which provides details how funds will be obtained and spent for a specified period of time.
- Annual budget are most common. Budget period range from one day to more than ten years. It is depending upon the firm's decisions.
- Financial budget will specify the needs and requirement for implementation of financial budget in company.
- It is not a tool for limiting expenditure but rather as a method for obtaining the most productive and profitable use of an organization core resources.
- It can be viewed as the planned allocation of firm resources which are based on forecasts of the future.

Types of budget

Common types of budget are listed below:

- Cash budgets
- Operating budgets
- Sales budgets
- Profit budgets
- Factory budgets
- Capital budgets
- Expenses budgets
- Variable budgets
- Flexible budgets
- And fixed budget

When an organization is face problems for this purpose a strategist use budgets which are especially important in guiding strategy implementation.

Limitations of Financial Budget

- Budgets are expensive and cumbersome to company
- Over budget and under budget can be caused problems to company
- Financial budget is the subjective for objectives
- It is tool and not an end in itself
- The real budget can be hidden inefficiencies if it based on solely precedents rather than on periodic evaluation of circumstances and standards.
- Budgets are sometimes used as instruments of tyranny i.e domination that result is frustration, resentment, absenteeism and higher turnover.
- To minimize the effect of budget , it is last concern, when managers should increase the participation of subordinates in preparing budgets.

Management / Usage of Funds

- Management or usage of funds refers to the investment of funds or asset mix decisions.
- Plans and policy are to be made by the company, plans and polices are listed below:
  - Capital investment
  - Fixed assets acquisitions
  - Current assets
  - Loans and advances
  - Dividend decisions
  - Relationship with shareholders.
- Management of funds related to efficiency and effectiveness of scarce resource utilization in firms in the process of strategy implementation.

Result of Implementations of Usage of Project

- Implementation strategy is the results in increase in capital work in progress and current assets.
- It plans and policy is not clear, the usage of funds is inefficient which will be leading to less than an optimum utilization of core resources
- It is also considered by firms to attract and retain shareholders interest in market.
- Dividend policy and bonus distribution policy is very important to usage funds in projects.

Management of funds

- Management of funds is also important area of financial strategies in firms.
- Management of funds basically refers to the decisions which are to the systemic aspects of financial management.
- The major policies and funds relating in business enterprise deals with the following issues:

  - The systems of finance
  - The systems of accounting
  - The systems of budgeting
  - The systems of managerial controlling
  - The systems of cash and credit
  - The systems of risk management
  - The systems of cost control and reduction
  - The system of tax planning and advantages
- Effective management of funds can be played a pivotal role in strategy formulation, it is to be aimed to achieved by company by optimum utilization of funds objectives, these are playing a central role for strategic action in company.
- Grand strategies like expansion, growth, retrenchment cannot escape from proper fund management in firms.
- Good fund management and efficient strategy implement will be brought result to company. Apart from the improper management of funds will be brought failure in strategy implementation in companies.
- Strategist responsibilities is the minimizing the conflict and make interest between the management and shareholders for effective utilization of funds, procurement of funds and allocation of funds.

Evaluating the Worth of a Business

Evaluating the worth of a business is the central and core role of the implementation strategy, it is integrative, intensive and diversification strategies are implemented and acquiring by the other firms in the market, Retrenchment strategy is the result of sale of division, portion of business in organization. Successful implementation strategies should be considered to evaluate the financial worth or cash value of a business.

Different Approaches determining the Worth of a Business.

Determining the worth of a business can be grouped into three main approaches in enterprise.

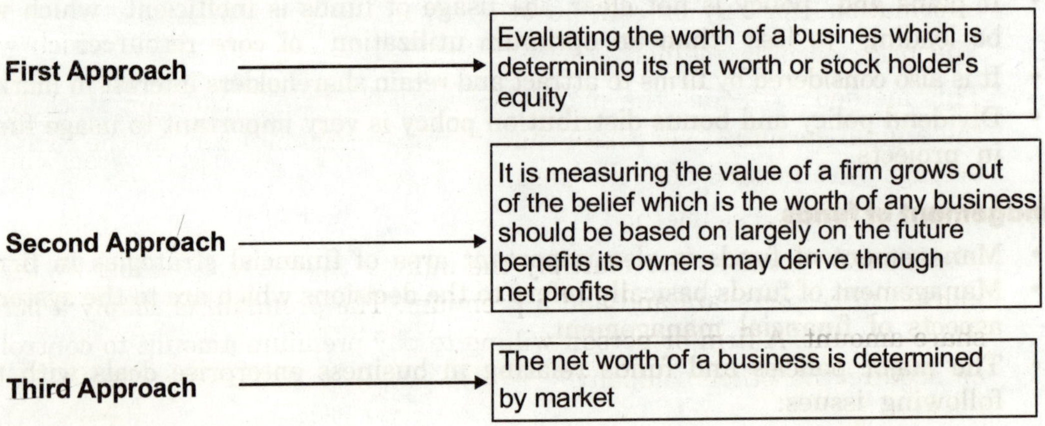

First Approach

- Evaluating the worth of a business which is determining its net worth or stock holder's equity.
- Net worth of company represents the sum of common stock, additional paid capital and retains earnings.
- After calculated the net worth, we shall do add or subtract an appropriate amount for goodwill and overvalued or undervalued assets.
- Its total value provides a reasonable estimate of a firm's monetary value.
- In the case, the firm has goodwill; it will be listed on the balance sheet, although it's intangible assets i.e. goodwill.

Second Approach

- It is measuring the value of a firm grows out of the belief which is the worth of any business should be based on largely on the future benefits its owners may derive through net profits.
- In another thumb of rule, it is to establish a business worth as five times the firm's current annual profit. For this purpose, we shall consider a five year average profit level can also used.
- When using this approach, the firm's normally surplus earnings and it shows in financial statements and minimize taxes to firms.

Third Approach

- The net worth of a business is determined by market.
- This approach involves three methods are listed below:

I. Firm's base worth on the selling price of similar company.

It deals with the potential problems in the forms of comparable figures are not available, it is not easy to locate, although the firm's has substantial information for buy or sell to other firms in the market.

II. The price earning method

This method is divide the market price of the firm's common stock by the annual earnings per share and multiply this number by the firm's average net income for the past five years.

III. Outstanding shares method

This method involves the multiply the number shares outstanding by the market price per share and add a premium. The premium is simply a per share amount. A firm or person willing to pay premium amount to control or acquire the other company.

5.7 PRODUCTION STRATEGY FORMULATION

- The production strategies are relating to production system, operational planning and control, and research and development.
- Production strategies are adopted which are affected to firm's nature of products or services, how these served to market, and the manner in which these strategies are served in markets.
- All theses influence to firm's production operations systems structure and objectives which are used to determine the operations plans and policies relating with the production.
- The operation system structure is concerned with the manufacturing or service and supply or delivery system , and operations system objectives , these are related to customer services and resource utilization which are determine the operations, plans and policies are set in firm's activities.

Production/Operation/Technical Issues

Production or operation or technical issues are as follows:

- To know the present raw material cost and availability
- Inventory control system of the organization.
- Location facilities; layout and utilization facilities.
- Technical efficiency and effective utilization of technical resource in the organization.
- Effective use and implementation of subcontracting.
- Degree of vertical integration in terms of value added and profit margin of the product.
- To know the efficient and cost benefit of production techniques.
- Effective utilization and implementation of operation control procedure: design, scheduling, purchasing, quality control and efficiency.
- To know the costs and technological competencies relative to industry and competitors.
- Research development, innovative, advance ethnological development.
- Patents, trademarks and similar legal protection for their organization products/ service.

Production System

- Production system is concerned with the capacity, location, layout, product or services design, work systems, degree of automation, extent of vertical integration.
- Production strategies are significant and play vital issues which are affecting the capability of the organization goals and objectives for achievement of both.

- Production strategy implementation are considered into account in the production system and used for decisions which are long term in nature. These are influence not the only operations capability of an organization. Apart from the ability to implement strategies and achieve strategic objective in company.

Operations Planning and Control

- Strategies are related to operations planning and control is concerned with aggregate production planning, materials supply, inventory cost and quality management and maintenance of plant and equipment in firm's level.
- It is the aim of strategy implementation, for this purpose, we have to see how efficiently resources are utilized and in what manner the day to day operations can be managed in the light of long term objectives.
- Operations planning and control provides to plan and control production process in company.
- It deals with the centralized the operations planning and decentralized the operation planning. It involves the testing, standardization and fabricating the equipment.
- Few companies are using the quality which is considered as the strategic tool. It helpful to design the test the quality inspection, standardization in terms of quality engineering.

5.8 LOGISTICS STRATEGY

- Logistics strategy is one of the important strategy to management for formulate logistic strategy at the supplies of goods and services to customer.
- It is process of integration of the flow of supplies of material by the organization to customer in this way achieve a level of services that ensure the right materials are available at right place, at the right time, of the right quality and at the right cost.
- It involves to the transportation of goods and services from company to customer place as it is low as possible consistent with safe and reliable delivery.
- Supply chain management helps to logistics and it enables to company to have constant contact with its distribution team that consists of trucks, trains, or any other mode of transportation.
- Emerging Technological changes and industrial initiatives are helpful to logistic strategy for successful development of logistics strategy formulation with infirm's.

Firms are effective logistic strategy will be involved for rising and finding major solutions to following questions are outlined:

- What are the sources of raw materials and components are available to firms?
- How many manufacturing locations owned by firm's?
- What are the products are produced or manufactured at each location?

- What is the mode of transport for goods and services which manufactured by company?
- What is the nature of distribution facilities of firms?
- What is the nature of materials handling equipment possessed? What is ideal to firms?
- What is the method for deploying inventory in the logistics network of firms?
- Is any transport vehicles either owned by company or not?

Improvement of Logistics

Effective strategy implementation results ensure that the following improvements for firms:

- Cost saving to company
- Reduced inventory system for company
- Increased the customer satisfaction
- To take competitive advantage

5.9 RESEARCH AND DEVELOPMENT STRATEGY

- Research and development can play significant role and integrated with part of strategy implementation.
- It refers to development of new products and improving the old products by adding new features to old products and services.
- Effective research and development strategy implementation results ensure that the quality products, quality services, and reduced the cost of products and services, satisfying the customer needs and requirements.
- Research and development department is one of the valuable department in firms, this department consists skillful resource persons who are perform tasks like transferring complex technology, adjusting processes to local raw materials, adapting process to local markets, and altering products to particular tastes and specifications.
- Product development, market penetration and concentric diversification strategies are required to develop new products and services successfully developed and also significantly improved to old products into new version products and bring effective and excellence of research development is required to all types of business operations in market.
- Technological developments are affected to company's products and services which are offered to the ultimate customers. It is affected to consumer and industrial products and services shorten product life cycles.

- Technological advancement will be taken by the company in form of increasing the profitability and enhance the customer base including existing and old and new customers in market, able to rival to rivalries in market.
- Majority of the survey shows that effective research and development strategy that ties external opportunities to enhance the internal strengths and these things linked with the objectives of firms.

Well Formulated Research Development Strategy Results

Well formulated research development strategy results enhance the opportunities from internal and externally from the company environment. The major results are outlined:

- It emphasis on product or process improvements
- It is basic or applied research
- To be leaders or followers in R&D
- It develop to robotics or manual type processes
- To perform R&D within the firm or to contract R&D to outside of firms.
- To use universal researchers or private sector researchers.

There must be effective interactions between R&D department and other functional departments in implementing different types of generic business strategies like focus strategy, leadership strategy and grand strategy. Avoid and minimize the conflicts between marketing, finance or accounting, R&D and information systems departments and make clear policies and objectives of company.

Proper Guidelines for Research and Development Strategies

Proper guidelines for research and development strategies are listed below:

- In the case, the company's technical progress slow, its result in market rate is moderate and significant barriers to possible new entrants, it can be clarified to company in house R&D is preferred for solution. In the case, research and development strategies are successful; it will result in a temporary products and process monopoly that can be exploiting by the company.
- In the case, the technology change is rapidly and the market is growing slowly in this case the research and development involves very risk due to lead to new development of an ultimately obsolete technology or one for which there is no market for products and services which offered by company.
- In the case, technology change is slow in spite of the market is growing quickly, in this case, there is not enough time for in house development. In this prescribed approach, it is to obtain R&D expertise on an exclusive or non exclusive basis from an outside firm.
- In the case, both technical progress and market growth are very fast. These circumstances, R&D expertise should be obtained through acquisition of a well established firm in the industry.

Research and Development Approaches

There are three approaches for implementation of R&D strategies:

First Approach →	Firm is to make technological products
Second Approach →	Firm is to an innovative imitator of successful products
Third Approach →	Firm is to be a low cost producer by mass producing products

First Approach

- Firm is to make technological products
- This strategy approach is the glamorous and exciting and dangerous one to firms.
- When competitor makes a technological products than only pioneer firms are fallen in marketing and rival firms seizing this initiatives.

Second Approach

- Firm is to an innovative imitator of successful products.
- It minimizing the risks and costs starts up in business.
- This strategy approach entails and allowing a pioneer firm have to develop the first version of the new product and to introduce to existing market.
- Excellent R&D personnel and Marketing department is the basic requirement to firms.

Third Approach

- Firm is to be a low cost producer by mass producing products.
- This approach is less expensive and products are recently introduced by the firms.
- A product prices is increased when a new product accepted by customers.
- This approach requires substantial investment for buying of plant and equipment, inspite of fewer expenditure compare first and second approach in R&D.

Research, Technology and Systems Delivered

Research, technology and systems delivered are essential requirement of the company. Research, technology and systems delivered are as outlined.

- Activities
- Costs and assets relating to product R&D,
- Process R&D
- Process design improvements
- Equipment design
- Computer software development
- Telecommunications system
- Computer assisted designs and engineering
- New data base capabilities
- Development of computerized support systems.

The R&D function develops new product and its process technologies. Technological innovation result is lower manufacturing costs and result in the creation of more attractive products that demand a premium price. It can affect primary manufacturing and marketing activities, and through them value creation.

5.10 HUMAN RESOURCE STRATEGY

Human resources management refers to recruitment, hiring, training, development and compensation of the employees of the organization. Human resource management activities are as follows:

- Activities
- Costs
- Assets associated with the recruitment, hiring training, development, and compensation of all types of personnel.
- Labor relations activities
- Developed of knowledge based skills and core competencies.

The human resource function ensures that the company or organization has the right mix of skill people to perform its value creation activities effectively.

- Human resource strategy play significant role in implementation of strategy in company.
- The job of human resource manager is changing rapidly as there companies that downsize and recognize employees requirements for projects.
- Strategic responsibilities of the human resource manager as listed below:
  - Assessing the staffing needs
  - And costs for alternative strategies proposed during strategy formulation and developing in firms.
  - Staffing plan for effectively implementing strategies in firms. This plan must consider how best to manager calculated to the individual costs in firm.
  - The plan must also include how to motivate employees and managers firms.

- The human resource department must develop performance incentives that clearly link between the performance and pay to employees in this way to achieve human resource strategies.
- It is process of empowering to implement human resource strategies; it is responsibilities of managers and employees in firm and their involvement in strategic management activities that yields the greatest benefits when all organizational members can be understood clearly and to know how they will benefit personally if the firm does well.
- It clearly linking between company duties and responsibilities and personal benefits is a major new strategic responsibility of human resource managers.
- Other new responsibilities for human resource managers may include: establishing and Administering an Employee Stock ownership plan (ESOP), instituting an effective childcare policy, and providing leadership for managers and employees in this way to allow them balance to work and family.

Human Resource Strategies Problems

- Well designed strategic management system can be failed if sufficient attention is not given to human resource dimension in firms.
- Human resource problems arises when business implement strategies can usually traced to three causes as listed below:
  I. Disruption of social and political structures
  II. Failure to match individuals aptitudes with implementation tasks
  III. Inadequate top management support for implementation activities

Human Strategy implementation poses a threat to many managers and employees in organization due to new power and status management relationships are anticipated and realized in firms. New formal and informal groups, values, beliefs, and priorities may be largely unknown by managers and employees, these things may become engaged in resistance behavior as their roles prerogatives and power in the firm change. Disruption of social and political structures that accompany with strategy execution, it must be anticipated and considered during strategy formulation and managed during strategy implementation process.

Major Tasks of Human Resource Strategy

Human resource strategies are concerning with matching managers with strategy specify that jobs have specific and relatively static responsibilities, although people are dynamic in their personal development it is commonly used methods that will be matched managers with strategies to be implemented in firm's. It includes the transferring managers task and duties for this purpose developing leadership workshops, offering career development activities, promotions, job enlargements and job enrichment to employees of the firm's.

Major Guidelines for Human Resource Strategy

A number of other guidelines can help to human resource managers and ensure that human relationship facilities in firms rather than disrupt strategy implementations efforts. Specifically, HR managers should do a form of chatting and informal questioning to stay abreast of how things are progressing and to know when to intervene to employees of the firm's. HR managers can be building proper support for strategy implementation. Managers are put efforts by giving few order, announcing few decisions , depending heavily on informal questioning and seeking to probe and clarify until a consensus emerges with human resource in projects. It is one of the key thrusts that needed should be taken in the form of rewarded that generously and visibly in firm's...

It is surprising that so often during strategy formulation shall consider individual values, skills, and abilities needed for successful strategy implementation in firms. It is very rare that a firm selection new strategies which are significantly altering an existing strategies possesses by the firm's at the right line and staff personnel in the light positions, for successful strategy implementation. These things are needed to match individual aptitudes with relevant strategy implementation tasks should be considered with strategic choice.

Inadequate support from strategies for implementation activities often undermines organizational success. Apart from chief executive officers, small business owners, and government agency heads must be personally committed to strategy implementation and expenses commitment highly visible ways in enterprise. Strategist formal statements about the importance of strategic management, it must consistent switch with actual support and rewards given for activities completed and should be objectives reached. Otherwise, stress will be created by inconsistency, it can cause uncertainty among manages and employees at all levels in business enterprises.

Perhaps the best method for preventing and overcoming human resource problems in strategic management, it is to activity which involved by many mangers and employees as possible in this process. Although, it is time consuming, this approach will be understanding, trust, commitment and ownership and reduces resentment and hostility. The true potential of strategy formulation and implementation presides by skilled and trained people in enterprise.

The firm's external opportunities and threats are on the one hand, and its internal strengths and weakness are on the other hand. In human resource strategic management, the competitive advantage may be in the form of low costs relationship in the industry or being unique in the industry along dimensions that are widely used by the customers in particular segments and society at large. And so that they can obtain a competitive edge by becoming a low cost leader or a differentiator puts a heavy premium on having a highly competent and commitment team for human resources.

According to Charles Greer

"In a growing number organizations, human resource are now viewed as source of competitive advantage, there is greater advantage that distinctive competencies are obtained through highly developed employed skills, distinctive organizational cultures management processes and systems".

The role of human resource enabling the organization effectively deals with the external environment challenges. The human resource management function has been accepted as a strategic partner in the formulation of organizations strategies, implementation of such strategies through human resource planning employment, training, appraisal, and compensation practices of employees, these are strongly influence on employee competence is very important to business enterprise.

The following points should be kept and focused in mind:

1. **Recruitment and selection:** in this process, the workforce will be more competent if a firm can successfully identity, attracts, and select and most competent applicants on market.
2. **Training**: in this process, the workforce will be more competent if employees are well trained to perform their job property.
3. **Appraisal of performance:** it refers to the performance appraisal is to identify and performance deficiencies experienced due to lack of competences. Such deficiencies, once identified, can often be solving through counseling, coaching or training in business enterprise.
4. **Compensation:** it refers in a firm can usually increase the competency of its workforce by offering pay and benefit packages that are more attractive than those of there competitors, this proactive enables organizations to attract and retain the most capable people in jobs.

Strategy and Human Resource Management

- The human resource strategy of business should reflect and support the corporate strategy.
- An effective human resource strategy include way in which the organization plans to develop its employees and provide them suitable opportunities and better working conditions so that their optional contribution is ensured .
- It implies to be selecting the best available personnel, in this ensuring a fit between the employees and the job and retaining, motivating, and empowering employees to perform well in direction of corporate objectives.

Strategic human resource management may be defined as the linking of human resource management with strategic goals and objectives to improve business performance and develop organizational culture that fosters innovation and flexibility. The success of an organizational depends on it human resource. This refers to how they are acquired, developed, motivated and retained. Organizational play an important role for organizational success. The pre supposes is an integrated approach towards human resource functions and overall business functions of an organization.

The human resource management practice of an organization may be important source of competitive advantage. Human resource strategy is focussed to the following points:

- Pre selection practices including human resource planning and job analysis in business enterprise.
- Selection practice refers to staff various positions in the organizations and predefined requirement and selection policies and procedures should be designed keeping in view the mission and the purpose of an organization.
- Post selection practices is to maintain and improve the workers job performance levels, human resources decisions that related to training and development, performance appraisal, compensation and motivation should be based on corporate strategy of the organization.

Strategic Role of Human Resource Management

The prominent areas where human resource manager can play strategic role are as follows:

1. ***Providing Purposeful Direction***
   - The human resource management must be able to lead people and the organization towards the desired direction.
   - It is involving right people for right job from the beginning.
   - The most important tasks of professional management is to ensure that the object of an organization has been internalized by each individual working in the organization.
   - Goals of an organization state the clear purpose and justification of its existence in business enterprise.
2. ***Creating Competitive Atmosphere***
   - Presents globalize market maintaining a competitive gain is the object of any organization.
   - There are two important ways of business can be achieved a competitive advantage over the others. The first is cost leadership which refers to the firm aims to become a low cost leader in the industry. The second competitive strategy is differentiation under which the firm seeks to be unique in the industry in terms of dimensions that are highly valued by the customers.
   - Putting these strategies into implementations that effect carries a heavy premium on having a highly committed and competent workforce.

3. ***Facilitation of Change***
   - The human resource will be more concerned with substance rather than form, accomplishments rather than activities, and practice rather than theory.
   - The personnel function will be responsible for furthering the organization not just maintaining it.
   - Human resource management will have to devote more time to promote changes than to maintain the status quo in business operations.
4. ***Diversion of workforce***
   - In the modern organization management refers to diverse workforce is a great challenge.
   - Workforce diversity can be observed in terms of male and female workers. Young and old workers, educated and unrelated workers. Unskilled and professional employees act.
   - Moreover, many organizations also have people of different castes, religious and nationalities.
   - The workforce in future will comprise more of educated and self conscious workers. They will ask for high people of degree of participation and avenues for fulfillment.
   - Money will no longer be the sole motivating force for majority of the worker. Non financial incentives will also play an important role in motivating the workforce.
5. ***Empowerment of human resource***
   - Empowerment means authorizing every number of a society or organization to take of his/her own destiny realizing his/her full potential.
   - It involves to be given more power to those who, at present, have little control what they do and little ability to influence the decisions being made around them.
6. ***Building core competency***
   - The human resource manager has a great role to play in developing core competency by the firm.
   - A core competency is a unique strength of an organization which may not be shared by others.
   - This may be in the form of human resource, marketing capacity, or technological capability.
   - If the business is organized on the basis of core competency, it is likely to generate competitive advantage. Because of this reason, many

organizations have restructuring their businesses around by divesting those businesses which do not match core competences implies leveraging the limited resources of a firm.

- It needs creative, courageous and dynamic leadership having faith in organizations human resource.

7. ***Development of works ethics and culture;***
   - Greater efforts will be needed to achieve cohesiveness because workers will have transient commitment to groups.
   - As changing work ethic requires increasing emphasis on individuals, job will have to be redesigned to provide challenge.
   - Flexible starting and quitting times for employees may be necessary.
   - Focus will shift from extrinsic to intrinsic motivation. A vibrant work culture will have to be developed in the organizations to create an atmosphere of trust among people and to encourage creative ideas by the people.
   - It is far reaching changes with the help of technical knowledge will be required for this purpose.

Human Resource Development Functions are as Outlined:

- Effective management of the human resource in the organization.
- Improvement of employee skill and morale.
- Labor relations costs compared to industry and competition from present industry scenario.
- Efficient and effective formulation and implementation and controlling of the policies.
- Effective utilization of incentive to motivate employees' performance.
- To know the ability to level peaks and valleys of employment.
- To regulate employee turnover and absenteeism.
- Specialized skills and experience.

CHAPTER 6

Strategy Implementation and Control

Contents

Learning Objectives

- Learning the concept of strategy implementation
- Understand strategy formulation and implementation
- To design the organization structure for implementation of strategy
- To know the strategic business units
- To evaluate the leadership role in strategy formulation and implementation and control in an organization
- Learn the corporate culture, types, and its environment in an organization
- To know the strategic control system in an enterprise

"Winning companies know how to do their work better"

Michael Hammer and James Champy

"A management truism says structure follows strategy. However, this truism is often ignored. Too many organizations attempt to carry out a new strategy with an old Structure"

"Weak leadership can wreck the soundest strategy; forceful execution of even a poor plan can often bring victory"

By – Sun zi

"An organization's capacity to execute its strategy depends on its "hard" infrastructure - Its organizational structure and systems- and on its "soft" infrastructure its culture and norms"

By – Amar Bhide

"The biggest levers you've got to change a company are strategy, structure, and culture. If I could pick two, I'd pick strategy"

By- Wayne Leonard, CEO, Entergy

"The ideal organizational structure is a place where ideas filter up as well as down, where the merit of ideas carries more weight than their source, and where participation and shared objectives are valued more than executive order"

Edson Spencer

"Leader lives in the field with his troops"

H – Ross Perot

"Weak leadership can wreck the soundest strategy; forceful execution of even a poor plan can often bring victory"

Sun Zi

6.1 INTRODUCTION

In this chapter, we shall discuss about the concept of strategy formulation, to know the relationships between strategy formulation and implementation of strategy, to study different issues in strategy formulation. Design the organisation structure for strategy formulation and implementation and control in terms of functional structrue, divisional structure, strategic business units, matrix structure and network structure. Strategy implementation and control in strategic business units and core competences are relating to value chain analysis, identifying the core competenaes and manages its links in business. It also involves leadership which is helpful to strategic implementation. While implementation of strategy in organization would be building a strategy which is supporting corporate culture for proper implementation and control. Finally strategic management is a continuous process in firms which decides what strategies will be required by enterprise. In this case, there must be translation of strategic thought into strategic action in enterprise and its process. Proper translation requires support of all managers and employees of business is the basic essential to enterprise. Improper implementation of strategy, it affects to entire organisation . It affects all the functional and divisional areas of a business.

6.2 INTER RELATIONSHIPS BETWEEN STRATEGY FORMULATION AND IMPLEMENTATION

- Strategy implementation is one of the managerial exercises of putting a new selected strategy into particular place in business enterprise.
- Strategy execution deals with the managerial exercise and it involves to supervision of organization for ongoing strategy formulation and execution in enterprise for survival, growth and development in organization.
- Strategy execution will be making work, it can be improving the core competences are implemented and showing measurable progress towards the achievement of the targets results.
- It is concerned with the translation a decision which converts into action that is pre purposeful and makes proper decision itself.
- Strategy implementation should be acceptable and to know the feasibility of the performance in organization.
- It involves to allocation of resources to new course of action which will be undertaken by company.
- It designs the organization structure and its activities for effective handling in organization.

Basic Elements of Strategic Management

Basic elements of strategic management involves to strategy formulation, implementation and control of strategy in enterprise or organization or company. Basic elements of strategic management described through the figure 6.1.

Figure 6.1: Basic Elements of Strategic Management

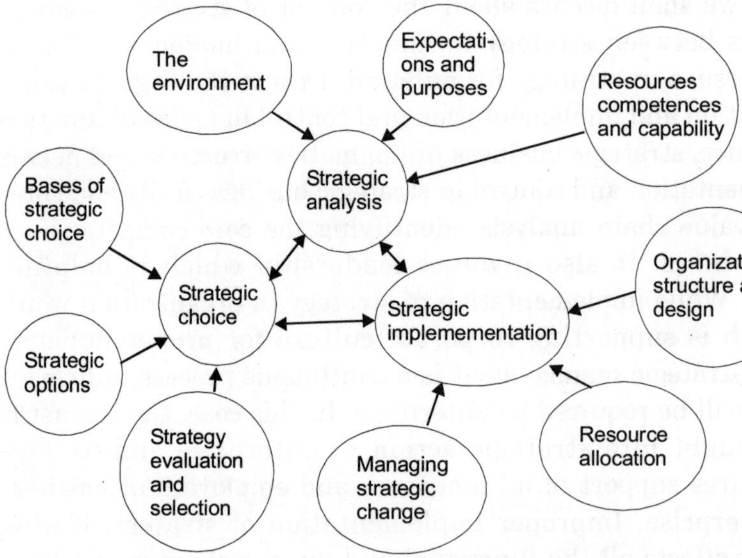

Figure 6.1 highlights the basic elements of strategic management are as outlined:

Step one is to Strategic analysis; it consists of the environment, expectations and purposes and resources competencies and capability.

Step second is to strategic choice; it principally combination of bases of strategic choice, strategic options and strategic evaluation and selection.

Third step is to strategic implementation: it composes of organization structure and design, resource allocation and control, managing strategic change.

Strategy Formulation and Implementation Matrix

There are so many differences between strategy formulation and implementation process. So many managers in enterprises fail to make distinguish between strategy formulation and implementation. Strategy formulation requires special skills and also strategy implementation also requires very different skills compare to strategy formulation. An organization is successful due to its credit goes to sound strategy formulation and implementation of strategy and control tool of strategy. In several cases, strategy formulation and implementation is failure due to lack knowledge, skills, and resources in project.

Figure 6.2: Strategy Formulation and Implementation Matrix

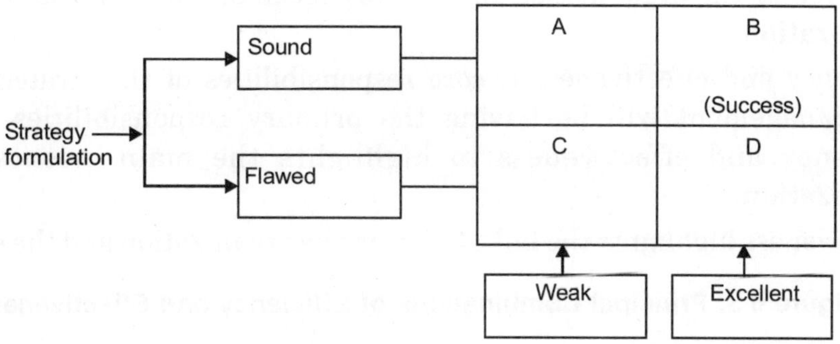

Figure 6.2 indicates the strategy formulation and implementation matrix in organization.

- This figure clearly identified the distinction between sound/flawed strategy formulation and excellent/weak strategy implementation.
- It identified the Square A, B, C, D
- Square A refers to the situation where a company seems to formulate a very competitive strategy, but it is showing difficulties, in the case of implementation it successfully. It happens due to the lack of experience, the lack of resources, missing leadership and so on. In these situations the company will be aiming at moving from A to B. In this case, project managers and team will be faced some difficulties for implementation of projects.
- Square B refers to the ideal situation where a company has been succeeded in designing a sound and competitive strategy and it has been successfully implement in enterprise.
- Square C refers to the reserved for companies but haven't succeeded in coming up with a sound strategy formulation and in addition are bad at implementing their flawing strategic model. In this case, it is ready to go success when it goes through business model redesign and implementation or execution with readjustment in projects.
- Square D refers to the situation where the strategy formulation is flawed; in this case, a company is showing excellent implementation skills. It finds itself in square D and the first thing is to redesign their strategy before readjusting their implementation or execution skills in projects.

Principal Combinations of Efficiency and Effectiveness Focus Strategy in Organization

- Efficiency and Effectiveness studying before we shall know about the reasons for failure like lack of strategic direction, guidance, suggestions and recommendations, lack of resources. These are created tendency to look inwards in times of stress. And for management to devote their attention to cost cutting and to shedding unprofitable divisions in business units in organization.

- Efficiency is the introspective to attain goals which achieved by each level employee in the organization in this way focus on efficiency and effectiveness organization.
- Efficiency and effectiveness is core responsibilities of the strategic managers, top management will be having the primary responsibilities towards the efficiency and effectiveness to highlights the main orientation of the organization.
- Effectiveness highlights the links between the organization and the environment.

Figure 6.3: Principal Combinations of Efficiency and Effectiveness

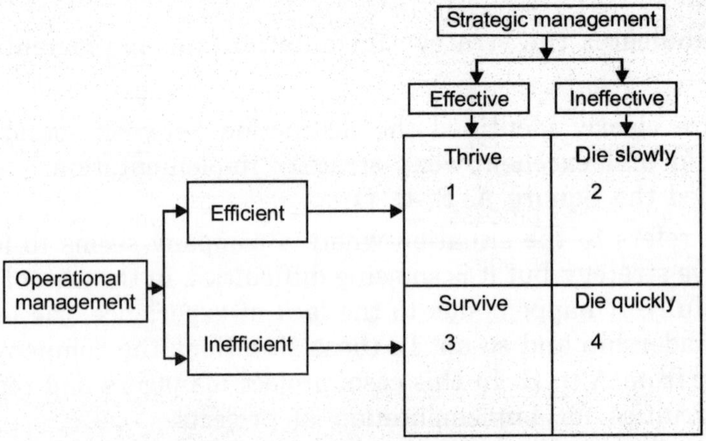

Figure 6.3 highlights the principal combinations of efficiency and effectiveness highlights operational management efficiency and inefficiency and also strategic management effective and ineffective situations in organization for thrive, die slowly, survive and die quickly circumstances in this way achieved with an efficient output and input ratio.

Cell 1 refers to thrive in organization, it finds and refers to well placed and it can be achieved what it aspires to achieve with an efficient output or input ratio.

Cell 2 refers die slowly, it is doomed, unless it can establish some strategic direction towards the efficient output or input ratio.

Cell 3 refers to survive, it is possible when increased the efficiency and effectiveness towards the output and input ratio in organization.

Cell 4 refers to Die quickly and it is doomed, in this situation organization take quick strategic decision.

Results of Efficiency and Effectiveness

Major results of efficiency and effectiveness in enterprise as outlined:

- It is in the form of dividend to shareholders

- Wages to employees
- Continued business to suppliers of goods and services
- Satisfaction on the part of customers and consumers
- Legal requirement fulfillment from the point of view of government.
- Responsible behavior towards society and environment from the perspective of pressure groups in the society.

Contrast between Strategy Formulation and Implementation

Major contrast between strategy formulation and implementation are outlined:

Exhibit 6.1: Contrast between Strategy Formulation and Implementation

Strategy formulation	Strategy implementation
• It is positioning forces before the action	• It is managing forces during the course of action
• It is focuses on effectiveness	• It is focuses on efficiency
• It is primarily intellectual process	• It is primarily and operational process
• It is required good intuitive and analytical skills	• It is required special motivation and leadership skills
• It requires coordination among a few individuals in project	• It requires combination among many individuals in project
• Formulation is primarily an entrepreneurial activity that based on strategic decisions making process	• It is mainly administrative task based on strategic as well as operational decision making

Strategic tools and concepts are very important for formulation of strategy which is not distinguish greatly for small, large, for profit, or non profit organizations. Therefore, strategy formulation varies significantly among different types and sizes of organizations. Meanwhile, implementation strategies requires in the following cases:

- Altering sales territories
- Adding new departments
- Closing facilities
- Hiring new employees
- Changing on organization pricing policy and its strategy
- Develop financial budgets
- Develop new employees benefits
- Establishing cost control procedures
- Changing advertising strategies
- Building new facilities

- Training new employees
- Transferring the managers among the divisions
- Building a better management information system

Above mentioned activities are differently greatly among the manufacturing, services, and government owned organizations.

Strategic Management Linkages

Strategic management linkages are very important for purpose of orderly study in organization. In real scenario of strategic formulation and implementation processes are interlinked with each other. There are two types of linkages exist between the strategy formulation and implementation phase as listed below:

I. Forward Linkages
II. Backward Linkages

Forward Linkages

- It deals with the impact of the formulation on implementation of strategies in enterprise.
- There are different elements are required for strategy formulation that starting with the mission and vision setting through environmental and organizational appraisal, strategic alternatives and choice to the strategic plan which determine and applicable to organization .
- It involves formulation of new strategies or reformulation of existing strategies, which may changes and have to be effected within the organization.
- For example, when organization structure undergone change, this time, formulation of new strategies are crucial otherwise undergone reformulation of existing strategies and try to make changes for dramatic improvement in organization structure for implementation of strategy.

Backward Linkages

- It concerned with the impact in terms of opposite directions in organization. i.e., Implementation is determined by the formulation of strategies. In this scenario, the formulation process is also affected by factors which are relating with implementation.
- It dealing with strategic choice, in this circumstance, strategist remembers the past strategic actions and process which determine and choose best choice strategy.
- Strategist tends to adopted past strategies which already implemented in organization. In this case, strategist take help from implemented strategy and design the appropriate strategies as per meet present requirement of the organization along with added special features in these strategies. These type

of incremental changes helpful to organization for very long time survival in the market.

6.3 ISSUES IN STRATEGY IMPLEMENTATION

There are so many issues are essential for implementation of project in real time scenario. Strategist task is very important to identify the different issues in different projects. These issues are based on strategist own experience, skills, knowledge, attitudes and abilities. The implement task help to strategist to put their skills, knowledge attitudes and abilities to test in terms of proper allocations of resources, design structures, formulate functional policies and take into consideration of leadership styles and how to deals with various issues in organization as listed below:

- It involves the strategic planning that set by organization, it proposes and put into action through implementation of project.
- Always strategies should lead to plans. For example, a company have been formulated grand strategies, which leads to modernization or organization plan that requires to goals, policies, procedures, rules, and steps to be taken in putting a plan into action for survival, growth, development.
- Project programmes which lead to the formulation of projects. A project programme is highly specific program, it determine the time schedule and cost involved in project. For this purpose, strategist to make budget for allocations of resource. Research and Development programmes may consist of several projects which is intentional to achieve specific and limited objective, these are required to allocations of funds, and is also set time schedule to finish projects.
- Projects have to require adequate infrastructure facilities which meet to day to day operations in an organization. It involves may be setting up new or additional infrastructure facilities, it requires new installation of newer systems, and several other activities that are needed for the implementation of strategies in business.

Implementation of strategies is not constraints to formulation of plans, programmes and projects resource is essential to all types of project. Each project properly designed the organization structure, systems requirements, planning tools, and strategic role of strategist to make plans and work as per planned and organized manner in projects.

Issues in Projects Implementation

Major issues which are relating to projects implementation as outlined in sequential manner:

Figure 6.4: Issues in Projects Implementation

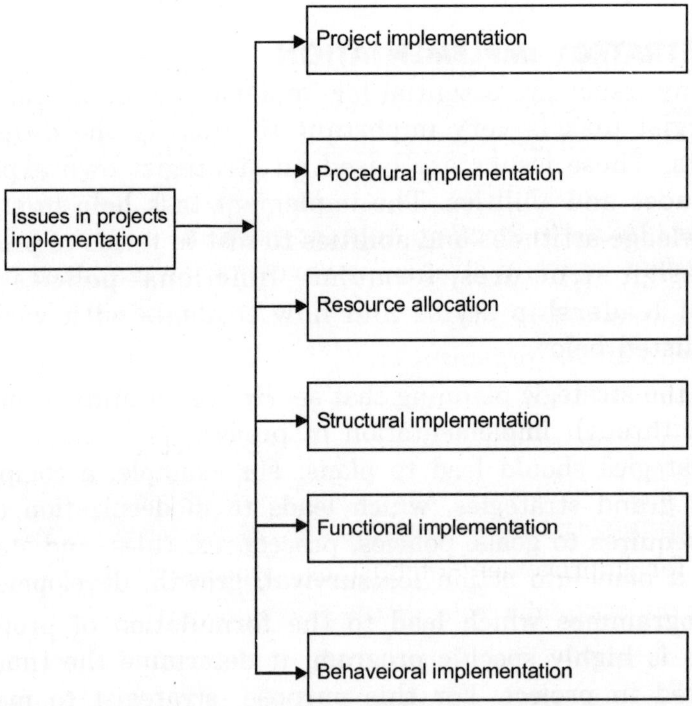

Figure 6.4 highlights the issues in project implementation are noted in the sequential, it does not mean that each of the issues in project implementation activities are necessarily performed one after another. Project implementation process activities can be performed simultaneously, in several cases, certain other activities will be repeated over time, in some cases, these activities are performed only once.

Strategic Responsibilities towards Project Implementation

- Strategic responsibilities are playing vital role in formulation of strategy and implementation of project in an organization.
- For strategy formulation and implementation strategy requires a shift in responsibilities from the divisional and functional strategic managers in an organization.
- Each project must be clearly defined the strategic role of divisional managers and functional managers in an organization.
- Improper design organization responsibilities have to create so many problems in project formulation and implementation.
- Decisions should be considered by middle and lower levels in projects in organizations, it is helpful to build good coordination and middle and lower level employees are participated in strategic decisions process.

- Managers and employees are motivated by themselves and perceived their self-interest along with organization interest otherwise both are coincide in projects.
- Divisional and functional managers are involved to formulation of strategy activities in an organization and provide equal importance to all categories of employees involved as possible in strategy formulation activities in an organization.

Central Management Issues in Strategy Implementation

Central management issues in strategy implementation are listed below:

- Establishing annual objectives
- Devising policies in an organization
- Proper allocation of available resource
- Ready to altering an existing organizational structure
- Restructuring and reengineering
- Revising rewarding and incentives policies in an organization
- Change only for improvement of business process
- Managers act as strategist role in an organization
- Development of support culture strategy in an organization
- Culture diversity and adoption and operation in an organization
- Effective development of human resource role in an organization
- Downsizing an organization, it is doing when it is necessary to organization.
- Strategic managers changes should direct to firm to move towards new directions for achievement, survival, growth and over all development of an organization in short-term and long-term in business.

Managers and Employees Participation in Project Implementation

- Managers and employees can be participated early and directly involved in strategy formulation and implementation decisions throughout an organization.
- They are participated for strategy implementation in this way buildup project design for implementation in an organization.
- Managers, employees and strategists genuine commitment is very important to finish implementation process in an organization.
- These personnel require a powerful motivate themselves and others in an organization.
- These personnel are busy towards strategy formulation and implementation activities in an organization.
- They try to learn new things and cop with the modern business environment.

- Strategist and employees should understand clearly mission and vision of the organization and clearly communicated throughout an organization.
- These personnel are discussed the following things:
    - Who are major competitors?
    - What are the major accomplishments?
    - What are the products and services offered to customers?
    - What are plans?
    - What is action plan?
    - What is the performance of an organization?
    - What are the major external opportunities?
    - What are the internal opportunities?
    - What is authority and responsibilities?
    - What is role in project?
    - What is cost of project?
    - What is time schedule of project?
    - What are hurdles in projects?
    - What are hierarchy position and its influence to an organization?

6.4 ORGANISATION AND STRATEGY IMPLEMENTATION

Nature of Strategic Change Management

To change is to move from the present to the future, from known information to relatively unknown information. Therefore, change can be defined as "to make or become different, give or begin to have a different form". For example post war recovery of Iraq and Afganistan. Change also refers to dissatisfaction with the old values, beliefs and systems and hence adapts to new values, beliefs and systems. The deficiency also reflects the inability of the system to respond to environmental changes. Change signifies a qualitatively different way of perceiving, thinking and behaving to make improvement over the past and present trends of the business management.

Change line context of an organization can be termed as a process of bringing about relatively enduring alteration in the present status of an organization or its components or interrelationships among the components and their differentiated and integrated functions in totally or partially. Therefore, changes in organization have attained greater adaptability and viability with reference to the current and emerging environmental developments in the world.

Strategic change in organization has signifies alteration in the objectives, goals and strategies, procedures for converting input into outputs, its specified features, structures and human resource. Changes in these are, however, inter-related in organization. Thus, it may include product and process restructuring, mergers and alliances, diversification and installing new systems. It may also mean change in attitudes and skills of organizational human resource, tasks and technology of the enterprise, alteration in customs responsive, norms and culture. These changes are essential and needed to business enterprise.

In view of its pervasive nature, change at anyone level is interrelated with changes at other levels of the enterprise. Therefore, it is essential for the management to assess organization with wide implications of any change is going to be affected. Further, these changes need to be reviewed on continuous basis to cope with ever changing environmental developments in business enterprise.

All changes are happened either in reaction to it as driving forces or a proactive. Changes have been planned and initiated by an organization. Therefore, reactive change happens in response to an event or series of events relating to business. The failure of existing process or system is a powerful mode for change in business. Reactive change being unplanned is hardly welcomed because it usually results in poorly coordinated, inefficient management. It plays havoc with virtually any strategic plan. Proactive changes take place when an organization's managers have concluded that a change would be beneficial to business. Proactive change is more orderly, more efficient because it is planned, structured and organized.

A change in organization is directed at the micro level. It focused on units /subunits /components with in an organization and brought in gradually are incremental changes. It is beneficial to an organization and built new skills and beliefs in the organization. These changes are efficient and acceptable by an organization. Many argue that such incremental development can be proactively managed; organization will keep in touch with the environment development and anticipate needs for change. This can be achieved through process of changing of current operating business system. Others argue that while it is not always possible to anticipate the need for major strategic changes, therefore, organizations react to external competitive or environmental pressures. Corporate managers may not perceive the need for major changes. In addition, adapt the existing paradigms and extent ways of operations.

However, incremental time changes may not be beneficial to the organization. Because such changes are based on the condition by the existing paradigms and routines of the organization even when the environmental developments are so cataclysmic and forceful systems and procedures in terms of basic assumptions, culture, technology etc. of the organization. These changes are transformational in character. Therefore, transformational change refers to change that cannot be handled within the existing paradigms and organizational change; it may be taken from the granted assumptions. Transformational change may also take from as result of either reactive or proactive process. If strategic drift has occurred or if external stakeholders are not happy due to the adequacy of current objective and strategy to meet external threat of the organization. For this situation, management may be in a forced transformational position. Likewise, if other changes happened in the organizational environment are very powerful to the business issues. The organization is constrained to go for transformation change. Where managers anticipate the need for transformational change, meanwhile they get time to act upon the desired change.

Change can be distinguished on basis of the degree of innovative is previously done in the organization. Innovation is brought changes in the organization. Innovation is different from change. Innovation occurs when an organization is the first time or early user of an innovative idea among its set of similar organizations in the business. Change brings modification of operating system of organization. Since innovation provides more excitement in change management. It is highly organized and systematic approach. It is exclusively concerned with reasoning what triggers change in the existing operating system and how affect the change in business. The management process programme is proactive, it monitors the continuously environmental developments for identifying the emerging opportunities and find out the suitable existing policies, strategies and programmes to exploit of these opportunities.

Another distinguishing characteristic of change management programme, it is engagement of the entire organization in the change process because people have always been and will remain important. Organization wide involvement of organizational people is crux of change management.

6.5 IMPLEMENTING STRATEGIC CHANGE: STEPS IN THE CHANGING PROCESS

The management of strategic change involves serious steps that managers must follow if the change process is to be succeeding. The major important steps are listed below:

Figure 6.5: Stages in the Change Process

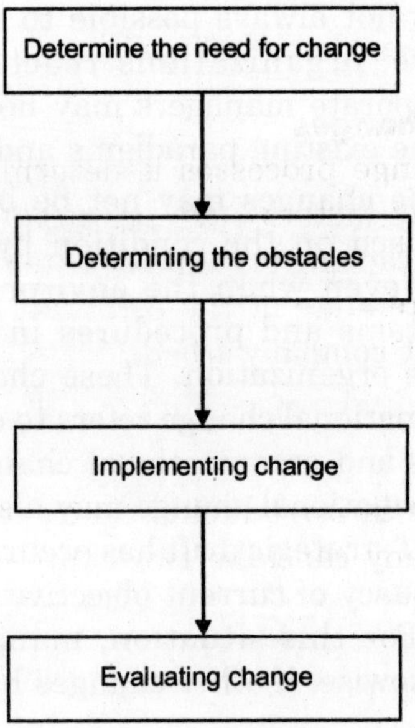

Figure –6.5 indicates the stages in the change process:

- Determining the need for change
- Determining the obstacles to change
- Implementing change
- Evaluating change

Determining the Need for Change

According to Sunbeam's turnaround suggests, the first step in the change process involves determining the need for change, analyzing the organisation current position and determining the ideal future state that strategic managers would like it to attain, we are conduct swot analysis, first we examine strengths and weakness. Once identified strength, weakness then determine the change of the management.

Figure 6.6: Indicated That a Model Change

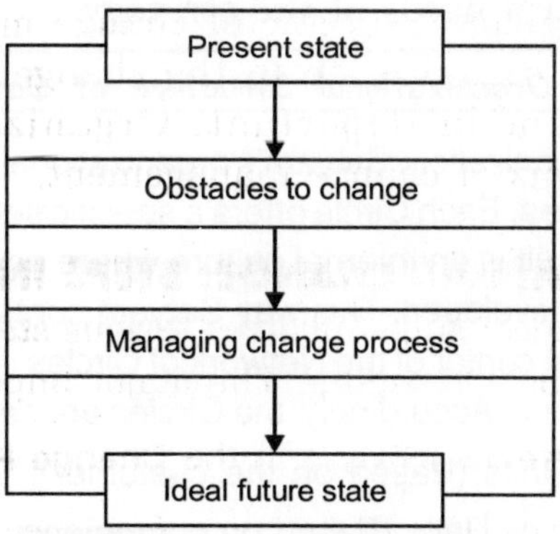

Figure –6.6 indicates the model of change that discussed as below:

Determining Obstacles to Changes

The second step in the change processes is determining the obstacles to change. Strategist must analyses the factors such as corporate, divisional, functional and individual. These factors are causing organization inertia and preventing the company from reaching its ideal future state at the corporate level strategy seemingly trivial ways may significantly affect company's behavior some corporate culture are easier to change than others.

Implementing Change

Implementing change stage is introducing and managing changes raises several questions generally, a company can take two main approaches to change. They are listed below:

- Top down change
- Bottom up change

In the case of Top down change approach CEO implementing change in the organization. Bottom up change approach, in the case low level management response to top level made changes in the organizational decision-making.

Evaluating Change

This is the last step in the changes process. It is to evaluate the effects of the changes in strategy and structure on organization performance. It is more difficult however, to assess the effects of changes in structure on company performance.

What is Structure?

Structure is the basic and simple concept: it is the division of task for efficiency and clarity of purpose in organization. It is coordination between the interdependent functional parts of the organization to ensure organizational effectiveness. Organization structure balances is to the need for specialization with the need for integration. It is providing for decentralizing and centralizing that consistent with the organizational and control needs of the strategy.

Case 6.1 : Organizational Structure of Satyam Industry

Satyam: A customer-centric organization. Satyam's organizational structure is inspired by a unique concept –the **Network of Circles.** Each Circle offers a specific set of business offerings based on its competency profile. The result is an internal culture where new ideas are nurtured and acted upon and new competencies developed. This way Satyam continuously provides services right across the IT value chain. At the center of the Network of Circles is the customer, whose business requirements are the driving force. Accordingly, the Circles are categorized as:

- Verticals Business Units (Based on the customer's line of business)
- Horizontal Competency Units (Based on competency requirements)
- Regional Business Units (Based on the regions the unit operates)

Questions

1. Explain the change structure in Satyam.
2. What vertical Business units?
3. What is Regional business units?

Reasons for Organization Structure

There are two reasons for organization structure due to changes in strategy as listed below:

(1) Organization structure largely explains how objectives and policies will be established.

(2) Why changes in strategy often require changes in structures that organization structure explains how resources will be allocated in an organization.

Chandler's Strategy - Structure Relationship

Chandler's strategy structure is very important to design the strategy and structure in organization. It is design in a different organization structure and its shows the relationship between strategy and organization structure to evaluate the different changes in strategy in different organizational structure.

Figure 6.7: Chandler's Strategy Structure Relationship

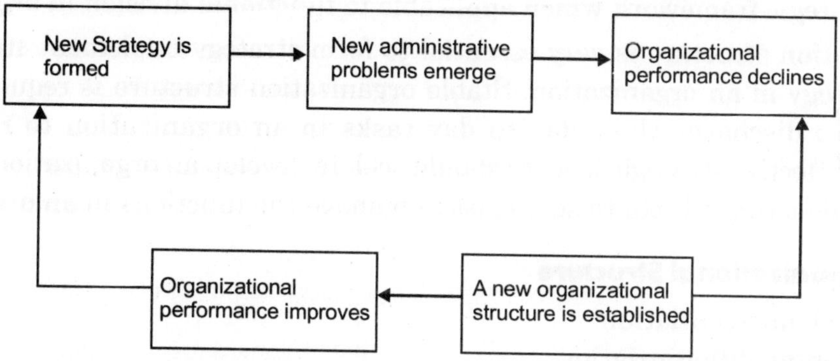

Figure 6.7 indicates the Chandler's strategy - structure relationship found a particular structure sequence to be often repeated as organizations grow and change strategy overtime. In this figure clearly highlights the there is no one optimal organization design or structure for given strategy or type of organization.

When we shall implement new strategy, it create so many administrative problems are emerged in terms of internal and external forces in environment. When an organization neglects its problems and mission and objects that time organizational performance is declined due to improper design of strategy – structure relationship. Strategist take care and design proper organization structure and suitable strategy structure relationship, it will be brought a new organizational structure should be established in enterprise. Well defined strategy and structure relationship creates very good work environment in this way organizational performance is improved in business.

What is Organizational Design?

Designing an organization's structure is the task of management who have the responsibility of designing, implementing and achieving the organization's mission. This is accomplished by dividing the work of the organization and then coordinating the various responsibilities. It defines how the organization's goals will be reached and how work will be done. This is a complex task, to assemble or alter a system. Designing an organization's frame work involves issues like complexity, formalization, centralization and determines what level of each will be required. It considers advance technology and environment to determine the appropriate structure to achieve organizational strategy.

Organizational structure is the company's formal configuration; it describes the roles, procedures, governance mechanisms, authority, and decision making process, responsibility, delegation of authority. It influence to an organization and its age and size and nature of businesses. These factors are influenced to strategist to form a new strategy and implement strategy in functional division. It acts as a design a strategic framework which applicable to functional division in organization.

Organization structure is very essential to form strategy implement strategy and control strategy in an organization. Stable organization structure is required by the companies to discharge their day to day tasks in an organization to finish task completely. Effective strategic leaders should seek to develop an organization structure and to provide a control tool to strategist to manage the functions in an organization.

Types of Organizational Structure

- Vertical differentiation
- Horizontal differentiation
- Integration and integrating mechanisms

6.6 VERTICAL DIFFERENTIATION

Vertical differentiation is an important element of an organizational structure. It is to specify the reporting relationships that link people, tasks and functions at all levels of a company or organization. It means that management chooses the appropriate number of hierarchical levels and the correct span of control for implementing a company's strategy effectively. The organizational hierarchy establish to span of control i.e. authority flows the top to bottom. The basic choice is a flat structure or tall structure.

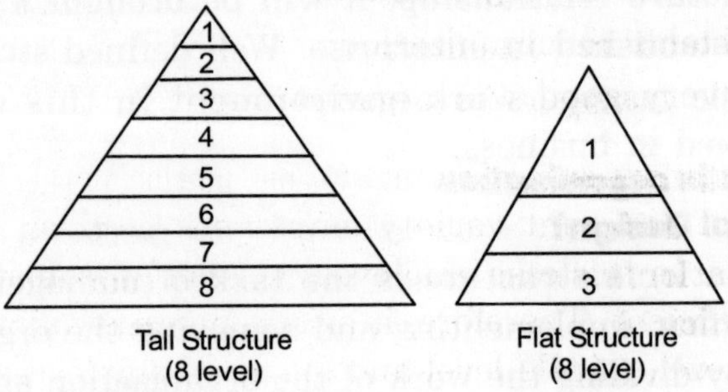

This chart indicate that the tall structure and flat structure, Tall structure have many hierarchical levels relative size. Flat structures have few levels relative to size

Figure 6.8: Problems with Tall Hierarchies

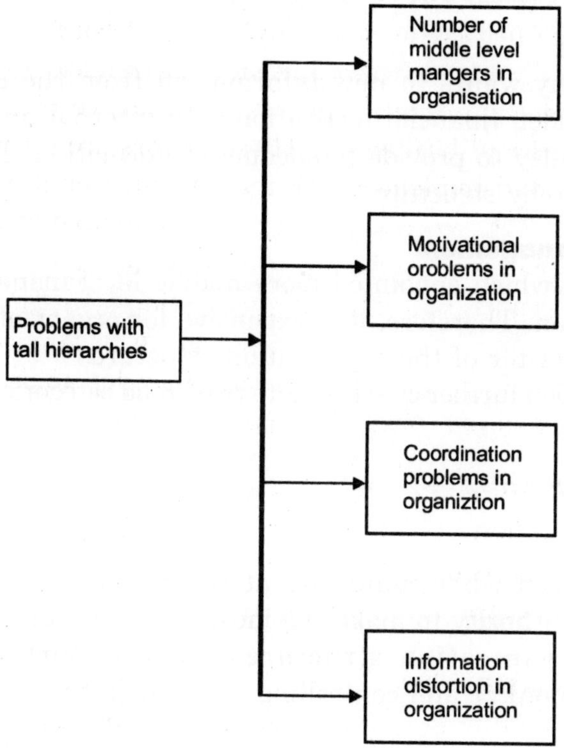

Problems with Tall Hierarchies

Figure 6.8 highlights the tall hierarchies' problems in organization. Tall hierarchies' problems are as listed below:

- Coordination problems in organization
- Motivational problems in organization
- Information problems in organization
- Number of middle managers in organization

Coordination Problems in organization

Organization consist of different variety employees perform their activities for accomplishment of goals. In this case employees are not coordinated to perform their duties effectively and efficient. Therefore, it arises in organization due to inadequate communication of top level, middle level and low level employees in organization.

Motivational Problems in Organization

Organizational hierarchy is essential to need for motivational aspects to motivate of employees who are perform their duties in organization. Praises, recognize and additional improvement of facilities and perk to employees these are the motives for employees in organization. Some times top management motivates their employees in terms of punishment. It is also one of the major problems of the organization structure.

Information Problems

Management hierarchy wants to new information from the customers, bankers, shareholders, debt holder, financial institution, and internal human resource of the organization. It has delay to provide to adequate information. Thus, it is one of the problems of the hierarchy structure.

Number of Middle management

Organization is a big, which appointed more middle level managers to manage and control the organization. Therefore, it is expensive for organization. This factor also one of the unhealthy factor of the organization structure.

Vertical differentiation further classified into two broad categories. They are as follows:

- Centralization
- Decentralization

Centralization

Authority is centralized when managers at the top levels of the organizational hierarchy retain the authority to make the most important decisions. Now days, the centralization of organization structure is not important to formulation, implementation and monitor and controlling of the objectives of an organization.

Decentralization

When the authority is decentralized, it is delegated to divisions, functional departments and managers at lower levels in the organization. Some important strategic factors are relating with the formulation, implementation and monitor and controlling the major objectives of an organization.

- Strategic managers delegate operational decision making responsibility to middle managers. Therefore, it reduces information overload to strategic managers in organization. In addition, strategic managers can spend more time on strategic decision-making process in organization for formulation, implementation and controlling the mission and vision of the organization.
- Managers of the organization become responsible for adapting the organization policy to suit local conditions, their motivation, and accountability to increase efficiency and productivity.

6.7 HORIZONTAL DIFFERENTIATION

Horizontal differentiation organization structure as follows:

- Simple structure
- Functional structure

- Divisional structure
- Strategic Business unit
- Matrix structure
- Product team structure
- Geographic structure

Simple Structure

Simple structure is suitable to small business enterprises. All strategic and operating decisions are centralized in hands of owner cum manager. This structure maximizes control by owners cum manager. Simple structures encourage employee involvement in more than activity.

Figure 6.9: Simple Structure

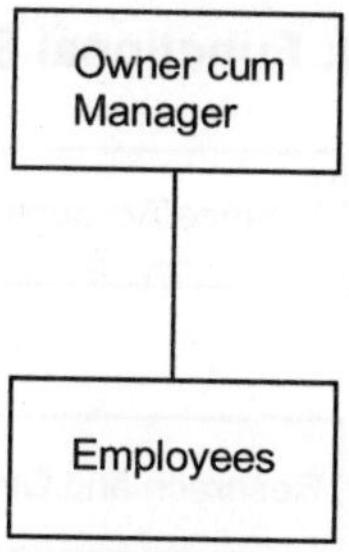

Merits

Exhibit-6.2: Merits of simple structure
• It Facilitate to control of all the business activities. • To make rapid decision making and to ability to change with market signals. • It is Simple and informal motivational control systems.

Exhibit-6.3: Disadvantages of Simple Structure
• It is very demanding on the owner cum manager. • It increasingly inadequate as volume expands. • It does not facilitate development of future managers. • It tends to focus owner cum manager on day-to-day matters and not on future strategy.

Functional Structure

Functional structure is the simplest and least expensive in organization design. Functional structure consists of several functions are as follows:

- Finance/accounting
- Research and development
- Human resource
- Marketing
- Production
- Engineering
- Sales and marketing.

Functional structure principally compose of a chief executive officer or a managing director and limited corporate staff with functional line managers in dominant functions like production, accounting, marketing, Research and Development, engineering and human resource. It provides facilities like communication and coordination among the line managers in an organization.

Figure 6.10: Functional Structure

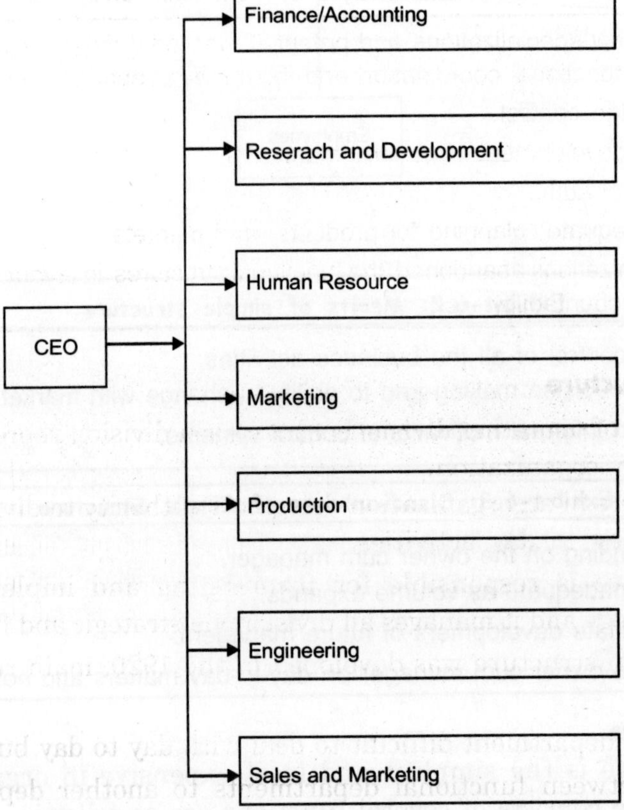

Advantages

Exhibit 6.4: Advantages of Functional Structure
• To efficiency through specialization • It is simplest and less expensive • To improve development of functional expertise. • To differentiate each division represents a separate business to which the top corporate officer delegates day-to-day operating decisions. • Functional structure promotes specialization of labour, encourages efficiency, minimizes the need for an elaborate control system and allows rapid decision making in an organization. • It is accurately monitor the performance of individual businesses. • It is simplifying control problems. • It improving the allocation of resource and stimulate managers of poorly performing divisions to seek ways to improve performance of an organization.

Disadvantages

Exhibit 6.5: Disadvantages of Functional structure
• It promotes narrow specializations and potential functional rivalry or conflict. • It is Difficulty in functional coordination and interns functional decision-making. • It creates staff-line conflict. • It limits internal development of general managers. • Poor delegation of authority • It involves inadequate planning for products and markets • Most of the organizations abandoned the functional structures in favour of decentralization and improved accountability

Multi- Divisional Structure

- It is composed of operating divisions where each division represents a separate business in an organization.
- Top level officers in an organization delegate's authority to divisional managers to discharge day to day activities.
- Corporate office is responsible for formulating and implementing overall corporate strategy and it manages all division via strategic and financial controls.
- Multi – division structure was developed in the 1920, main reasons are listed below:
    - Functional department difficult to deal with day to day business activities.
    - Conflict between functional departments to another department.
    - Costs are not properly allocated individual units.
    - It is not possible analysis individual products profit contribution.

- Top management become over involved in solving short run problems like coordination, communications and conflict management.

New innovative structure issues are outlined:

- Creating separate divisions, and each divisions is representing a distinct process in business.
- Each division consists of its functional hierarchy in an organization.
- Division managers are responsible persons for day to day business operations in an organization.
- Small corporate offices determine the long term strategic direction of the firm and exercise overall control over the multi divisions.

Divisional organizational structure

An organization programme diversifies its product /service line. It covers broad geographic areas and utilized unrelated market channels, or begins to serve distinctly different customer groups and a divisional structure is needed for organization. The divisional structure can be organized in the following manner.

- By geographic area
- By product or service
- By customer
- By process

Divisional Structure by Geographic Area

- Divisional structure by geographic area is appropriate for organizations whose strategies are needed to be tailored to fit the particular needs and requirement of customers in different geographic regions in world.

Functional managers is responsible for formulating and implementing overall corporate strategy and manages divisions via strategic and financial controls.

- It is suitable only multinational organization which divisions are dispersed across the world. This type of structure allows local participation in decision making and brings to be improved coordination and cooperation within a region.

Divisional Structure By product or service

- This structure most effective for implementing strategies in an organization having specific products and services which are needed special emphasis.
- It widely used when an organization offers only a few products and services when its services and products differ substantially.
- It allows to strict control over and give attention to product lines for this purpose required skills management force and reduced to top level management control.

Divisional Structure by Customer

- In this structure, a few customers are vital importance and many different services are provided to these customers, and it is very suitable to implement divisional structure of implementing strategies.

- This structure allows an organization to cater effectively to the requirements of clearly defined customer groups. For example, publishing companies often organize their activities around customers groups like colleges, schools, etc.

Divisional Structure By process

- It is similar to a functional structure.
- It activities are organized according to the work, it is actually performed.
- Divisional structure by process is evaluated on the basis of accountable for profit or revenues.

Advantages

Exhibit 6.6: Advantages of Divisional Structure

- It focuses on coordination and necessary authority down to the appropriate level for rapid response.
- It should clearly defined roles in an each division.
- It frees chief executive officer for broader strategic decision-making.
- It places strategy development and implementation in closer proximity to the divisions unique environment.
- It sharply focuses accountability for performance.
- It retains functional specialization within each division.
- It is good training ground for strategic managers.
- Division managers are responsible for sales and profit levels in an organization.
- It creates career development opportunities for managers and it allows to control of local situations that leads to a competitive climate within organization and allows new businesses and added to new products easily.

Disadvantages of Divisional Organization Structure

Exhibit 6.7: Disadvantages of Divisional Organization Structure

- It fosters potentially dysfunctional competition for corporate level resources.
- To problem with the extent of authority given to division managers.
- To potential for the policy inconsistencies between divisions.
- It problems of arriving at a method to distribute corporate overhead costs that is acceptable to different division managers with profit responsibility.
- It is costly due to each division requires functional specialists who must be paid highly salaries because these managers are highly qualified.
- Duplication of staff services, facilities and personnel in each division in an organization.
- It requires an elaborate, headquarters driven control system.
- Divisional structure is not suitable to small firms.

Figure 6.11: Divisional Organizational Structure President

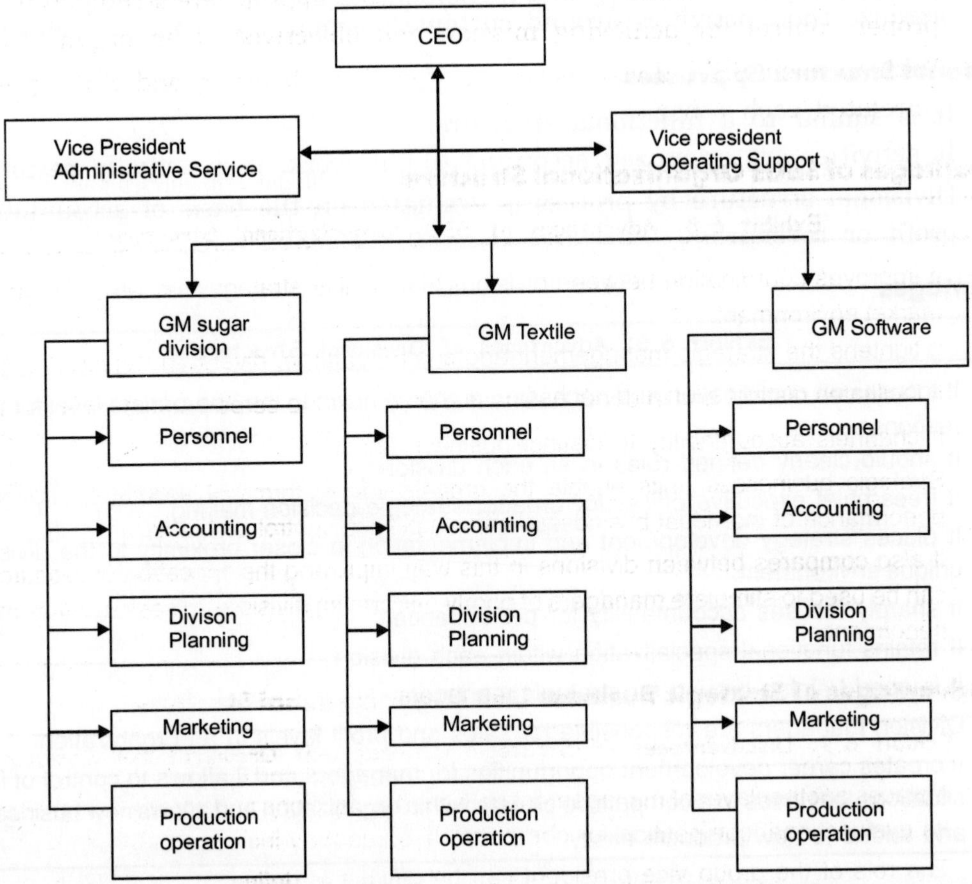

6.8 STRATEGIC BUSINESS UNITS

Some organizations encounter difficulty in controlling their divisional operations as the diversity, size, and number of these units continues to increase. And corporate management may encounter difficulty in evaluating and controlling it's numerous, often multi industry divisions. Under these conditions, it may become necessary to add another layer of management to improve strategy implementation, promotion synergy, and gain greater control over the diverse business interests. It can be achieved by grouping various divisions' in terms of common strategic elements. These groups commonly called strategic business units (SBUs).

- It consists of at least three levels, first level is a corporate headquarters at the top, second level is a strategic groups and third level is a divisions grouped by relatedness within each SBU.
- It consist of operating units where each unit representing a separate business to which top corporate officer delegates responsibility for day to day operations and business unit strategy to its managers.

- It provide to delegation to strategic business unit managers are responsible for formulation of strategy and implementing appropriate strategies and make proper control for achieving mission and objectives of an organization.
- With in each SBU, divisions are related to each other, and SBU groups are unrelated each other

Advantages of SBUs Organizational Structure

Exhibit 6.8: Advantages of SBUs Organizational Structure
• It improves coordination between divisions with similar strategic concerns and product / market environment. • It tightens the strategic management and control of large, diverse business enterprises. • It facilitates distinct and in depth business planning at the corporate and business levels. • It channels accountability to distinct business unit. • Strategic businesses units enable the organization in terms of accurately monitor the performance of individual businesses and simplifying control problems. • It also compares between divisions in this way improving the allocation of resource and can be used to stimulate managers of poorly performing divisions to seek ways to improve performance.

Disadvantages of Strategic Business Unit Organizational Structure

Exhibit 6.9: Disadvantages of Strategic Business Unit Organizational Structure
• It places another layer of management between the divisions and corporate management. • Its dysfunctional competition for corporate resource may increase. • The role of the group vice president can be difficult to define. • It is difficult in defining the degree of autonomy for the group vice presidents and division managers.

6.9 MATRIX ORGANIZATIONAL STRUCTURE

The matrix organization provides for dual channels of authority, performance responsibility, evaluation and control. It is essentially; subordinates are assigned to both a basic functional area and a project or product manager. The matrix form is included to combine the advantages of functional specialization and product / project specialization.

- In matrix structure, functional and product forms are combined simultaneously at the same level of the organization.
- It is the most complex of all designs due to it depends upon both vertical and horizontal flows of authority and communication.

Figure 6.12: Matrix Organizational Structure

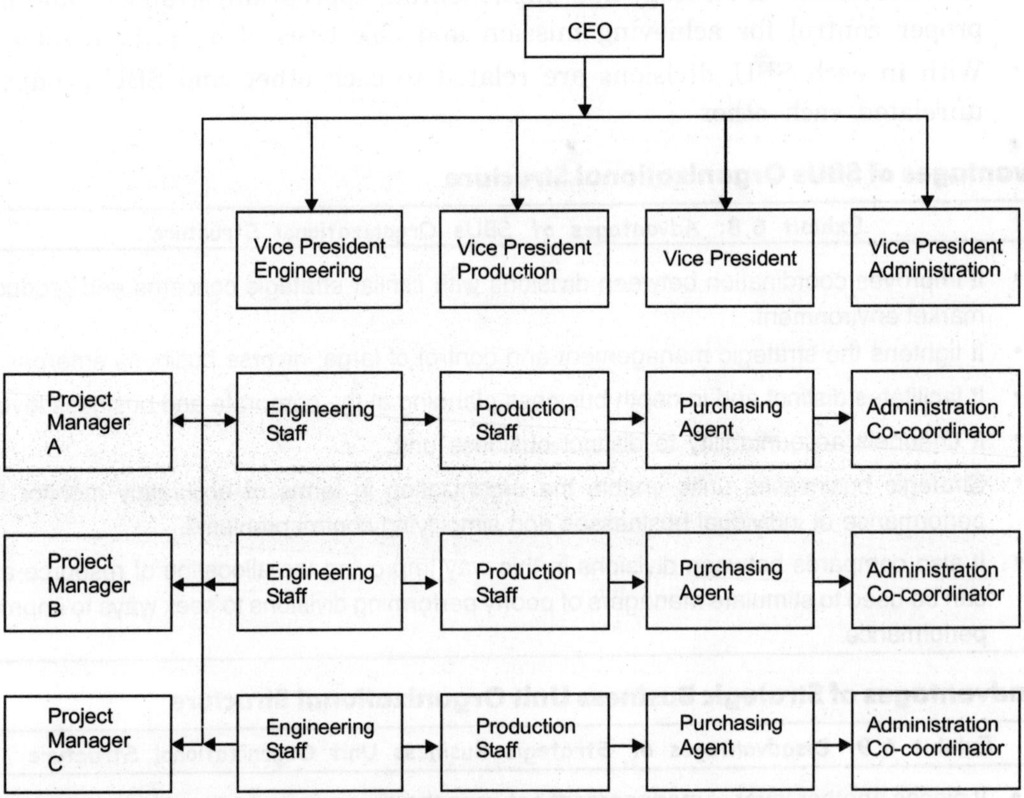

Advantages of Matrix Organizational Structure

Exhibit - 6.10: *Advantages of Matrix Organizational Structure*
• It accommodates a wide variety of project oriented business activity. • It provides good training ground for strategies managers. • It maximizes efficient use of functional managers. • It fosters creativity and multiple sources of diversity. • It is broader middle management exposure to strategic issues for the business. • It project objectives are very clear in an organization. • It is to be effective structure for planning, training, clear mutual understanding of roles and responsibilities and mutual trust and confidence. • It is very useful to external environment especially it's technological and market aspects is very complex and changeable.

Disadvantages of Matrix Organizational Structure

Exhibit 6.11: Disadvantages of Matrix Organizational Structure
• It acts as dial accountability can create confusion and contradictory policies. • Necessities tremendous horizontal and vertical coordination. • It produce conflicts revolving around duties, authority and resource allocation. • It goals are vague and technology used in project that is poorly understand.

Difference between Old Organization Design and New Organizational Design

Old organization design	New organizational design
• It is one and large corporation	• It is multi-business units and cooperative relationships
• It require vertical communication	• It require horizontal communication
• It is needed centralized top down decision making	• It is decentralized
• it involves quality teams	• it involves autonomous work teams
• it as a functional work teams	• it as cross functional work teams
• it requires minimal training	• it needs extensive training
• It specialized job design focused on individual	• It is value chain team focused job redesign
• It is vertical integration	• It is outsourcing and virtual organizations

Development of Matrix Structure

Davis and Lawrence have proposed three distinct phases for development of matrix structure.

Figure 6.13: Development of Matrix Structure

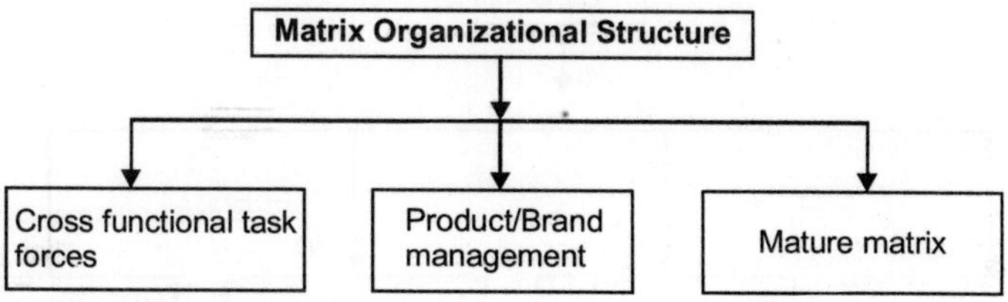

Figure 6.13 highlights Development of Matrix Structure are listed below:

- Cross-Functional task forces
- Product/Brand management
- Mature Matrix

Cross Functional Task Force

- It is temporary cross functional forces which are initially used when a new product line is being introduced in an organization.
- In this task force, project manager is in charge as the key horizontal link.

Product/Brand Management

- In the cross functional task forces become more permanent, the project manager becomes a product or brand manager and a second phase begins.
- In this arrangement, it is primary organizational structure, but in this case, product brand or brand managers act as the integrators of semi permanent products or brands in an organization.

Mature Matrix

- It is the third and final phase of matrix development involves a true deal authority structure in an organization.
- In this case, both the functional and product structures are permanent.
- All employees in organization are connected to both a vertical functional superior and horizontal product manager.
- In this mature structure, functional and product managers have equal authority and must work well together to resolve disagreements over resources and priorities.

Product Team Structure

Product team structure is a major structural innovation in recent years. It has similar advantages to a matrix structure but is much easier and for less costly to operate because of the way people are organized into permanent cross-functional teams.

Figure 6.14: Product Team Structure

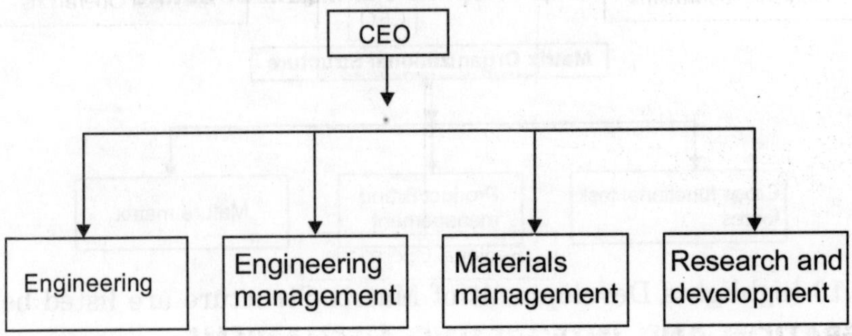

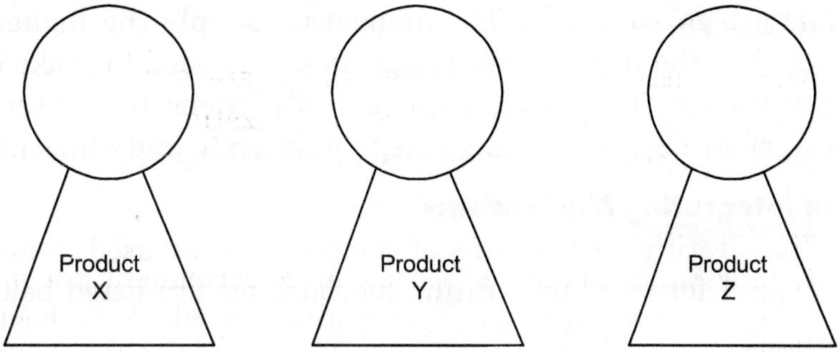

Geographic Structure

Company operates as a geographic structure; geographic regions become the basis for the grouping of organizational activities. For instance, a company may divide its manufacturing operations and establish manufacturing plants in different regions of the country. Service organizations like store chains or banks may organize their sales marketing activities on a regional, rather than national level to get closer to their customer.

Geographic structure provides more control than a functional structure because there are several regional hierarchies carrying out the work previously performed by a single centralized hierarchy.

Figure 6.15: Geographic Structure

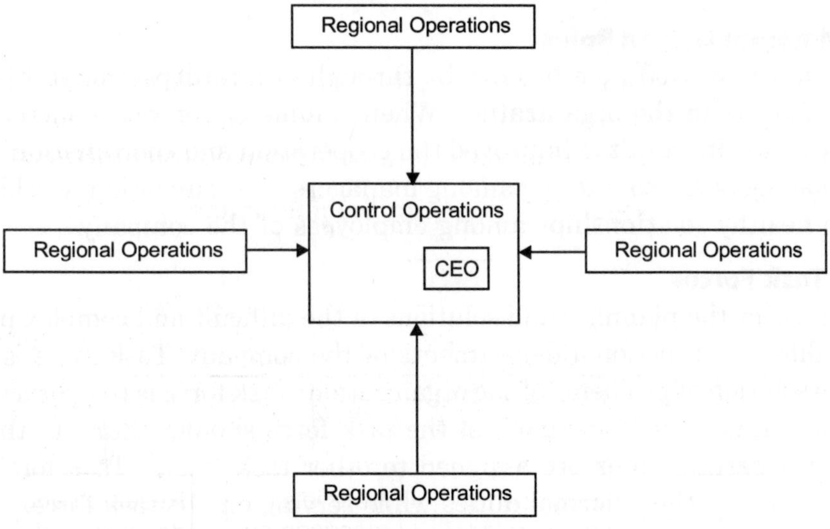

6.10 INTEGRATION AND INTEGRATING MECHANISMS

The level of integration and integrating mechanisms are necessary for organization structure to work effectively and efficiently. Integration refers to the extent to which an organization seeks to coordinate its value creation activities and make them independent. The design issues can be summed up simply the higher a company's level of differentiation, the higher level integration is needed to make organizational structure work efficiently. Therefore, company only integrates its task activities to the extent necessary to implement its strategy effectively and efficiently.

Types / Forms of Integrating Mechanisms

Forms / types of integrating mechanisms of company can be used to increase its level of integration. Types / forms of integrating mechanisms are listed below:

- Direct contact
- Liaison roles
- Task forces
- Teams
- Integrating roles
- Integrating departments
- Matrix

Direct contact

Chief executive officer has directly contacted among managers from different divisions or functional department can work together to solve mutual problems. Different functions managers have tend to equal authority for accomplishment of goals and objectives of the organization with cooperation and motivation.

Interdepartmental Liaison Roles

A company has improved its efficiency by through of interdepartmental liaison roles of among managers in the organization. When volume of contact is increased two or more departments, its result is improved the cooperation and coordination. Therefore, functional managers are contacting among managers of organization, weekly, monthly. It builds up healthy relationships among employees of the company.

Temporary Task Forces

Task force involves the planning and solutions of the difficult and complex problems. It arises from different functional departments of the company. Task force is a just like committee to solution of problems of the organization. Task force is temporary, therefore, once the problem is solved, members of the task force should return to their normal roles in their departments or are assigned to other task forces. Task force members also perform many of their normal duties while serving on the task force.

Permanent teams

Task force solves the problems effectively and efficiently an organization must establish permanent integrating mechanisms like as a permanent team. Example – product development committee.

Integrating Roles

Integrating roles means, a functional/divisions managers job is a full time. Who is normally a senior manager with a great deal of experience in the joint needs of the two departments? The job is to coordinate the decision process among departments/divisions so that the synergetic gains from cooperation can be obtained.

Integrating Department

The permanent integrating department is established at corporate head quarters. This department consists of mainly of strategic planners and may indeed be called the strategic planning department. Corporate head quarter's staffs in a divisional structure can also be viewed as an integrating department from the divisional perspective.

Matrix Structure

Lastly, differentiation is high and the company must be able to respond quickly to the environment, a matrix structure becomes the appropriate integrating device.

Institutionalizing the strategy

Three organizational elements provide the fundamental and long term for institutionalizing the company' strategy are as follows:

- Structure
- Leadership
- Culture

Matching Structure and Control Analysis at the Functional Level

Matching structure and control analysis strategy at the functional level are as below:

- Manufacturing functions/divisions
- Research and development functions/divisions
- Marketing division/functions
- Human resource division
- Accounting and finance division
- Customer welfare division
- Production departments

These are the matching structure of the functional level. Functional level strategies are discussed in the earlier chapter. Therefore, there is no need to discuss again these aspects in this chapter.

Matching Structure and Control at the Business Level

Matching structure and control at the business level are as below:

- Generic business level strategies
- Cost leadership strategy and structure

- Differentiation strategy and structure
- Implementing a combined differentiation and cost leadership strategy
- Focus strategy and structure

These are the matching structure of the business level. Business level strategies are detailed to discuss in the earlier chapter. Therefore, there is no need to discuss this topic in this chapter.

Designing a Global Structure

Global structure is consisting of the following areas:

- Multi domestic strategy and structure
- International strategy and structure
- Global strategy and structure
- Transnational strategy and structure

6.11 MULTIDOMESTIC STRATEGY AND STRUCTURE

A company pursues a multi domestic strategy; it generally operates business with a global area structure.

Figure 6.16: Global Area Structure

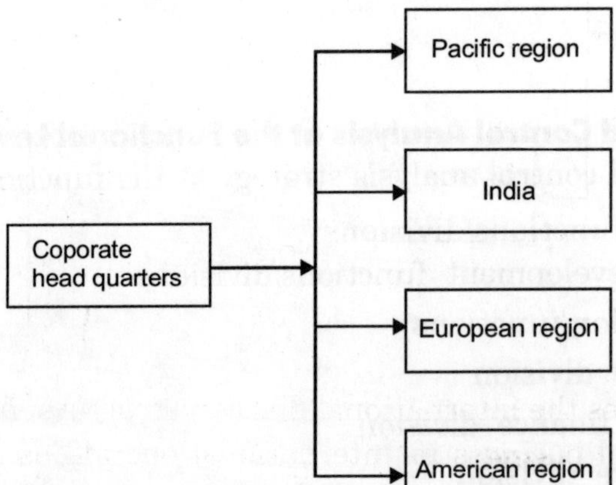

Figure 6.16 highlights the multi domestic area structure. A company duplicates all values like value creation activities and establishes a foreign division in every country or world in which it operates. Authority can be decentralized to managers in each foreign division and they devise the appropriate strategy for responding to the needs of the local environment. Corporate head quarter is much farther away from the scene of operations. It makes sense to decentralize, control and grant decision authority to managers in foreign operations. Managers at global headquarters use market and output controls as listed:

- Rate of return
- Growth in market share
- Operation costs evaluate the performance of foreign divisions.

On the basis of these comparison in global level and they can make global capital allocation decisions and global transfer of new technical knowledge.

INTERNATIONAL STRATEGY AND STRUCTURE

A company has adopted international strategy to enter into international market for global expansion. Normally, the company shifts to this strategy when it begins selling its domestically made products in foreign markets.

Figure 6.17: International Division Structure

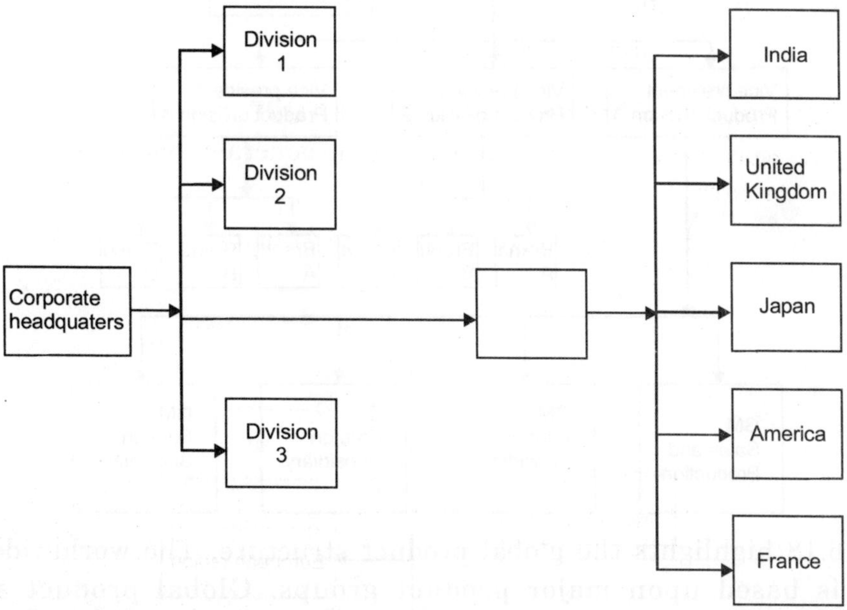

Figure 6.17 indicates the international division structure. A company has managed as a separate divisional business in International operations. International company has provided the authority and responsibility to managers for coordinating domestic product divisions and foreign market. The international division also controls the foreign subordinate, market the products and decides how much authority to delegate to foreign management.

6.12 GLOBAL ORGANISATIONAL STRUCTURE

Growing of international business operations and increasing of business competitive environment. Its result is global organizational structure. It further classified into five categories. They are as follows:

- Global products structure
- Global area structure
- Global functional structure
- Global customer structure
- Hybrid/mixed structure

Global Product Structure

Figure 6.18: Global Product Structure

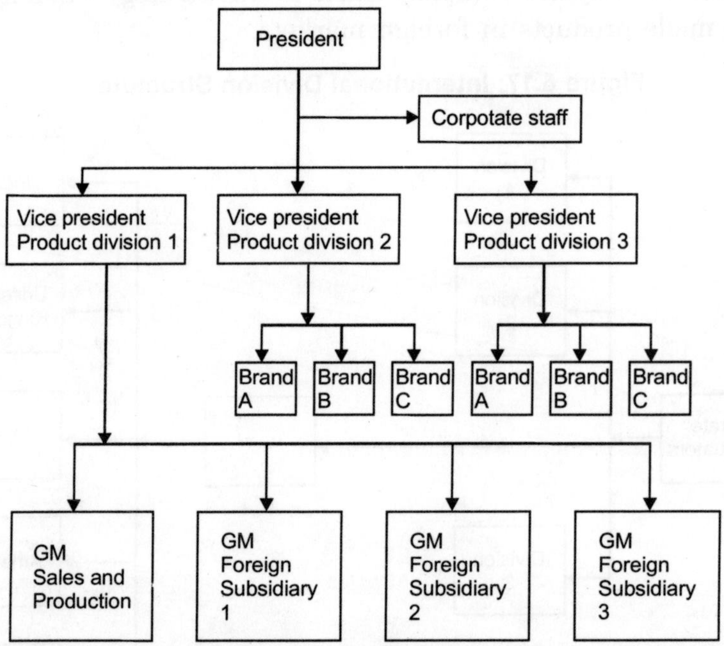

Figure 6.18 highlights the global product structure. The worldwide product structure is based upon major product groups. Global product structure responsibilities are involved for all functions for marketing a specific product group or class throughout the world. It can be delegated to a group within each product division. Therefore, there is a corporate staff at the headquarters to provide wide expertise and provide some degree of assistance to each product division; the product divisions have a good deal of autonomy with their own functional staff.

Company's international activities like product-oriented structure are allocated among the various product divisions. Therefore, the significance of the overseas operations varies substantially. Some of the firm's products maybe more amenable to export or import markets than others or the management of some division may simply have more international experience than do managers in other divisions.

The global product structure has the advantage of focusing upon and optimizing the firm's production strengths. The managers of different product divisions have developed a great deal of knowledge that relates to the following:

- Products
- Competitors
- Production facilities
- Market
- Customer characteristics

They develop familiarity with the environmental constraints of products and how best to position these products in various markets for variety of users. The product managers can also develop a worldwide perspective regarding sales and marketing for their groups.

Advantages of Global Product Structure

Exhibit - 6.12: Advantages of Global Structure·
• This structure suitable for firms with very diverse product lines catering to different end users in different distributional channels. • The greater diversity of the firm's products, end users and distribution channels are the more attractive.

Disadvantages of Global Product Structure

Exhibit - 6.13: Disadvantages of Global Product Structure
• Global structure suffers from manifold weakness. • It absence of central international focus there maybe lack of communication and coordination among different the product division. • Duplication of operational efficiency and often creating confusion among customers. • Corporate management actively encourages international development, not all product divisional managers may be interested in developing their overseas potential.

The Global Area Structure

This form of global organization is based on upon a geographical orientation, either the geographical location of customers or of the company's productive facility. Figure 6.19 indicates the global area structure. The firm is organized on the basis of geographical areas of its international markets. The configuration of the geographical structure depends on the markets in which a multinational corporation operates but typical divisions occur according to major market area like India, North America, Europe, Middle East, and South America. Under the global area structure, all of the firm's activities relating to any products or service that is bought, sold or produced within a region, are under the control of the regional group head who reports directly to the president of the firm.

Advantages of the Global Area Structure

Exhibit 6.14: Advantages of the Global Area Structure
• This form of organization follows the marketing concept in as much as individual areas and markets are given concentrated attention. • Geographical -oriented corporate structure, a multinational firm can place greater emphasis on the specific needs, market characteristics and market requirements of the individual market areas. The firm can pay concentrated attention to satisfy local demands and there by improve its market share.

Figure 6.19: The Global Area Structure

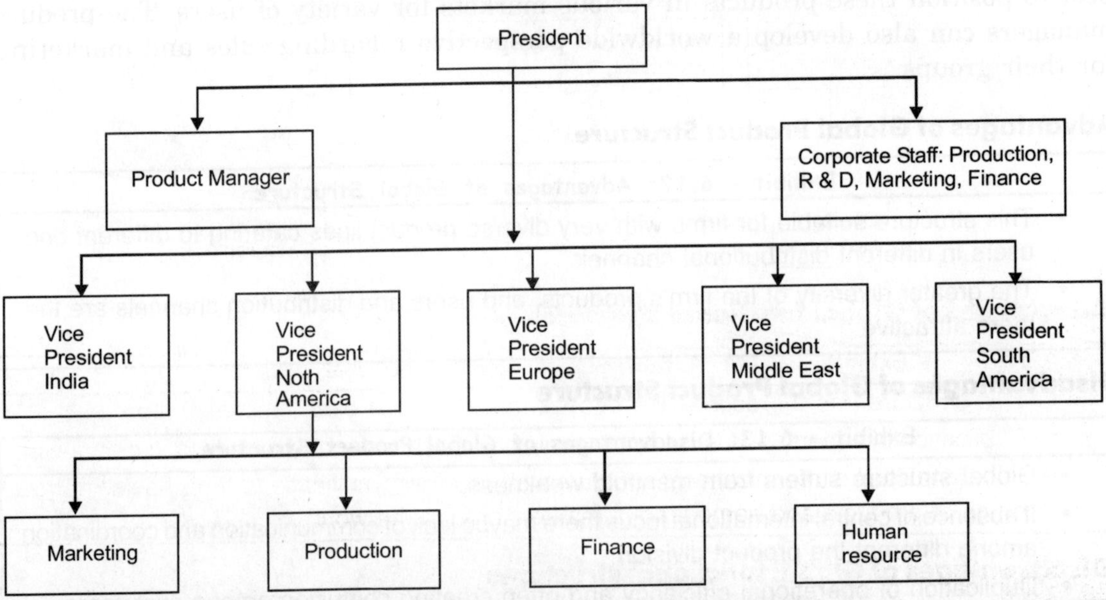

Exhibit - 6.15: Disadvantages of the Global Area Structure
• The major weakness of this form of global organization is that by emphasizing regional operations, it fails to facilitate the development of the coordination of functional or product line activity worldwide. • The firm misuses the opportunity of economies of scale introduction or in raw-materials sourcing. • It failure to learn regional operation of the organization factors like as production, development, and marketing on a global basis. • Another draw back to this type of structure is that it requires the allocation of considerable resources to establish regional headquarter headed by area managers. • There are certain problems involved in this form of structure. It involves duplication of specialists in the different divisions, since such services are not centralized in the geographically structured company. • The geographical orientation tends to give the managers in such group a geographical rather than a company wide perspective.

The Global Functional Structures

Under this structure, global operations of the firm are organized primarily on a functional basis. Figure 6.20 indicates the global functional structure.

Figure 6.20: The Global Functional Structure

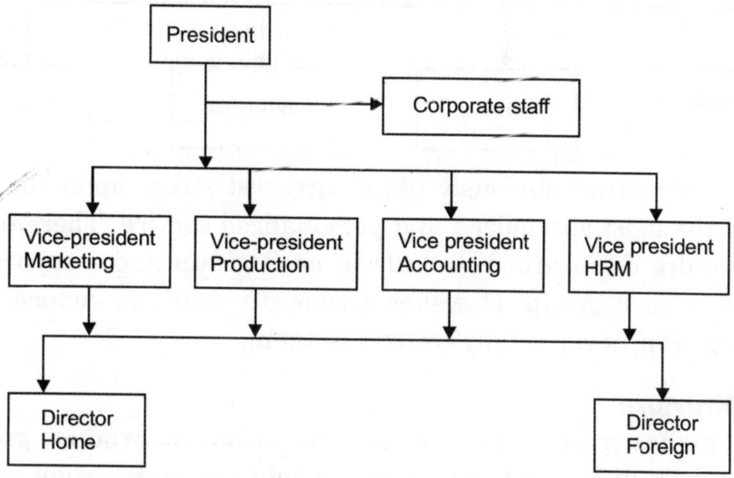

Advantages of Global functional structures

Exhibit - 6.16: Advantages of Global functional structures
• This structure has the economies of scale gained within each functional area. • Duplication of expert service is kept to a minimum with consequent savings in manpower. • Functional form of organizational structure finds favor with multinational firms having narrow range of products and homogenous markets around the world.

Disadvantages of Global functional structures

Exhibit - 6.17: Disadvantages of Global functional structures
• Problem of coordination between functions or divisions of the company. • Lack of flexibility for a firm attempting to market number of products in a number of markets • Managers in this form organization develop too narrow a perspective in emphasizing their own functions rather than the overall welfare of the company.

The Global Customer Structures

Sometimes firms may organize its global operations according to the customer goods. Figure 6.21 indicates the global customer structures. The global customer structures as listed below:

- Individuals
- Business
- Governments
- Corporate staff

Figure 6.21: Global Customer Structure

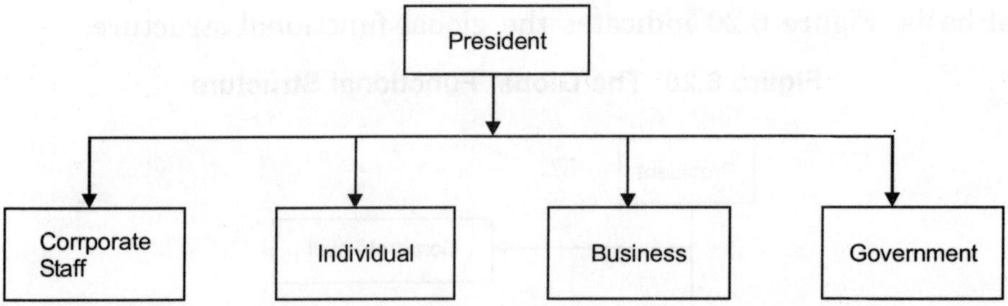

This form of structure obviously places greatest stress upon the customer and can be provided the most specialized and personalized service. Therefore, however, it also tends to require duplication of skills in each group and a separation between such specialists in each group. However, corporate staff can reduce some of these disadvantages but can never totally overcome them.

Global Matrix Structure

This structure makes it very difficult for the different product groups to trade information and knowledge and obtain the benefits of corporation. Sometimes the potential gains from sharing product, marketing and research development knowledge between products groups are very high.

Figure 6.22: Global Matrix Structure

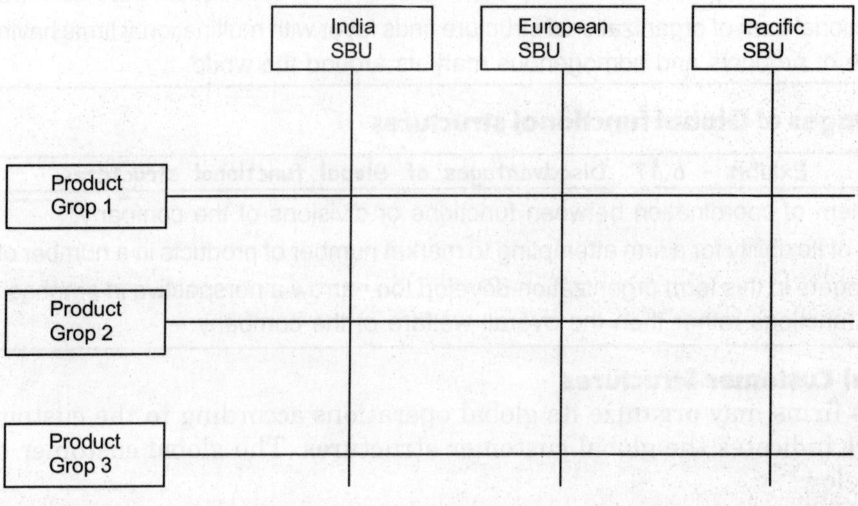

Matrix structures work help to companies to develop strong international organizational culture to facilitate communication and coordination among managers.

Network Structures

- It newer and radical organization design.
- Network structures involves many activities are outsourced to partners.
- It is consist of a series of projects groups or collaborations lined by constantly changing non hierarchical and cobweb like networks.
- When firm environment is unstable that time this net work is useful to an organization.
- Network organizations structures consists of series of independent firms or business linked together by computers in an information system that designs, produces and markets a product or services.

Advantages

- It provides an organization with increased flexibility and adaptability to cope with rapid technological change and shifting patterns of international trade competition thereby enhance their strengths.
- It allows to company to concentrate on its distinctive competencies to provide services to their client.
- Net working firms are supplying the skill and trained employees to their clients and achieve client's mission and vision.
- Networking companies are provided services through contract with client.
- It arrangement of newly evolving that typically are in response to social and technological advances.

Disadvantages

- The availability of numerous potential partners can be a source of trouble to networking companies.
- Some time agreement is failure due to unable provide services and want to separate suppliers or distributors may keep the firm from discovering any synergies by combining activities.
- Few networking companies are offering highly specialize few functions only, so that it is also disadvantages to network companies.
- This type of companies runs the risk of choosing the wrong functions and thus it become non competitive.

6.13 STRATEGIC BUSINESS UNITS AND CORE COMPETENCE

Strategic business units and core competence are outlined as:

- Strategic business units are playing significant role in multinational organization.

- Most of the modern organizations are organized their business into appropriate strategic business units in world.
- It is the relevant, suitable to multiproduct and multibusiness enterprise.
- It provides separate strategic planning treatment to each one of its products and businesses.
- It is a grouping of related business activities in an enterprise that is amenable to composite planning treatment to all business activities in an organization.
- In scientific sense, it is a multibusiness enterprise groups its multitude of businesses into a few distinct business units.
- It is to provide effective strategic planning treatment to each one of its products or business offered by an enterprise.
- Strategic business units firms are handling business planning on a territorial basis since their structure was territorial; this structure is the outcome of a manufacturing or distribution logistics.

Characteristics of Strategic Business Units

There are three most important characteristics of strategic business units are outlined:

- It is a single business or collection of related businesses which offer scope for independent planning and that feasibly stand alone form the rest of the organization.
- It has own set of competitors in market.
- Strategic managers in SBUs who has responsible for strategic planning and profit performance and control of unnecessary activities which are harmful to strategic business units.

Strategic Business Units Planning Difficulties

Strategic business units in territory planning rise to two kinds of difficulties are listed below:

- A number of territorial units handled the same products; the same product was getting varied strategic planning treatments in an enterprise.
- A given territorial planning unit carried different and unrelated products, products and dissimilar characteristics are getting identical strategic planning treatment in organisation.

Concepts of Strategic Business Units

- It is underlying the grouping principle that relating all products and services falling under one strategic business units.
- It helps to a multibusiness corporation in scientifically grouping its businesses into a few distinct business process units.
- It provides the right direction to strategic planning by removing the vague and confusion often experienced in multibusiness grouping enterprise.

Strategic Business Units and Its Benefits

- Strategic business units help to organization for strategic planning that is based on the scientific method of grouping the business activities.
- It brings improvement in territorial grouping of business and these units based on strategic planning.
- It is the grouping of related businesses which can be taken into for strategic planning that distinct from the rest of the businesses. Each unit in strategic groups will be getting equal priority among the products and services in an organization.
- It task is relating to anglicizing and segregating the assortment of business or portfolios and regrouping them into few, well defined, distinct and scientifically demarcated business units . If product or businesses are related from the standpoint of 'function' are assembled together as consider as distinct SBUs.
- In the case, unrelated products, businesses is any group are separated from the main business, if they assigned to any other SBU that applying the criterion of functional relation, these are assigned accordingly. Otherwise, these are made into separate SBUs.
- In removing the vagueness and confusion from the strategic business units and its products and services in an enterprise.
- It also provides right facilities to set correct strategic planning to each unit in strategic business units.
- SBU is separate businesses from the strategic planning point of view. It means each strategic business units mission, objectives, competition, and strategy will be distinct from one to another.
- Each strategic units will have own set of competitors and its own distinct strategy in an enterprise.
- Each SBU CEO is responsible for strategic planning for their Strategic business unit and its performance in terms of profitability, growth, development and also considers controlling factors in an organization.

Strategic Issues in Strategic Business Units

Strategic issues in strategic business units at corporate levels are first whether the corporate body wishes to have a related set of SBUs or not ; and if so, on what basis. Strategic issues are relatedness in turn has direct implications on decisions about diversification relatedness may exist in different ways as listed way:

- Strategic business units may build on similar technologies or all provide similar sorts of products and services offered to customers.
- It can be served to similar or different market even if different technologies or products and different customer.
- Competences and competitive advantages in SBUs are different and similar to strategic business units.

6.14 THE VALUE CHAIN

The primary analytical tool of value chain is identifying the separate activities, functions and business process of the organization that are performed in designing, producing, marketing, delivering and supporting a product and service. The chain of value is creating activities like, it takes to provide a product or service activities that starts with raw materials supply and continues on through conversion of the raw material into finished product or service, after the distribution of goods and service to ultimate user of the product or service.

Basic Concept of Value Chain

A company's or organization value chain identifies the primary activities and supporting activities create the value for end user of the product and service.

The value chain of the organization creates the value for the product and service. It is measured by the amount that buyers are willing to pay for a product or service. Organization is profitable, it creates, exceeds the value for the product or service. The value creation functions are as listed below:

- General administration
- Operations,
- Material management
- Research and development
- Human resource
- Infrastructures
- Procurement
- Marketing

These functions gain to competitive advantage of an organization. Company or organization must perform value creation functions at a lower cost.

The Value Creation Process

The value creation process chain concept popularized by Michael Porter

Figure 6.23: The Value Chain Process

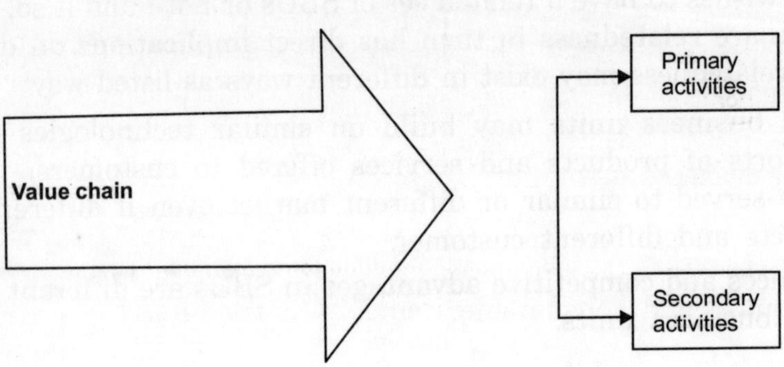

The figure 6.23 indicates the value chain process.

The value creation process chain is classified into two processes. They are as outlined:

- Primary Activities
- Supporting Activities

Figure 6.24: Company Value Chain

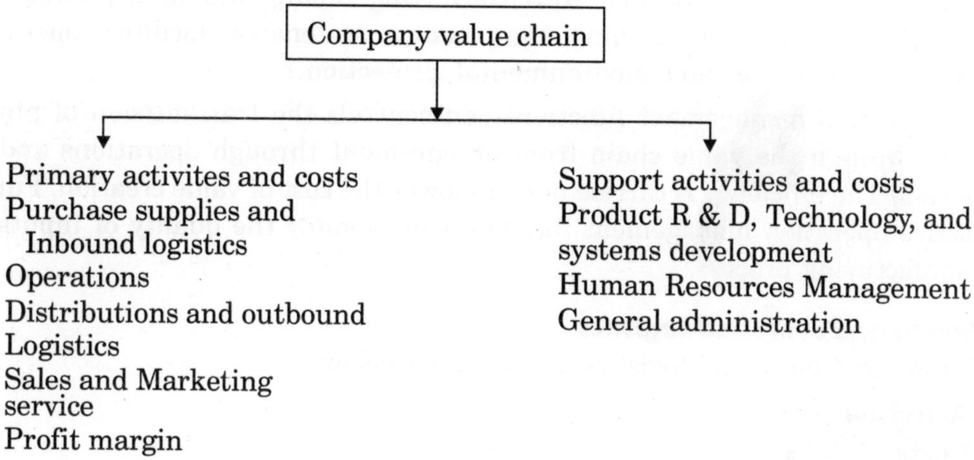

Figure 6.24 indicates company value chain. The company value chain consists of the primary activities and the supporting activities of the company. Company value chain activities are as listed below:

Primary Activities

Primary activities are as outlined:

- Purchased supplies and inbound logistics
- Operations
- Distribution and outbound logistics
- Sales and marketing
- Services

Purchased Supplies and Inbound Logistics

Purchased supplies and inbound logistics activities are as outlined:

- Activities
- Costs
- Assets associated with purchasing fuel
- Raw materials
- Past components
- Merchandise and consumable items from vendors

- Receiving, storing and disseminating inputs from suppliers, inspection
- Inventory management

Operations

Operations activities are as below:

- Activities
- Costs and assets associated with converting inputs into final product form (production, assembly, packing, equipment, maintenance, facilities, operations, quality assurance, and environmental protection.)

The operation management functions can controls the transmission of physical materials through the value chain from procurement through operations and into distribution. The efficiency is carried out can lower the cost of value creation. Further, an effective operation management function can monitor the quality of inputs into the manufacturing process.

Distribution and outbound Logistics

Distribution and outbound logistics are as listed below:

- Activities
- Costs
- Assets dealing with physically distributing the product to buyers (finished goods warehousing, order processing, order picking and packing, shipping, delivery vehicle operations, establishing and maintaining a net work of dealers and distributors).

Sales and Marketing

Sales and marketing activities are as listed below:

- Activities
- Costs
- Assets related to sales force efforts
- Advertising and promotion market research and planning
- Dealer /distribution support

Service

Service activities are as outlined:

- Activities
- Costs
- Assets associated with providing assistance to buyers such as installation, spare parts delivery, maintenance and repair, technical assistance, buyers inquires and complaints.

Supporting Activities

Figure 6.25: Supporting Activities

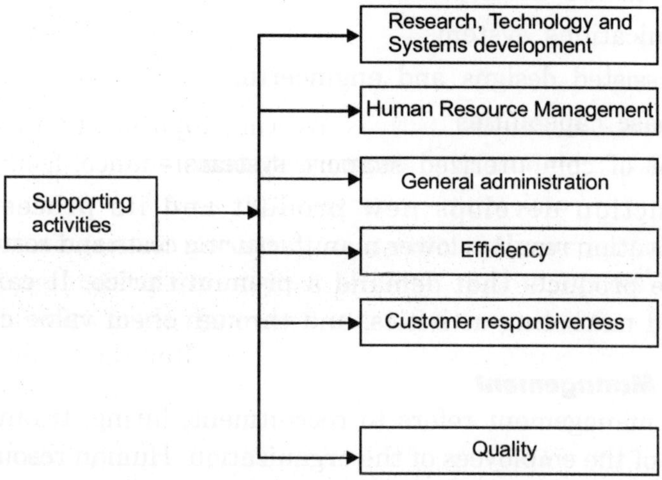

Figure 6.25 highlights the supporting activities of the company or organization. It indicates to cross functional goals and value chain. Supporting activities are known as functional activities of the organization. Supporting activities are as listed below:

- Research, Technology and Systems Development
- Human resource management
- General administration
- Efficiency
- Quality
- Innovation
- Customer responsiveness

Support Activities

Support activities are listed below:

- Research, technology and systems delivered
- Human resource management
- General administration

Research, Technology and Systems Delivered

Research, technology and systems delivered are essential requirement of the company. Research, technology and systems delivered are as outlined.

- Activities
- Costs and assets relating to product R&D,
- Process R&D

- Process design improvements
- Equipment design
- Computer software development
- Telecommunications system
- Computer assisted designs and engineering
- New data base capabilities
- Development of computerized support systems.

The R&D function develops new product and its process technologies. Technological innovation result is lower manufacturing costs and result in the creation of more attractive products that demand a premium price. It can affect primary manufacturing and marketing activities, and through them value creation.

Human Resources Management

Human resources management refers to recruitment, hiring, training, development and compensation of the employees of the organization. Human resource management activities are as follows:

- Activities
- Costs
- Assets associated with the recruitment, hiring training, development, and compensation of all types of personnel.
- Labor relations activities
- Developed of knowledge based skills and core competencies.
- The human resource function ensures that the company or organization has the right mix of skill people to perform its value creation activities effectively.

General Administration

General administration refers to administration of the organization. The general administration activities are as listed below:

- Activities
- Costs
- Assets relating to general management
- Accounting and finance
- Legal and regulatory affairs
- Safety and security
- Management information systems
- Forming strategic alliances and collaborating with strategic partners and other overhead d functions.

Infrastructure is the final supporting activities of the company or organization value chain. It has a somewhat different character from the other support activities. Infrastructure is the company's or organization wide context within which all the other value creation activities take place. It includes the company's or organizational structure, control systems, and culture.

Value creation activities are as Superior efficiency, quality; innovation and customer responsiveness are achieving goals of the company or organization. These activities are requires strategies for formulation, implementation and monitor, guide and controlling of value chain activities of the organization or company.

Steps in Value Chain Analysis

Value chain analysis can be broken down into a three sequential steps are as follows:

- Break down a market/organization into its key activities under each of the major headings in the model.
- Assess the potential for adding value via cost advantage or differentiation, or identify current activities where a business appears to be at a competitive disadvantage.
- Determine strategies built around focusing on activities where competitive advantage can be sustained.

6.15 MATCHING STRUCTURE AND CONTROL AT THE CORPORATE LEVEL

Matching structure and control at the corporate level are as below:

- Related diversification
- Unrelated diversification
- Vertical integration
- Mergers
- Internal new ventures

We shall refer to earlier chapter.

Concept of Corporate Culture

A concept of corporate culture refers to the following factors:

- A company's values
- Beliefs
- Business principles
- Traditions
- Ways of operating
- Internal environment of the company
- Assumptions
- Norms
- Rules and regulations
- Policies and procedure of the corporate

Corporate Culture

Case 6.2. : Satyam' Corporate Culture and Philosophy

Core Purpose:

"To leverage information, knowledge and technology to enhance human endeavor." Satyam develops and deploys intelligent applications in technology for diverse situations meeting varying requirements. Satyam helps businesses and organizations push the limits of excellence, and helps optimize their strengths. Satyam's core values are expressed in the way teams are built and the manner in which they operate and achieve results. These values have been identified based on internal strengths of the organization. They are the guiding parameters for all organization-wide initiatives. **Belief in People:** Satyam believes its true strength lies in the potential of its Associates. Associates work in an atmosphere of trust and confidence. Every individual Associate is a leader. This leadership is expressed in the way tasks are assigned and taken up, the freedom with which work styles are negotiated and high standards of quality set independently by each and every Associate. A high degree of operational freedom helps Associates exercise their creativity and expertise in approaching tasks and achieving Customer Delight. **Entrepreneurship:** At Satyam, it's ideas that drive people. A variety of programs help Associates create tangible value, constantly encouraging Associates to convert ideas into market value, in the true spirit of entrepreneurship. **Customer Orientation:** As a customer-centric enterprise, we are very sharply focused on delivering not only what the customer demands but also providing them with the weapons to compete with. In other words we deliver business competitiveness. All this eventually leads to Customer Intimacy. **Pursuit of Excellence:** Achieving excellence in anything we do is a part of our corporate DNA. It is not just lip service. Rather a process driven strategy that allows us to benchmark everything against the global best and then surpass it, so that we set the benchmark for others to follow. In the process we are always a couple of steps ahead of our nearest competitor. Satyam adheres to stringent Quality processes that meet and exceed international standards that are continuously monitored. **Corporate Social Responsibility:** As a larger expression of its Mission and Core Values, Satyam is actively involved in a variety of public service projects in education, environment and public health. Working through Alambana, an umbrella organization that brings together committed Satyam associates and their spouses, the Company contributes to social causes and organizes initiatives for social change, primarily in the areas of education, environment and healthcare

Questions

1. Explain the culture and philosophy of Satyam.
2. Describe the corporate social responsibility
3. What is customer orientation?

Source: Satyam

Corporate culture is the set of important assumptions. Every company has its own culture it's followed by all the members of the company. Corporate culture is similar to an individual's personality, principles, concept and trade practice ethical opinion actions within the company or organization.

Basic Elements of Corporate Culture

Organization culture is the set of important assumptions are sufficiently central to the life of the organization or company. Basic elements of corporate culture are as listed below:

- Basic Assumptions and Beliefs
- Cultural artifacts
- Values
- Norms

Basic Assumptions and Beliefs

Basic assumptions and beliefs are important to the corporate world. In addition to know, how it actually works, basic assumptions and beliefs derive from personal experience and are reinforced by it in the company. Corporate staff is relying to some degree on the judgment and expertise of others this based on the basic assumptions and beliefs. They trust or can identify with to help them and to decide what to believe or not believe. It underpins the various aspects of organizational activity and represents the core ideology of the business. Some examples of basic assumptions and beliefs underlying organizational culture:

- Market oriented communication system
- Customer orientation
- Employee participation, open communication and security
- Entrepreneurism, self discipline and control

Cultural Artifacts

Cultural artifacts are the visible manifestation of culture. It reflect in the physical and social environment of the organization like its structure systems, subsystems, symbol and plaques etc., an important cultural artifacts are public documents, media reports and stories about the organization, its rituals, ceremonies, rules, procedures and observable behavior of its members. Therefore, these cultural artifacts form a system of support and maintenance for the set of prevailing beliefs.

Values

Values refer to conception of what members of an organization regard as desirable. They are the deep-rooted feelings about ideas and physiology, desires and preferences, emotions and beliefs that influence the members' reaction and responses to any situation. Corporate culture involves shared values, social ideals, or normative beliefs about proper behavior in various situations. Organizational values are reflected in terms of beliefs, emotions, desires, preferences and behaviors of the members of the organization. It stated reasons therefore, in neutral value, orientation emotions are not expressed freely. However, organizations are having affective value generation and encourage free expressions among the people and the groups. In specific value orientation interactions between people, are direct, purposeful, precise, and transparent and authority relationship are confined to work situation. Organizations are espousing diffuse value that encourage maintaining relationships among the organizational people outside the organization also.

Norms

Norms are the paradigms, the informal rules of the game telling employees what they are supposed to be saying, believing, and doing and what is right and what is wrong. For example, as per the IBM norms employees should attentively listen to their demands. Norms are generally passed on to new employees by word of mouth and enforced by the social approval or disapproval of one's behavior in terms of its congruence or in congruence with prevalent norms.

Contents of Corporate Culture

Corporate culture contents that ultimately derive from three major sources are as follows:

- It influence to the business environment in general and the industry in specifically.
- Founders, leaders, directors and corporate employees bring a systematic pattern of assumptions with them when they join the corporate world. These assumptions are dynamic in terms of personal experience, regional, ethnic, religious, occupational and professional communities from which they came.
- Realty and experience of human resource of the corporate world to make and use the solution and coping with the basic problems of corporate culture world.

Strengths of Corporate Culture

The strength of a culture has influenced the intensity by which organization members comply with it as they go about their day-to-day activities. The specific feature of culture that determine the basic strengths of corporate culture are as follows:

- Strong culture companies
- Weak culture companies
- Unhealthy culture
- Adaptive culture
- Thickness culture
- Extent of sharing culture
- Clarity of ordering culture

Strong Culture Companies

A strong culture is a valuable asset when it matches strategy and dreaded liability when it does not. Strong culture companies refer to company conduct its business according to clear and explicit set of principles and values. Strong culture is the strength and one of the features of the culture. Therefore, strong culture companies typically have creeds or values statements and executives regularly stress the importance of using these values and principles as the basis for decisions and actions taken throughout the organization. There are three important factors contribute to the development of strong culture factors. They are as listed below:

- A founder or strong leader who establishes values, principles and practice that are consistent and sensible insight of customer needs, competitive conditions and strategic requirements of the business.
- A sincere, long standing company commitment to operating the business according to these established traditions, thereby creating an internal environment that supports decision-making and strategies based on the cultural norms.
- A generic concern for the well-being of the organization's three biggest constituencies like customers, emplcyees and shareholders. Continuity of leadership, small group rise, stable group membership, geographic concentration and considerable organizational success all contribute to the emergence and sustainability of a strong culture.

Weak Culture Companies

Weak culture companies refers to company culture, there is little cohesion and glue across organization units – top executives don't repeatedly expose any business philosophy or exhibit commitment to particular values or extoll uses of particular operating practices. Because of a dearth of common values and ingrained business approaches. Organization members typically have no deeply felt senses of corporate identity. In weak culture there are no traditions, beliefs, values, common bonds or behavioral norms. It provides little or no strategy implementation assistance that the management can use as levers to mobilize commitment to executing the choosen strategy.

Unhealthy Cultures

Unhealthy culture refers to companies they are adopted number of unhealthy cultural characteristics which can undermine a company's business performance. Unhealthy culture characteristics are as follows:

- A political internal environment allows and influencing managers to operate autonomous 'fieldoms' and resist needed change.
- The second unhealthy cultural trait, one that can plague companies suddenly confronted with fast changing business conditions, is hostility to change and to people who champion new ways of doing things.

- Unhealthy characteristic is promoting managers who are good at staying within their budgets, exerting close supervisory control over their units can handling administrative detail as opposed to managers who understand vision, strategies and culture building and who are good leaders, motivators and decision makers.
- The last trait of unhealthy culture is a version to looking outside the company for superior practices and approaches.

Adaptive culture

Adaptive culture is a valuable competitive asset. Sometimes is a necessity for organization; in fast changing environments for instance, today's dot com companies are classic example of adaptive culture.

In adaptive cultures, members share of confidence that the organization can deal with whatever threats and opportunities come down the pike: they are receptive to risk taking, experimentation, innovation, and changing strategies and proactive whenever necessary to satisfy the legitimate interests of stakeholders, customers employees, shareowners, suppliers and the communities where the company operates.

Thickness culture

Thick cultures have many, thin culture has few cultures with many layers of implement shared beliefs and values generally have a stronger influence behavior.

Extent of Sharing culture

Some of important assumptions are more widely shared than others. Few are completely shared in the sense that every members of the organization has internalized them. Culture with more widely shared beliefs and value has a more pervasive impact because they guide more people.

Clearly or Ordering culture

Some organizational cultures and shared with beliefs and values which are clearly ordered. Cultures whose shared assumptions are clearly ordered have a more pronounced effect on behavior because members of the organization are sure of which values should prevail in cases of conflicting interests.

Deciphering a Culture

Reading a culture is an interpretive subjective activity. One cannot decipher a culture simply by relying on what people say about it other evidence, both historical and current, must be taken into account to infer the culture.

Figure 6.26: Frame Work for Deciphering Culture

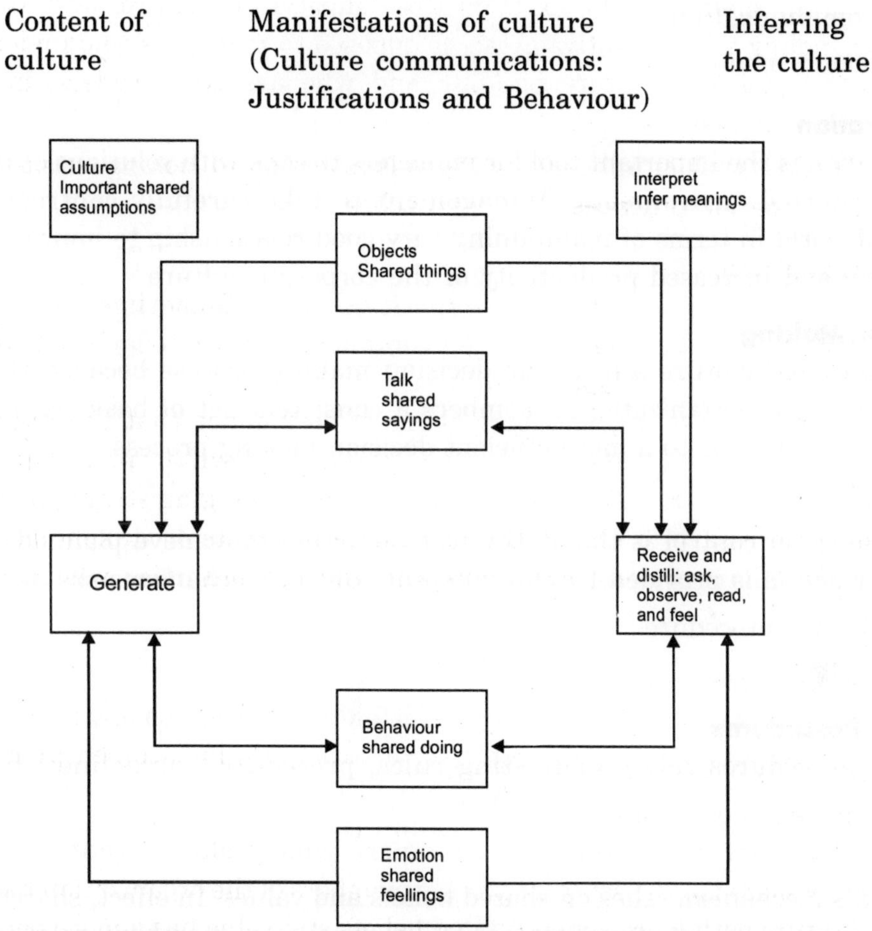

Figure 6.26 indicates the frame work for deciphering culture. It presented systematic method to help decipher or infer an organization culture. Each important shared assumption creating an organizations culture may be inferred from one or more shared things, shared sayings and feelings, the important point is to distill from these various cultural manifestations a much more concise set of important shared beliefs and values.

CULTURE INFLUENCES TO ORGANISATION

We need to examine five basic processes that lie at the heart of any organization - they are as outlined below:

- Cooperation
- Decision making

- Control
- Communication
- Commitment

Cooperation

Cooperation is the important tool for managers to cope with solutions of the problems in the internal environment. Management to take carefully contracted with the external world in terms of maintaining very good relationship to improvement of the efficiency and increased productivity of the corporate culture.

Decision Making

Organizational culture affects the decision making process because shared beliefs and values give organizational members a consistent set of basic assumptions and preferences. It leads to a more efficient decision making process.

Control

The essence of control is the ability to take action to achieve planned results. The basic for action is provided by two different control mechanisms are as follows:

- Formal procedure
- Clans

Formal Procedures

Formal procedures rely on adjusting rules, procedures, guidelines, budgets, and directives.

Clans

The clan's mechanism relies on shared beliefs and values. In effect, shared beliefs and values constitutes on organizational 'compass' that members rely on to choose appropriate course of action clan control derives from culture.

A strong culture facilitates the control process by enhancing clan control. Clan control is highly efficient, but again, efficiency and effectiveness should not be confused.

Communication

Communication should be clear and clarity to understand by one person to another i.e. communication. Corporate culture reduces these dangers of miscommunication into ways are as follows:

- There is no need to communicate in matters for which shared assumptions already exist.
- Shared assumptions provide guidelines and cues to help interpret messages that are received.

Therefore, a strong culture encourages efficient and effective communication. Communication is the lifeblood of organizations.

Commitment

A person feels committed to an organization when he or she identifies with it and experiences some emotional attachment to it. A variety of incentives like as salary, prestige, and personal sense of worth. Strong culture encourages efficient and effective commitments.

Building Ethics into culture

An ethical corporate culture has a positive impact on a company's long-term strategic success; an unethical culture can undermine it. Values and ethical standards must not only be explicitly stated but must also be ingrained into the corporate culture. Implementing the values and code of ethics entails the following actions:

- To incorporation of the statement of values and the code of ethics into employee training and educational programmes.
- To explicitly attention to values and ethics in recruiting and hiring to screen out applicants who don't exhibit compatible character traits.
- To communication of the values and ethics code to all employees and explaining compliance procedures.
- To management involvement and oversight from CEO down to first line supervisors.
- To word of mouth indoctrination
- To strong endorsements by the CEO

Strategic Leadership

Strategic manager has to play significant different leadership role as listed below:

- Visionary
- Chief entrepreneurial and strategist
- Chief administrator and strategy implementer
- Culture builder
- Resource acquirer and allocator
- Capabilities builder
- Process integrator
- Coach crisis solver
- Task master
- Spokesperson
- Negotiator
- Motivator

- Arbitrator
- Consensus builder
- Policy maker
- Policy enforcer
- Mentor
- And head cheer leader

Some times, it is useful to be authoritarian and hardnosed; sometimes it is best to be a perceptive listener and a compromising decision maker, sometimes strong participative, collegial approach works best; and sometimes being a coach and adviser is the proper role.

Strategic leader act as many occasions call for a highly visible role and extensive time commitments. While others entailed a brief ceremonial performance with the details delegated to subordinates.

Strategic Managers have five leadership roles to play in pushing for good strategy execution is as follows:

- He has closely monitoring progress of the top management and studies the overall changes in organization for this purpose he is learning what obstacles lies in the path of good execution.
- To promote a culture and esprit de corps that mobilizes and energizes organizational members to execute strategy in a competent fashion and perform at high level.
- To keep the organization responsive to changing conditions alert for new opportunities, bubbling with innovative ideas, and ahead of rivals in developing competitively valuable competencies and capabilities.
- To exercise ethics leadership and insisting that the company conduct its affair like a model corporate citizen.
- To push corrective actions to improve strategy execution and overall strategic performance.

Leadership Role in Implementation

Leadership role is vital for formulation, implementation and control of strategy in an organization. Leadership roles are provided new opportunities, challenges, development of existing and new strategies in an organization. Strategic leaders are effectively and able to use the strategic management process for design the strategic programme for formulation of strategy and implementation of strategy in an organization.

Figure 6.27: Strategy Design And Implementation: Interrelationships of Elements

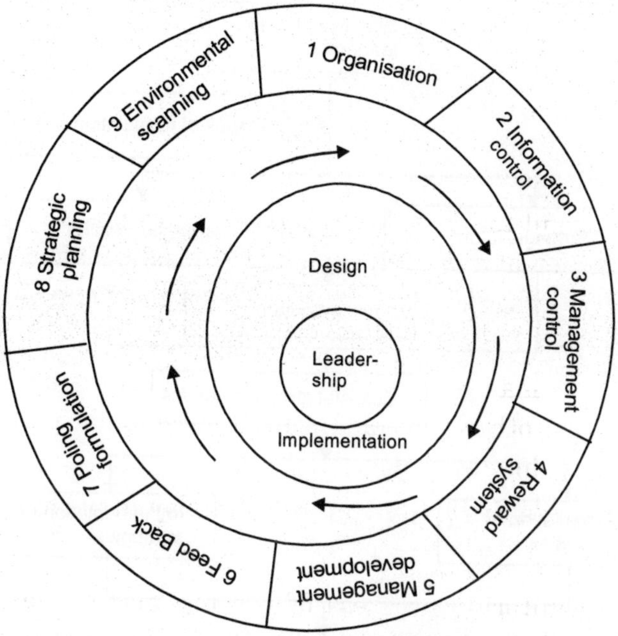

Figure 6.27 highlights the strategy design and implementation with interrelationship of elements like organization, information system, management control, reward system, management development, and environment at scanning, strategic planning, policy formulation and get feedback.

- Strategic leadership focus on the ability to anticipate, envision, maintain flexibility and manpower to be used for design strategic programme.
- Strategic leader should exhibit skills like ability to guide an organization, analysis of competitive scenario in market, how to buildup effective team and strategic groups for accomplishment mission and vision.
- To know how to tackle changes in different environment scenario.
- To cooperate and cooperation among the human resource in an organization.
- To take feedback and forecast to future and its result.
- To posses modern skills like technical, human, conceptual skills and to know when to use these skills for proper control in an organization issues like expansion of business, mergers, acquisition and strategic alliance and diversification of business activities.
- Strategic manager's ability to manage human skills and critical task in an organization.

Figure 6.28: Effective Strategic Leadership

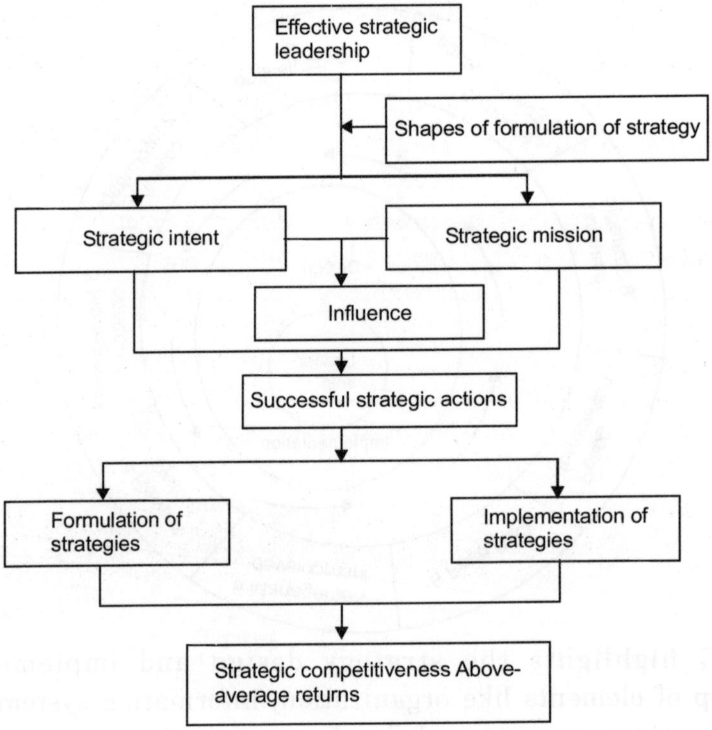

Strategic leaders are those who refers to top management in an organization, it consists of board of directors and chief executive officer in company and also consist of strategic business units division managers in an organization.

Strategic Leaders Responsibilities

Strategic leader's responsibilities are listed below:

- Effective managing the human resource and effectively and efficiently managed firms business operations.
- To sustain high level achievement in terms of profit, growth and expansion of business activities in firms.
- To make bold and planned, organized decisions for accomplishment major tasks in enterprise.
- To make effective feedback via face to face communications in enterprise.
- Decision making responsibilities which cannot be delegated.

Two leadership issues in an organization

- The role of the chief executive officers (CEO)
- The assignment of key managers

6.16 STRATEGIC LEADERS

Dhirubhai H. Ambani

Founder Chairman, Reliance Industries Limited, India

December 28, 1932 - July 6, 2002

Major Group Companies: Reliance Industries Limited, India's largest private sector company.

Description of Group's Business: The Reliance Group founded by Dhirubhai H. Ambani (1932-2002) is India's largest business house with total revenues of over Rs 99,000 crore (US$ 22.6 billion), cash profit of Rs 12,500 crore (US$ 2.8 billion), net profit of Rs 6,200 crore (US$ 1.4 billion) and exports of Rs 15,900 crore (US$ 3.6 billion). The Group's activities span exploration and production (E&P) of oil and gas, refining and marketing, petrochemicals (polyester, polymers, and intermediates), textiles, financial services and insurance, power, telecom and infocom initiatives. The Group exports its products to more than 100 countries the world over. Reliance emerged as India's Most Admired Business House, for the third successive year in a TNS Mode survey for 2003.Reliance Group revenue is equivalent to about 3.5% of India's GDP. The Group contributes nearly 10% of the country's indirect tax revenues and over 6% of India's exports. Reliance is trusted by an investor family of over 3.1 million - India's largest.

Birthplace: Chorwad, village in Saurashtra (Gujarat), India

Father's Name: Hirachand Govardhandas Ambani

Mother's Name: Jamunaben Hirachand Ambani

Career: At the age of 17 went to Aden (now part of Yemen) and worked for A. Besse & Co. Ltd., the sole selling distributor of Shell products.

In the year 1958 returned to Mumbai and started his first company, Reliance Commercial Corporation, a commodity trading and export house.

In the year 1966, as a first step in Reliance's highly successful strategy of backward integration, he started the textile mill in Naroda, Ahmedabad.

In the year 1975, a technical team from the World Bank certified that the Reliance textile plant was "excellent by developed country standards."

In the year 1977, the company went public.

Credited with a number of financial innovations in the Indian capital markets. Today, the Reliance Group has one of the largest family of shareholders in the world. With an investment of over Rs 36,000 crore (US$ 9 billion) in petroleum refining, petrochemicals, power generation, telecommunication services and a port terminal in a three-year time frame, has steered the Reliance Group to its current status as India's leading textiles-petroleum-petrochemicals-power-telecom player.

Achievements: Voted India's 'Top Businessman' in the 'Best of India' poll conducted by Zee News, August 2003.

Petrotech Society conferred posthumously the 'Lifetime Achievement Award' for his outstanding contribution to Downstream Petroleum Industry in India, January 2003. Rated as one of 'India's Most Admired CEOs' for the fourth consecutive year in the *Business Barons* - Taylor Nelson Sofres - Mode Survey, July 2002. Conferred the 'Lifetime Achievement Award' by India HRD Congress, February 2002. Conferred 'The Economic Times Award for Corporate Excellence for Lifetime Achievement', August 2001. Felicitated by the Municipal Corporation of Greater Mumbai with a citation at a civic reception, December 2000. Conferred the 'Man of the Century' award by Chemtech Foundation and Chemical Engineering World in recognition of his outstanding contribution to the growth and development of the chemical industry in India, November 2000. Conferred the 'Indian Entrepreneur of the 20th Century' award by FICCI (Federation of Indian Chambers of Commerce and Industries), for his meticulous scripting of one of the most remarkable stories of business endeavour of the 20th century, March 2000. Thrice (in the years 2000, 1998 and 1996) nominated as one of the 'Power 50 - the most powerful people in Asia' by *Asiaweek* magazine. Voted as the most admired Indian of the millennium in the field of Business & Economics in 'Legends - A Celebration of Excellence' poll audited by Ernst & Young for Zee Network, January 2000. Voted as 'Creator of Wealth' of the Century in *The Times of India* poll, January 2000. Chosen as one of the three 'makers of equity' by India Today in their special millennium issue entitled '100 People Who Shaped India in the 20th Century', January 2000. Chosen by the Indian Merchants' Chamber as "An Outstanding Visionary of the 20th Century" in recognition of his unique achievements and contribution in the development of industry and capital markets in India, December 1999. Voted as 'Indian Businessman of the Century' in *Business Barons* Global Multimedia Poll, December 1999. Amongst 'The Power 50 - India's 50 most powerful decision-makers in Politics, Business & Finance', *Business Barons,* August 1999. Declared 'Most Admired Indian Business Leader' by *The Times of India,* Indiatimes.com poll, July 1999. The only Indian industrialist in 'Business Hall of Fame' in *Asiaweek,* October 1998. Awarded the Dean's Medal by The Wharton School, University of Pennsylvania, for setting an outstanding example of leadership, June 1998. Chosen as 'Star of Asia' by *Business Week,* USA, June 1998. Leading business magazine *Business Barons* placed him in its list of 'India's 25 Most Influential Business and Financial Leaders', June 1998. Awarded the Companion Membership of the Textile Institute, UK, an award which is limited to 50 living members who have "substantially advanced the general interests of the industries based on fibres", 1994. Chosen 'Businessman of the Year 1993', *Business India,* January 1994. **Family:** Wife: Kokilaben.Four children: two sons, Mukesh, who is Chairman & Managing Director and Anil, Vice-Chairman & Managing Director of Reliance Industries and two daughters, Dipti

Salgaocar who lives in Goa and Nina Kothari, who resides in Chennai.Reliance gets an award for Corporate Social Responsibility -naïve population, low cost for technical services, and use of English as the primary business and medical language is ideal for completing trials rapidly and cost efficiently. "RCRS expects to leverage the India advantage with its value proposition to deliver world-class clinical research services to global pharmaceutical, biotechnology, medical device and nutraceutical organisations", said Mr. K.V. Subramaniam, Sr. Executive Vice President, Reliance Industries Limited

Source: Reliance Industries Limited

N. R. Narayana Murthy - Chairman of the Board and Chief Mentor

N. R. Narayana Murthy is the Chairman of the Board and Chief Mentor of Infosys Technologies Limited. He founded Infosys in 1981 along with six other software professionals and served as the CEO for 20 years before handing over the reins of the company to co-founder Nandan M. Nilekani in March 2002. Under his leadership Infosys was listed on NASDAQ in 1999. He served as the Executive Chairman of the Board and Chief Mentor from 2002 to 2006.

Mr. Murthy is the chairman of the governing body of the Indian Institute of Information Technology, Bangalore. He is a member of the Board of Overseers of the University of Pennsylvania's Wharton School, Cornell University Board of Trustees, Singapore Management University Board of Trustees, INSEAD's Board of Directors and the Asian Institute of Management's Board of Governors. He is also a member of the Advisory Boards and Councils of various well-known universities – such as the Stanford Graduate School of Business, the Corporate Governance initiative at the Harvard Business School, Yale University and the University of Tokyo's President's Council.

Mr. Murthy has led key corporate governance initiatives in India. He was the Chairman of the committee on Corporate Governance appointed by the Securities and Exchange Board of India (SEBI) in 2003.

Mr. Murthy serves as an independent director on the board of the DBS Bank, Singapore, the largest government-owned bank in Singapore and on the boards of Unilever, NV and Unilever, plc. He is a member of the Asia Pacific Advisory Board of British Telecommunications plc., and a member of the Board of New Delhi Television Ltd. (NDTV), India. He serves as a member of the Prime Minister's Council on Trade and Industry, and as a member of the Board of Directors of the United Nations Foundation. He is an IT advisor to several Asian countries. He is also a member of the Board of Trustees of TiE Inc. (Global), a worldwide network of entrepreneurs and professionals dedicated to fostering entrepreneurship.

Mr. Murthy is the recipient of numerous awards and honors. The Economist ranked him 8th among the top 15 most admired global leaders (2005). He was ranked 28th among the world's most-respected business leaders by the Financial Times (2005). He topped the Economic Times Corporate Dossier list of India's most powerful CEOs for two consecutive years – 2004 and 2005.

TIME magazine's "Global Tech Influentials" list (August 2004) named Mr. Murthy as one of the ten leaders who are helping shape the future of technology. In 2006, TIME magazine again voted him as one of the Asian heroes who have brought about revolutionary changes in Asia in the last 60 years. He was the first recipient of the Indo-French Forum Medal (2003), awarded by the Indo-French Forum in recognition of his role in promoting Indo-French ties. He was voted the World Entrepreneur of the Year – 2003 by Ernst and Young. He was one of two people named as Asia's Businessmen of the Year for 2003 by Fortune magazine. In 2001, he was named by TIME/CNN as one of the 25 most influential global executives, selected for their lasting influence in creating new industries and reshaping markets. He was awarded the Max Schmidheiny Liberty 2001 prize (Switzerland), in recognition of his promotion of individual responsibility and liberty. In 1999, BusinessWeek named him one of their nine Entrepreneurs of the Year, and he was featured in BusinessWeek's 'The Stars of Asia' for three successive years – 1998, 1999 and 2000.

Mr. Murthy was born on August 20, 1946. He holds a B.E. from the University of Mysore and an M. Tech. from the Indian Institute of Technology, Kanpur. He has been conferred honorary doctorates by well-known universities in India and abroad.

Source:www.infosys.com

Ratan N. Tata

Heading the Tata Group since 1991, Ratan N Tata is the Chairman of Tata Sons, holding company of the Tata Group, and major Group companies including, Tata Motors, Tata Steel, Tata Consultancy Services, Tata Power, Tata Tea, Tata Chemicals, Indian Hotels, Tata Teleservices and Tata AutoComp. He is also Chairman of two of the largest private sector promoted philanthropic trusts in India. During his tenure, the Group has further expanded its global reach, with its revenues growing over sixfold to Rs 97,000 crore ($21.9 billion).

Mr Tata joined the Tata Group in December 1962. After serving in various companies, he was appointed the Director-in-Charge of The National Radio & Electronics Company Limited (Nelco) in 1971. In 1981, he was named Chairman of Tata Industries, the Group's other holding company, where he was responsible for transforming it into the Group's strategy think-tank and a promoter of new ventures in high-technology businesses.

He is associated with various organisations in India and abroad in varying capacities, some of which are:

- Chairman, government of India's Investment Commission
- Member, Prime Minister's Council on Trade and Industry
- Member, National Hydrogen Energy Board
- Member, National Manufacturing Competitiveness Council

- Serving on the International Investment Council set up by the president of the Republic of South Africa
- Serving the International Business Advisory Council of the British government to advise the chancellor of the exchequer
- Member, International Advisory Council of Singapore's Economic Development Board
- Member, Asia-Pacific Advisory Committee to the board of directors of the New York Stock Exchange
- Member, International Advisory Boards of the Mitsubishi Corporation, the American International Group and JP Morgan Chase
- President, Court of the Indian Institute of Science, Bangalore
- Chairman, Council of Management, Tata Institute of Fundamental Research, Mumbai
- Member, Board of trustees of the Rand Corporation, Cornell University and University of Southern California, and the Foundation Board of the Ohio State University
- Chairman, Advisory Board of RAND's Center for Asia Pacific Policy
- Member, Global Business Council on HIV / AIDS and the programme board of the Bill & Melinda Gates Foundation's India AIDS initiative

Mr Tata received a Bachelor of Science degree in architecture from Cornell University in 1962. He worked briefly with Jones and Emmons in Los Angeles, California, before returning to India in late 1962. He completed the Advanced Management Program at Harvard Business School in 1975.

The government of India honoured Mr Tata with one of its highest civilian awards, the Padma Bhushan, on Republic Day, January 26, 2000. He has also been conferred an honorary doctorate in business administration by the Ohio State University, an honorary doctorate in technology by the Asian Institute of Technology, Bangkok, and an honorary doctorate in science by the University of Warwick

Source:www.tata.com

Azim H. Premji

Chairman, Wipro

In 1966, at the age of 21, Premji took on the mantle of leadership of Wipro. He began his stint in Wipro with a simple Vision – to build an organization on a foundation of Values.

Under his leadership, the fledgling $2 million hydrogenated cooking fat company has grown to $3 billion IT, BPO and R&D Services organization, serving customers across the globe. Wipro is the largest third party R&D Services provider in the world. Business Week ranks it among the top 100 Technology companies globally today. Forbes counts Wipro in its list of Fab 50 Firms of Asia. Wipro's growth continues be driven by its core Values.

Over the years, Azim Premji has received many honors and accolades, which he believes are recognitions for each person who has contributed to Wipro. Financial Times included him in the global list of 25 people who are "dramatically reshaping the way people live, work or think" and have done most to bring about significant and lasting social, political or cultural changes (October 2005, November 2004). Time listed him (April 2004) as one amongst 100 most influential people in the world. He was named by Fortune (August 2003) as one of the 25 most powerful business leaders outside the US, Forbes (March 2003) listed him as one of ten people globally, who have the most "power to effect change" and Business Week (October 2003) featured him on their cover with the sobriquet "India's Tech King". He was adjudged as the Business Leader of the Year 2004 by the Economic Times. In 2005 he became the first Indian recipient of the Faraday Medal.

The Indian Institute of Technology, Roorkee and the Manipal Academy of Higher Education have both conferred honorary doctorates on him, while XLRI, Jamshedpur has conferred the Sir Jehangir Ghandy Medal for Industrial and Social Peace, Visvesvaraya Technological University conferred Sir M. Visvesvaraya Memorial Award in Sept 2000 and the Institute of Electronics and Telecommunication Engineers in the year 2000 conferred its highest honor the Honorary fellowship. He is a non-executive Director on the Board of the Reserve Bank of India. He is also a member of the Prime Minister's Committee for Trade and Industry in India. In January 2005, the Government of India conferred upon him the Padma Bhushan, one of the highest civilian awards in the country.

Premji firmly believes that ordinary people are capable of extraordinary things. He believes that the key to this is creating highly charged teams. He takes a personal interest in developing teams and leaders. He invests significant time as a faculty in Wipro's leadership development programs.

Premji has a fanatical belief in delivering Value to the Customer through Innovation and leading-edge quality processes. This belief has driven Wipro's pioneering efforts on Quality, culminating in the system called the "Wipro Way". Wipro was the first Indian Company to embrace Six Sigma, the first Software Services Company in the world to achieve SEI CMM Level 5 and the world's first organization to achieve PCMM Level 5 (People Capability Maturity Model). Wipro is also the pioneer in applying Lean methodologies to Software development and maintenance with more than 300 lean projects. The belief in Innovation has translated into the attempt to institutionalize Innovation at Wipro, and complement the spark of creativity with methodical, deliberate and sustainable processes to drive and facilitate Innovation.

In the year 2001, Premji established the Azim Premji Foundation, a not-for-profit organization with a Vision of significantly contributing to quality primary education for every child, in order to build a just, equitable and humane society. The financial resources to this foundation have been personally contributed by

Premji. The current programs of the Azim Premji Foundation engage 3.2 million children in more than 17,000 schools across India. In October 2006, the Foundation was recognized as the Corporate Citizen of the year by the Economic Times.

Azim Premji is a graduate in Electrical Engineering from Stanford University, USA.

Source:www.wipro.com

Management Profile - B. Ramalinga Raju

Mr. B. Ramalinga Raju

Chairman of Satyam Computer Services Ltd

Chairman - NASSCOM Mr. Ramalinga Raju is the Founder and Chairman of Satyam Computer Services Ltd. (NYSE:SAY). Satyam Computer Services was incorporated in 1987. The Company went public in 1992 and has since grown to become one of India's pre-eminent IT companies with a truly global presence, servicing over 144 Fortune 500 and over 390 multinational corporations.

Raju has been described by various media and other eminent people as a Visionary, a Global Business Leader, Technology and Management Thinker. Raju's vision for the company envisages an organization that is respected for its entrepreneurial spirit, global standards of quality and delivery, and the professionalism and commitment of over 21,000 people working in 45 countries across five continents. Raju has an MBA from Ohio University. He is also an alumnus of the Harvard Business School. Raju has won several awards and global accolades, which include Ernst & Young Entrepreneur of the Year for Services in 1999, Dataquest IT Man of the Year in 2000, and CNBC's Asian Business Leader - Corporate Citizen of the year award in 2002. He is the recipient of the Andhra Pradesh Akademi of Sciences' Professor Y Nayudamma Memorial Gold Medal in 1999 for his outstanding contribution in the field of computer technology. Raju has been playing a key role in shaping policy on information technology in India and abroad. He is presently the Vice-Chairman of the National Association of Software and Service Companies (NASSCOM), Chairman of IT Committee in Federation of Indian Chambers of Commerce and Industry (FICCI), and a member of the International Advisory Panel of Malaysia's Multimedia Super Corridor. He speaks at several forums in India and abroad on behalf of the industry and the country. Raju shares a social vision and has set up several trusts to aid greater social equity and providing opportunities for the under-privileged. He has been instrumental in setting up Byrraju Foundation and Satyam Foundation. Byrraju Foundation aims to aid a process of rural transformation through enhancing the health, education and the living standard of the people. It impacts close to a million people. Satyam Foundation works in the area of urban transformation. Raju is the driving force behind the Emergency Management Research Institute (EMRI). The EMRI is instituted to provide Emergency Response Services addressing about one million calls per day across India, in line with similar services (911) in the USA.

Source: http://www.nasscomfoundation.org

Role of Strategic CEO

The chief executive officer is the catalyst in strategic management. CEO is most closely identified with and ultimately accountable for a strategy's success. In most corporate world, particularly larger ones, CEOs spend into 80 percent of their time developing and guiding strategy.

The nature of the CEO role is both a symbolic and substantive in strategy implementation as follow:

- The CEO is a symbol of the new strategy. CEO actions and the perceived seriousness of his other commitment to a choosen strategy, particularly if the strategy represents a major change, except a significant influence on the intensity of subordinate managers commitment to implementation.
- The organization mission, strategy and key long term objectives are strongly influenced by the personal goals and values of its CEO. To the extent that the CEO invests time and personal values in the choosen strategy. He or she represents an important source for clarification, guidance and adjustment during implementation.
- Major changes in strategy are often quality followed by a change in CEO. Successful strategy implementations directly linked to the unique characteristics, orientations and actions of the CEO

Exhibit-6.18: Key consideration in Managerial Assignments to Implement Strategy

A new strategy subject issue	Advantages	Disadvantages
• Using the existing executives to implement	• Already know key people, Practice and conditions. • Personal qualities better known and understand by associates.	• Less adaptable to major strategic because of knowledge, attitdes values.
	• Have established relationships with peers, subordinate, supplies etc.	• Past commitments may hamper hard decisions required executing a new strategy
	• Symbolizes organizational commitment to individual careers.	• Less ability to become inspired and credibly convey the need for change.
• Bringing outsiders to implement a strategy	• Outsiders may already believe Inland have "lived" the new strategy	• Often costly, both in terms of compensation and learning to work together.

Contd....

	• Outsider is unencumbered by internal commitments to people	• Candidates suitable In all respects (exact experience) may not be available leading compromise choices.
	• Outsiders come to the new assignment with heightened commitment and enthusiasm.	• Uncertainty in selecting the right person. • The "morale" costs when an outsider takes a job. • Several insiders wanted.
	• Bringing an outsider can send powerful signals throughout the organization that change is expected.	• "What to do with poorly free" problem.

Source: Adapted from Boris Yavitz and William H.Newman, Strategy in action (New York: Free Press, 1982) and Paul J. Stonich, Implementing Strategy (Cambridge, Mass: Ballingr, 1982) chap.4.

Four Managerial Assignment Situations

Four managerial assessment situations are

- Selective blend
- Turnover
- Stability
- Reorientations

Figure 6.29: Four Managerial Assignments

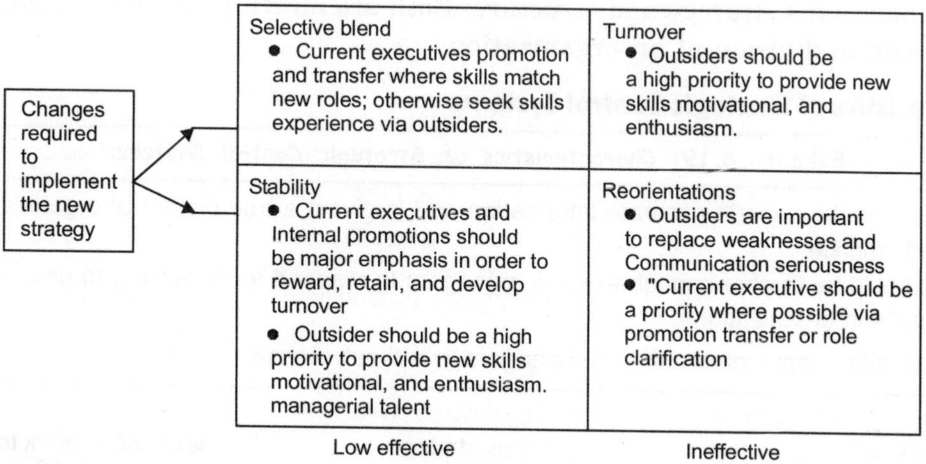

Figure 6.29 indicates the four managerial assignment situations like selective blend, turnover, stability and reorientation.

Strategic Control Systems

We shall examine the main operational control system; monitoring performance and evaluating deviations, strategic control systems allow top managers to monitor and evaluate the performance of divisions, functions, and employees and to take corrective action to improve their performance. Strategic control is the process of establishing the appropriate types of control system at the corporate, business and functional levels in a company which allow the strategic managers for guiding and evaluating the strategy in the organization.

Control strategy can be characterized as a form of 'steering control' ordinarily, a significant time span occurs between initial implementation of a strategy and achievement of its intended results. During that time, numerous projects are undertaken, investments are made, and actions are undertaken to implement the new strategy. In addition, during that time, both the environmental situation and firm's internal situation are developing and evolving. Strategic control is necessary to steer the firm through these events. They must provide the basis for correcting the actions and directions of the firm in implementing its strategy to development and changes in its environment and internal situation take place.

Strategic Control System

Strategic control systems are vital aspect of implementing strategy of an organization. The primary function of strategic control systems is to provide information for management. Information needs to control its strategy and structure. Strategic control systems are the formal target setting, monitoring, and evaluation and feedback systems. It provides information to management about the organization's strategy and structure. Both are meeting strategic performance and mission and vision of an organization.

Characteristics of Strategic Control Systems

Exhibit- 6.19: Characteristics of Strategic Control Systems·
• It should be provide accurate information and is giving a true picture of organizational performance. • It should be flexible enough to allow managers to respond as necessary to unexpected events in organization. • It should supply information to managers in a timely sense.

Steps /Process in Designing an Effective Control System in Organization

Figure 6.30: Steps or Process in Designing in Effective Control System in Organization

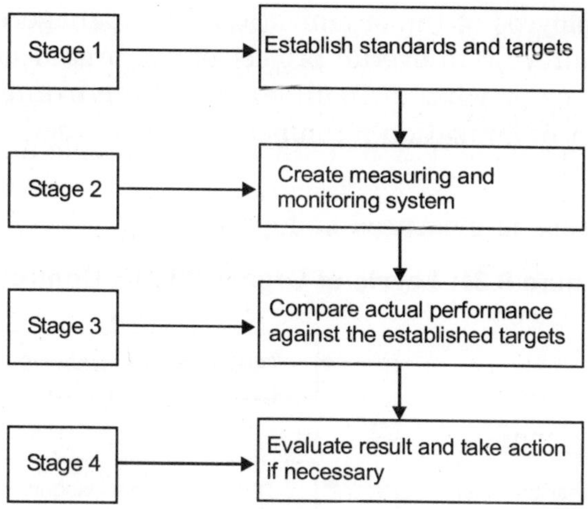

Figure 6.30 highlights the steps or process in designing in effective control system in organization. There are four stages involved for designing an effective control system of an organization. They are as follows:

- Establish standards and targets
- Create measuring and monitoring system
- Compare actual performance against the established targets
- Evaluate result and take action if necessary

Establish Standards and Targets

Establish standard and targets is the first stage in design an effective control system. Company managers select standard targets to evaluate its performance. Standard targets are major objectives and goals of the company. It is accomplished and monitoring by managers of company or organization.

Create Measuring and Monitoring Systems

This is the second stage of the establishing strategic control systems. Company has established procedures for assessing work goals at all levels in the organization. Either work goal achieved or not achieved. Organization task is the difficult task to measure and monitoring task force of an organization.

Compare Actual Performance Against the Established Targets

Strategic management is to select the best decision out of the set of decisions. Therefore, strategist should estimate future targets on the basis past and present performance the organization. Therefore, in this stage, comparison is essentially needed to the past, present and future performance of the organization.

Evaluate result and Take Action if Necessary

Evaluate result and take action if necessary is the last stage of the evaluating, monitoring and guided to the strategy to the CEO, managers and finally response from the low level employees of the organization. Top managers spent huge time for policy making and monitoring to overall project of the organization. Strategy always leads to achievement even with difficult external environment. This goal is to continually enhance an organization's competitive advantage.

Levels of Control

Organization performance is measured at four levels

Figure 6.31: Levels of Organizational Control

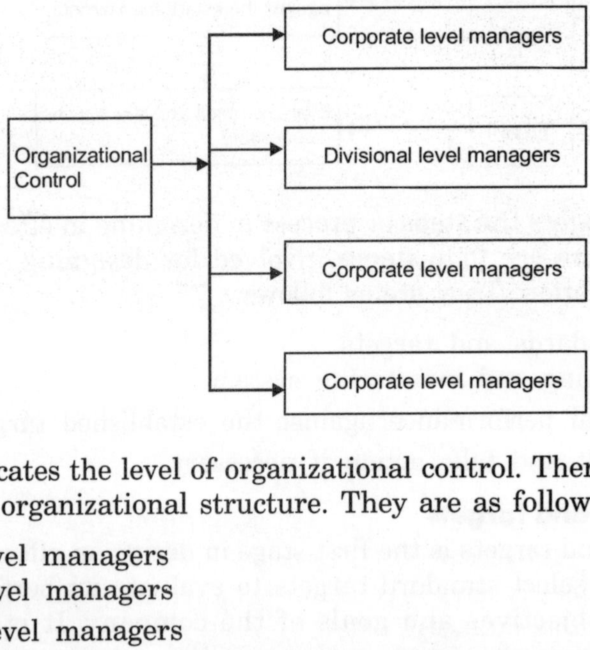

Figure 6.32 indicates the level of organizational control. There are four levels are involved to control organizational structure. They are as follows:

- Corporate level managers
- Divisional level managers
- Functional level managers
- First level managers

Managers at the corporate level are most concerned with overall and abstract measures of organizational performance like profit, return on investment or total labor force turnover. The main aim is to choose performance standards. It measure overall corporate performance. Similarly, managers at the other levels are most concerned with developing a set of standards to evaluate business or functional level performance. These measures should be closely tied with possible task force activities and accomplishment of the corporate objectives.

Types of Strategic Control

There are six types of strategic control. They are as listed below:

- Premise control

- Implementation control
- Strategic surveillance
- Special alert control
- Market control
- Output control

Premise Control

Strategy is based on assumed or predicted conditions. These predictions or assumptions are planning premises. Company's strategy can be designed around these predicted conditions. Premise control can be designed to check systematically and continuously. Whether premises set during the planning and implementation process are still valid or not valid. If a vital premise is no longer valid, therefore, then the strategy may have to be changed and premise can be recognized and revised for the better changes and acceptable.

Premises are primarily concerned with two factors are listed below:

- Environmental factors
- Industry factors

Environmental Factors

A company has little or no controllable over environmental factors. But these factors exercise considerable influence over the success of the strategy. Environmental factors like Inflation, technology, interest rates, regulation, demography and social changes etc. These factors are influenced to strategy formulating, implementation and control and monitoring of premises.

Industry Factors

Industry factors like competitors, suppliers, substitutes and barriers to entry. These are a few examples to affect the performance of industry. Industry factor differ from one industry to another industry. A company should aware of the factors that influence to success for particular industry.

Premises are some major and some minor. Premises are often make about numerous environmental and industry variables, therefore, to attempt to track every premise may be must select premises and variables on the basis likely to change and would have a major impact on the company and its strategy.

The key premises should be identified during the planning process. The premises should be recorded and responsibly for monitoring, then should be assigned to the persons to departments who are qualified sources of information.

Implementation Control

The implementation control phase is an important phase of strategic management. It locates in the series of steps, programmmes, investments and moves undertaken over a period to implement to strategy. In this stage, special programmes are undertaken by company to implement and control for accomplishment of objectives. A company function areas initiate several strategies that are relating to managers convert broad strategic plans into concrete actions and results for specific units and individuals for implementing strategy.

Implementation control can be designed to assess whether the over all strategy should be changed in light of unfolding events and results associated with incremental steps and actions. There are two basic factors involved for implementation control. They are listed below:

- Monitoring strategic thrusts/projects
- Milestone reviews

Monitoring Strategic Thrusts /projects

It involves implementation of strategies in companies that undertaking several new strategic projects or thrusts. These projects or thrusts provide a source of information to manager. Strategic manager can obtain the information from the feedback. It helps to determine either the overall strategy can be progressed as planned or it needs to be adjusted to change.

There are two important approaches are useful in enacting implementation control. It focuses on monitoring strategic projects. They are as listed below:

- The planning process of projects or thrusts.
- Monitoring strategic projects or thrusts.

Milestone Reviews

Managers are attempted to identify critical milestone in organization. It will occur over the time period. Strategy can be implemented in a critical milestone like major resource allocations. In each critical case, it review and full-scale reassessment of the strategy and advisability of continuing or refocusing the direction of the organization or company.

Strategic Surveillance

Strategic surveillance can be designed to monitor a broad range of events inside and outside the company or organization. They are likely to threaten the course of the company's or organization's strategy. It should be encouraged in form of monitoring a source of information.

Special Alert Control

Another type of strategic controls is a special alert control. A special alert control can be needed to thoroughly and often rapidly reconsider the company's or organization basic strategy. It is based on a sudden and unexpected event.

Market Control

It is an important objective of output control. It is helpful to strategist to analysis, monitoring the marketing performance of organization. Market control focus on the performance of one company to compare with another company in terms of stock market price and return on investment. These things help to appraise financial performance of the company or organization.

Output Control

This is the last type of control system designs of the company or organization. Output control concentration on output like divisional goals, functional goals, individual goals which monitoring, evaluating and guided by the strategic managers. Strategic manager aims to establish projects with execution of different types of control systems for measuring and improving efficiency of the organizational strategic objectives.

6.17 OPERATIONAL CONTROL SYSTEMS

Strategic control concerns with "steering" with company's future direction. Strategic control can be useful to top management in monitoring and steering the basic strategic direction of the company. Therefore, operating managers also need appropriate control methods at all levels for strategy formulation and implementation and control operational system of an organization or company. The primary aim of the operating level can be allocated and use of the company's resources.

Operational control systems can guide, monitor and evaluate progress in current objectives of the company. Effective operational control systems must take into four steps. They are as below:

- Set standards of performance
- Measure actual performance
- Identify deviations from standards
- Initiate corrective action or adjustment

Types of Operational Control Systems

There are three types of operational control systems. They are as listed below:

- Budgeting systems
- Scheduling
- Key success factors

Budgeting Systems

Budgeting systems provide to efficient resource allocation among the divisions / functions of the company. A budget involves to simply resource allocation plan, helps managers for coordination operations and facilitates managerial control.

Types of Strategic Budgets

There are three types of Strategic budget are listed below:

- Revenue budgets
- Capital budgets
- Expenditure budgets

Revenue Budgets

Companies are prepared revenue budget to monitor their sources of revenue /income of the organization. The revenue budget has provided important information for the daily management of financial resources and key feedback as to whether for strategy is working. A revenue budget is particularly important as a tool for control of strategy implementation. It has provided an early warning system about the effectiveness of the company's strategy.

Capital Budgets

Capital budgets look for specific expenditures for plant, equipment, machinery, inventories and other capital items are needed during the budget period. Always Organization looks for strong sales. It can only to a strong growth of the organization. Capital is required for diversification/retrenchment of its current operations to generate additional resources. It carefully plans the acquisition and expenditure of funds for effective control. A company additional to prepare another two budgets as mentioned below:

- Cash budget: It forecasts receipt and expenditure of the organization.
- Balance sheet: it forecasts the status of assets, liabilities and net worth at the end of the budget period.

Expenditure Budgets

Expenditure budget aim to record all expenditure belongs to division /function of the organization. Expenditure budgets introduction is necessary to company to control and implementation of strategy in various operating units of the company. It can set standards to assess expenditure of the all divisions /functions of the organization. It can provide an effective communication link between top management and operating managers. It provides another warning system which alerting management to problems in the implementation of the company's strategy.

Scheduling

Scheduling is the key factor in the success of the strategy. It is simply a planning tool for allocating the use of a time-constrained resource or arranging the sequence of interdependent activities. Scheduling offers a mechanism with which to plan for, monitor and control these dependencies.

Key Success Factor

Key factors are very important to implementation of the project. Successful key factors are listed below:

- Improved productivity
- High employee morale
- Improved product /service quality
- Growth in market share
- Completion of new facilities

Monitoring Performance and Evaluating

Organization carefully watches all goals, objectives that discharged by employees of the organization. A successful measure is a monitoring all activities of divisions / functions. It can be the best way reduced the errors and mistakes and brings very good productivity. Then we shall accomplishment of the objectives of the organization. Control can be needed all activities of the company.

6.18 STRATEGIC REWARD SYSTEM

Strategic reward system is also important to implement, control and monitoring the activities of the organization. Top-level executives want strategic reward in terms of

- Praise
- Recognition
- Morale support

While in the case of middle level and low level management employees want strategic reward in terms of;

- Piecework plans
- Commission systems
- Bonus plans
- Profit sharing systems
- Employee stock option systems

These benefits provide to employees to control and monitor the organizational activities.

CHAPTER 7

Reaching the Strategic Edge

7.1 INTRODUCTION

Business organization evolves the different kind of strategies adopted in businesses and in responses to the environment force that are relating to business enterprises. Today business scenario is to be time of diversification, it is strategic buzzword in business world and different organizations are believed in entering into new business irrespective of any relationship with their existing business. Then the basic ideology of business shifted from diversification to core competencies in competitive business world. There are several changes in the basic requirement of strategic ideology.

7.2 BUSINESS PROCESS REENGINEERING

- It refers to dramatic changes in business, take an example; a person waiting in a queue in a post office or bank, a person may feel need for improvement in processes.
- In case of queue the process begins with your stepping into the queue, and ends with receiving the desired items or service and improves to getting service.
- Apart from this, it is applicable to business trends and business people to make dramatic changes only for bring changes for improvement of business activities.
- These steps are process of the activities that finds change to business but not only business and also personal those have providing services that performs to complete the transaction with quality , efficiency and effectively.

Buying a ticket is a simple business process example in business. There are other business processes involved in daily business operations like purchasing raw material ,logistics movements of finished products, developing new products etc., that are much more tricky to deal with enterprise. Business processes are simply a set of output for another person in business enterprise.

Business process requirement is to be in order to have a better appreciation of activities in business. The term 'BPR' really means as it would be pertinent to have preliminary knowledge of businesses processes. What is a business process in firm and how it differs from other processes in firm; it is question that may be improvement for change come to mind. Business process or business activities are not discrete or unrelated piece of work in firm. They are part of recurrent work process in firm with in which they are located, sequenced and organized in firm.

What is the Business Process?

A business process is a set of logically related tasks or activities oriented towards achieving a specified outcome in firm. It is as "a process is a collection of activities which creates an output of value to the customer and often transcends departmental or foundational boundaries.

For example, one common process can be founded almost in every organization, it is like order fulfillment. Order fulfillment process begins with procuring an order and ends with delivery of goods to the ultimate customer. It also includes all other related activities in between order processing to delivery of goods to customers. Apart from this; Other basic processes may include developing a new product or services like launching a new product in the market, procuring goods from suppliers, preparing the organization's budget, processing and paying insurance claims and so on in business.

Business process principally comprises a combination of number of such independent or interdependent processes as listed below:

- Developing new product
- Customer order processing
- Bill payment system

Typically a business process involves a number of steps performed by different people in different departments in firm. The structural elements constitute a process that provide the basis for its analysis , appraisal , and redesign for achieving higher levels of efficiency and effectiveness in firm activities and enhance its economy and speed and quality of output.

A set of interconnected process principally comprises a business system. The performance of business enterprises and its outcome are interrelated operation in business firm, its constituent work processes in firm efficiently and effectively for improvement in process. The redesign processes provides powerful tools for improving the performance in a business enterprise.

Core Business Process

- Some process turns out to be extremely for the success for survival of the enterprise.
- BPR focuses to critical business processes that go on in any company.
- BPR are the core business processes of the company. A core business process creates value by the capabilities, it provides to the competitiveness.
- Core business process is critical in a company evaluation by its customer's real time.
- They are vital for success in the industry sector within which the company is positioned to get success for dramatic changes in improvement.
- They are crucial for generating competitive advantages for a firm in the market place.

While some core business processes are easily identifiable in business enterprise, some core business process may not always be immediately apparent in company. The following instance, serves to show that core processes need to be carefully interns of their bearing on a firm competitiveness.

- In case of insurance industry, the actual works leads to a balance of competitive premiums for customers and profit after claims for the company; it refers to core business process in insurance industry.
- In case of banking industry, the activities that help mobiles deposits and generates funds for advances to customers, it refers to core business process in banking industry.
- In case of electronics and semi conductor industries, new product development, it refers to core process in electronics and semi- conductor industries.
- In the case of fast moving consumer goods industry, marketing and brand management, it refers to core process in fast moving consumer goods,

The core processes of a company may change over a period of time according to the shifting requirements of its competitiveness in business. Since the main objective of reengineering is to be provided competitive advantage to the enterprise, it is extremely important to identify those core processes which need organization business vision , mission and drive form. These processes are to be the best in the world in order to realize that vision in company.

An imperative need to be felt for process change is one of the reasons of company. It is the most requirement of the process to organization and changes are engaged and have been developed by their functional units over a period of time that have to be evolved on basis of series of unplanned decisions. Seldom there has been any serious effort to systematically analyze the processes and measures their effectiveness towards the organizational efficiency to bring dramatic changes for improvement in process quite often the individual departments or units of a company aim at optimizing their own performance disregarding the resultant effect on other areas of operation. This may lead result in a sub optimal performance for the organization as a whole. The overall business processes in an organization that extending over several departments. It may be quite lengthy, time consuming, costly and inefficient. Also the existing business process and work patterns are largely obsolete and irrational in business enterprise activities.

If fragmentation of work processes in business enterprise makes it difficult to improve the quality of work performance and also develops a narrow vision among the employees in company. As a result, the employees tend to focus more on the narrow goals of their own department at the cost of larger goals of the organization as to be considered a whole. This results show in terms of piecemeal accomplishment of tasks without looking at the overall goal. As the small fragments of work move from one person to other person and from one unit to another unit When it delays keep on mounting and it enhances the chances of errors, in this a situation, the emerging critical issues often remain unattended to firm as they do not fit into the narrow definitions of tasks or roles of an individual department in business enterprise.

Firms must remember that, most of the existing work processes are developed before advantage of computers and it revolution which brings major changes due to technological development. Even after the massive penetration of information technology, results suitable to most organizations have usually applied the technology only in a limited way to automate their existing business process. . This has resulted only in some sort of mechanizations of the existing work methods without bringing in any appreciable change in the process and output in firm's activities.

For instance, established Japanese industries as well as new entrepreneurial ventures in Japan prove that it is possible to achieve a much higher level of process performance by redesigning the process. In this example, it has been possible to double the speed in the form of normal production, utilized assets several times more productively and respond to customer's needs and expectations much more rapidly. This can be achieved by effecting a total change in the processes instead of a piecemeal change in industry. It is, therefore, imperative to many organizations that results to the decline. Changing the process or redesigning the process may be the only viable alternative for turnaround of business operation in company. It must break force from their primitive and archaic work processes that drag them down in business activities in company operation. Business issues are emerging from the foregoing discussions in industry that is to be needed for change to firms.

Different forms of business process reengineering

Totally business process reengineering is to be considering in the following ways:

- The operational excellence of a company, it is a major basis for its competitiveness in its operation.
- The business strategy of a company, it can be oriented towards leveraging its operational excellence into the market place.

- A customer focused organization that needs to be realigned in terms of a process orientation.
- Process need to manage in company, not functions in company.
- It is totally considering new ways of redesigning processes in company for this purpose each and every concept assumption, purpose, and principle, needs to abandoned temporarily.
- Continuous improvement is an efficient approach in a company when a company is far behind the industry standards, and needs rapid quantum leaps in performance.
- Company's changes should be dramatic improvements in performance; it is the prerequisite for overcoming competition.
- It is how to compete and it is more important than it is deciding about where to compete.

Definition of BPR

The term Business Process Reengineering (BPR) refers to the analysis and redesign of workflows and processes both within and between the organizations.

- There is orientation of the redesign effort is radical, i.e., it is a total reconstruction and rethinking of a business process in it's entirely applicable in business, this unconstrained by its existing structure and pattern.
- Its objectives are to be obtained quantum gains in the performance of the process in terms of time, cost, output, quality, and responsiveness to customers in business operations.
- The redesign effort aims at simplifying and reformation a process by eliminating all unnecessary and non value adding steps, activities and transactions; these are reducing significantly the number of stages or transfer points of work, and speeding up the work flow through the use of IT systems.

BPR is an important approach to unusual improvement in terms of operating effectiveness through the redesigning of critical business processes and supporting business systems in company's operating environment.

- It is revolutionary redesign of key business processes that involves examination of the relevant and irrelevant process itself.
- It looks at the minute details of the process, like why the work is done, who does it, where is it done and when it is done. BPR is mainly focus on the process of producing the output. This output is the result in organization process.
- The term Business Process Reengineering means starting all over, starting from scratch in firm, i.e., 'reengineering'.
- In other words, it means that pulling aside much of the age old practices and

procedures of doing a thing developed over hundred years of management experience.

- It implies forgetting how work has been done so far, and deciding how it can best be done now.

Reengineering begins with a fundamental rethinking. In doing reengineering people must ask some most basic questions about their organizations and about their operations. They try to find out answers to such questions like

- "Why do we do what we do?
- And why do we do it the way we do?

An attempt to find out answers to above mentioned questions may startlingly reveal certain rules, assumptions and operational processes as obsolete and redundant. Apart from Reengineering does not begin with anything give or with any assumptions.

- Reengineering thinking process begins with a totally free state of mind without having any preconceived notion in the minds of consultants who are responsible person for reengineering in firm.
- Reengineering first time determines what a company must do. And then it decides on how to do it.
- Reengineering ignores, what is the existing process and how concentrates on what is should be reengineering. If something is not required to be done in firm, in this case, it is outright discarded.

Key Elements in Reengineering Process

- Reengineering involves radical redesigning of process is another key element in firm.
- Radical redesigning refers to going to the root of the problem areas and not attempting to make any superficial changes in firm.
- Radical redesign involves completely discarding all existing structures and procedures and evolving completely new ways of doing the work.
- Reengineering involves about business reinvention in terms of not business improvement, business enhancement or business modification.
- The next key concept is lies behind reengineering; it aims at achieving dramatic improvement in performance in firm.
- In the case, an organization feels to need for marginal improvement in any area of operation at any point of time in firm, and it can be achieved by conventional methods of adjustments in operating process for this process reengineering is not the answer in firm's.
- Reengineering is representation for replacement of the old process by altogether new one to achieve dramatic improvement in the performance.

Focus in Reengineering Process

Reengineering process follows from the above and also from the characteristics of the definition of reengineering process. Its main focus is on the process in firms in the following ways:

- It is an attempting to improve performance in firms.
- Most people in business focus their attention in terms of particular tasks, jobs, people, structure, but fail to pay adequate attention on the process.
- Business process as already mentioned earlier, it has defined as the series of activities that utilizes various inputs to create output that are valued by customers in business.
- All the processes in an enterprise enjoy not equal importance in creating customers value.
- A firm must try to identify the generic business processes that significantly add to the value for its output to the customer and should try to focus on reengineering processes in this way to improve its competitive position.

Generic Business Processes of a Firm Needing Redesign

'The generic business processes of a firm needing redesign can be classified into three broad categories as outlined:

- Processes pertaining to development and delivery of products and services. These may be included research, design, engineering manufacturing and logistics, besides purchasing or procurement and materials management.
- Process involving interfaces with customers. These usually include marketing, advertising, order fulfillment, and service.
- Process principally consists of management activities: these include strategy formulation, planning and budgeting, performance measurement and reporting, human resource management, and building infrastructure.

In this above mentioned context of these generic business processes, BPR may be viewed as a means of solving business problem through an imaginative leveraging of IT capabilities in enterprise.

Rationale of BPR

- Improving business process in enterprise is a paramount for business operation that is to be competitive scenario in today's market place.
- Over the last decade, several factors have accelerated which are needed to improve business processes in enterprise.
- The most obvious and important is technology in business processing. It influence to new technologies like information technology are rapidly bringing the new capabilities to businesses. Thereby raising the strategically options and the need to improve business processes dramatically for improvements in enterprise,

- Indian companies have been forced to improve their business processes due to increased competition in Indian economy.
- More companies have entered the market place, it results that competition has become harder and harder. Meanwhile, more companies have entered the market place; major changes are required to just stay even in market. It has become a matter of survival for most companies who are in competitive race in market.
- Majority cases, Customers are also demanding better products and services in market. If they do not get what they want from one supplier, that time, they have ready to choose many suppliers in market. In this circumstance, they are ready to try to be opted new brands in markets.

Implementing BPR in Organization

- It is a crude sense; companies began business process for improvement with a continuous dramatic improvement model in enterprise.
- It is attempts to understand model and measure the current processes, in this way to make performance improvements.
- Therefore, some companies are making reengineering efforts under the assumption of the current processes that are some time may be wrong and irrelevant to enterprise. Under this perspective designers of businesses process disassociate themselves from existing processes.
- This can be helped in looking at the problem; it should be in a clean mind and free of any biases in enterprises.

BPR Approach

- The BPR approach begins with defining the scope and objectives in the reengineering project.
- Persons have entrusted with the tasks of BPR that have to undertake research in the light of scope, employees, competitors and new technology etc.
- Strategist and researcher can be helped to design to BPR that is in a position to create a vision for the future and design new business processes in this way achieve to BPR objectives. They are creating a plan of action that based on the gap between the current and proposed processes in enterprise. Technologies and structures.

Steps in BPR

Steps in BPR are listed below:

Determining Objectives and Framework

- It refers to the objectives which are the desired end results of the redesign process that management and organization attempts to realize in enterprise.

- It will provide the required focus, direction, and motivation for the research design, process in enterprise.
- It helps in building a comprehensive foundation for the reengineering process in enterprise.

Identify Customers and Determine Their Needs

- In this step, the designers have to understand customers, their profile, and their step in acquiring, using and disposing a product in enterprise.
- It main purpose is to redesign business process that clearly provides added value to the customer in enterprise in this way identify and determine customer needs..

Study the Existing Process

- In this step refers to the existing processes that will provide an important base for the red signers in enterprise.
- The purpose of study of existing process is to be gained and understand of what and why of the targeted process.
- In this step, some companies go through the reengineering process with clean perspective without laying emphasis on the past performance.

Formulate a Redesign Process

- In this step refers to information gained through the earlier steps, these steps are translated into an ideal redesign process.
- Formulation of redesign plan is the real crux of the reengineering efforts of enterprise.
- In this step, focus towards the customers redesigned concepts. These concepts are identified and formulated in enterprise.
- In this step involves alternative processes that can be used to operationally for new process.

Implement the Redesign

- In this step refers to enterprise is easier to formulate new process than to implement them.
- For Implementation of the redesigned process, it require the application of other knowledge that gained from the previous steps, it is key steps to achieve dramatic improvements in enterprise.
- It is the joint responsibility of the designers and management to involve for operationally the new process in enterprise.

The Role of Information Technology in BPR

- Rapid development of information technology has emerged during the past few years had a very large impact in the transformation of business process.

- Various studies have shown and conclusively established the role relating with information technology in the transformation of business processes.
- Information technology is going to play a magnificent role in changing the business processes during the year to year, it has been established beyond doubt in enterprise.
- A reengineering business process, characterized by IT in terms of assist speed, accuracy, adaptability, and integration of data and service points. It is focused to meet the customer needs, requirements and expectations are quickly and adequately thereby enhancing client satisfaction level in business.
- Globalization and competition call for better management in terms of faster response to change and adherence to globally accepted standards of quality of services.
- Information technology IT is a critical factor in the success of bringing this change.

Impact IT systems are identified as listed below:

- Compression of time
- Overcoming restrictions of geography
- Restructuring relationships

IT – initiatives have provided business values in three distinct areas are listed below:

- Efficiency – by way of increased productivity
- Effectiveness – by way of better management
- Innovation – by way of improved products and services.

Above mentioned these changes bring about a radical change in the form of quality of products and services, thereby improving the competitiveness and customer satisfaction.

Central Thrust of BPR

- It refers to improvement on quality and cost follows after improvement.
- BPR is continuous improvement process in enterprise.
- BPR is a multidimensional approach in improving the business performance in enterprise.
- Its thrust area may be identified as "the reduction of the total cycle time of a business process in enterprise".
- BPR aims at reducing the cycle time by keeping the process in this way eliminating the unwanted and redundant steps and by simplifying the systems and procedures and also by elimination the transit and waiting times as far as possible.
- Even after redesigning of a process, BPR always maintains a continuous effort for more and more improvements in business operation.

Figure 7.1: Customer Time Cycle

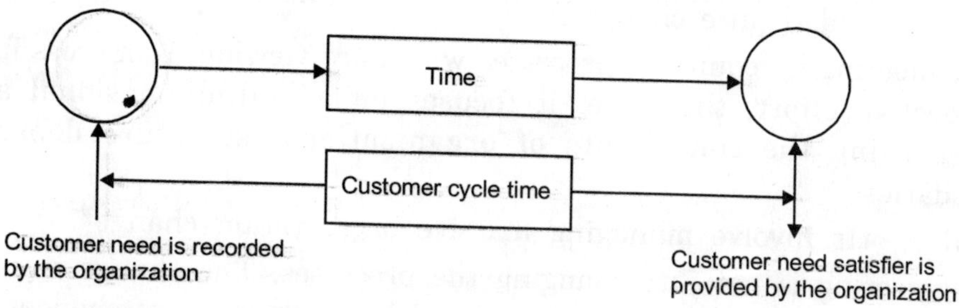

- Reengineering does not mean any partial modification or marginal improvement in the existing work processes in enterprise.
- It is a revolutionary approch towards radical and total redesigning of the business processes in enterprise.
- Meanwhile reengineering may lead to restructuring to organization.

The basic principles will be differentiating to reengineering from any other drive in the form of improving organizational efficiency; it may be briefly summarized as listed below:

- At the core of reengineering process lies the concept of discontinuous thinking in enterprise.
- Reengineering does not have any scope for any partial modification or marginal improvement in the existing business process in enterprise.
- It aims at achieving excellence and a breakthrough in performance by redesigning the process entirely and radically in enterprise.
- It requires challenging task that are the necessity of existing rules and procedures and discarding the same to evolve altogether new processes.
- BPR approach recognizes the most of the existing rules and procedures of work methods which are based on certain assumptions about technology, people and the goals of the organization.
- Assumptions may not be valid any more time in enterprise , apart from the many of these systems and procedures have failed to reap the benefit of massive development of information technology during the past few years in industry.
- BPR recognizes "the vast and expanding potential of IT for the most rational, simple, and efficient redesign of work structure".
- BPR aims at utilizing information technology for evolving a new process, instead of automating the existing processes in enterprise.
- Reengineering starts with the processes it does not end in organization.
- The fundamental and radical changes that take place in organization meanwhile reengineering is the process.

- It own implication on other parts of the organization which almost on every part of it and require changes.
- Reengineering is requires a processes which are viewing from cross functional perspective effort, therefore, it focuses on a multidimensional approach disregarding the constraints of organizational structure departmental boundaries.
- "BPR efforts involve managing massive organization change".
- Reengineering is not just changing the processes. The change is considered process; it is almost always accompanied by a whole lot of changes in other areas too.
- It also considers work changes from and existing task oriented to new processes oriented. In this process, people have the choice of making their own decisions instead of being directed towards changes in organization.
- "Functional departments find their existence as redundant. Practically every aspect of the organization changes beyond recognition". It is also involved changes in functional department process.
- Faster and efficient redesigned business process in organization has to provide to a firm with many more opportunities for trying, testing, modifying and learning in organization,

In above mentioned view, results to the massive organizational changes that involved in reengineering, it is imperative process in organization. A reengineering drive is supported by the vision and commitment in the organizational top leadership to see and to make changes through successful completion of its process.

Problems of BPR

Problems of BPR as listed below:

- Reengineering is a major and radical improvement in business process so it is one of the problems for firms to find new changes in business process.
- Only a limited number of companies are able to implement business process and have enough courage for implementation BPR, it posed serious challenges problems to organization.
- It disturbs established hierarchies and functional structures in this way to creates serious repercussions and involves resistance among the workforce in organization.
- Reengineering takes time for dramatic changes in organization.
- BPR is the expenditure task to organization.
- It is very to make dramatic changes at least in the short run in organization.
- It may not to be reluctant many companies that are to go through the exercise in business activities.

- Some times, there can be loss in revenue during the transition period of enterprise.
- Setting of targets is tricky and difficult in organization, if the targets are not properly set or the whole transformation not properly carried out in organization, reengineering efforts may turn out as a failure.

7.3 BENCHMARKING

We shall explain benchmarking with an example: Two men were passing through a jungle. They saw a tiger at a distance. One of them immediately started running away. Not use the other claimed 'we cannot outrun him. We are sure to be killed. The first person replied 'I need to outrun you and not him.

- This example clearly applicable to business world and its competition scenario; similarly, in cut throat competition, it is important for organization to gain edge over their competitors for this purpose benchmarking helps organization to get ahead of competition in market via its products and services.
- The organization possesses it involves a large amount of information that helps them in taking strategic and other important decisions.
- Companies ready to translate this mentioned information to knowledge and use it their planning and decision making for win in the goals and objectives in enterprise...

Dictionaries defines the term 'benchmark' as a standard or a point of reference against which things may be compared and by which something can be measured and judged. In this definition clearly indicates the following issues in benchmarking:

- In this sense, it may be compared to the concept of control as the similarities do exist at a naïve level in organization.
- The concept of benchmarking is much broader than mere controlling as there are major strategic dimensions involved in business process in organization.
- The term benchmarking has presumably been adapted from physical sciences wherein it refers to surveyor's mark, it made on a stationary object at preciously determined position and elevation and used as reference point to measure altitude in enterprise.

Historical Background of Benchmarking

- The scientific studies conducted by Frederick Taylor in the latter part of the nineteenth century.
- It is represented an early use of benchmarking concept, however, the term benchmarking has got popularity much later in the seventh decade of twentieth century.

- Initially, the concept evolved in companies operating in an industrial environment. Over a period of time it covered other spheres of business activity in business world.
- In recent years, different commercial and non commercial organizations are discovering the value of benchmarking and are applying it to improve their processes and systems in business environment.

What Is Bench Marking?

- In simple words, the term benchmarking is an approach of setting goals and measuring productivity that based on best out of need to have information against which industry practices.
- It can be developed performance which can be measured out of need to have information... For example, a customer support engineer of a television manufacturer attends a call within forty eight hours. If the industry norm is that all calls are attended with in twenty five hours, then twenty four hours can be benchmark.
- Benchmarking helps to be improving performance in industry for this purpose it involves learning from best practices and the processes by which they are achieved in organization.
- It involves regularly comparing different aspects of performance with the best practices in organization.
- It can be involved for identifying gaps and finding out novel methods, it does not only reduce the gaps but to improve the situations, therefore, the gaps are positive for the organization.

Benchmarking is not panacea for all problems in enterprise business process. Rather, it studies the circumstances and processes which help to organization in terms of superior performance. In this process, Better processes are not merely copied. Efforts are made to learn, improve and evolve them to suit the organizational circumstances in industrial environment. Further, benchmarking exercises are also repeated periodically, therefore, the organization does not lag behind in the dynamic environment in business.

- Benchmarking is a process of continuous improvement in search for competitive advantage.
- It measures a company's products, services and practices against those of its competitors or other acknowledge leaders in their field.
- For example, Xerox pioneered benchmarking process in late 70's by benchmarking its manufacturing costs against those of domestic and Japanese competitors and got dramatic improvement in the manufacturing cost. Subsequently ALCOA, Eastman Kodak, IBM adopted benchmarking.
- Firms can be use benchmarking to achieve improvement in diverse range of management function like:

- Maintenance operations
- Assessment of total manufacturing costs
- Product development
- Product distribution
- Customer services
- Plant utilization levels
- Human resource management

The Benchmarking Process

Benchmarking processes lack standardization. Apart from this, few common elements are as identified below:

1. ***Identifying The Need For Benchmarking and Planning***
   - This step will define objectives the benchmarking exercise.
   - It will also involve the type of benchmarking.
   - It will find organizational identity realistic opportunities for improvements.
2. ***Clearly Understanding Existing Business Process***
   - This step will involve coming information and data on performance.
   - This will include mapping processes.
   - In this step, information and data is collected by different methods for example, interviews, visits, and filling of questionnaires.
3. ***Identify Best Practice***
   - In this step, identify best practice for design the selected frame work.
   - To find best processes that is identified. These may be within the same organization or external to them.
4. ***Compare Own Processes and Performance with that of others***
   - In this step, it comparing gaps in performance between the organization and better performers is identified.
   - It further involves gaps in organization. In performance is analyzed to seek explanations. Such comparisons have to be meaningful and credible. Feasibility of making the improvements in the light of the conditions that apply within the organization is also examined.
5. ***Prepare a report and implement the steps necessary to close the performance gap***
   - A report on the benchmarking initiatives containing recommendations is prepared. Such a report includes the action plans for implementation.

6. ***Evaluation***

- business organization evaluate the results of the benchmarking process in terms of improvements vis a vis objectives and other criteria set for the purpose.
- It also periodically evaluates and reset the benchmarks in the light of changes in the conditions that impact the performance.

7.4 TOTAL QUALITY MANAGEMENT

- The total quality management (TQM) focuses on improving the quality of a company's products and services and stress that all company operations should be oriented toward this goal.
- "Total Quality Management is a people - focused management system that aims at continual increase in customer satisfaction at continually lower real cost".
- TQM is a total system approach and integral part of high level strategy: it works in across all departments and its functions, involving with all employees including top to bottom, it extends backward and forward and to consist the supply chain and the customer chain.
- It stresses learning and adaptation to continue to change for modification and dramatic changes for improvements for organizational success.

The TQM Concept

The quality management (TQM) concepts were first developed by a number of American consultants, including Wetware Deming, Joseph Juran, and A.V.Feigenbaum. The TQM Philosophy greatly emerged under the Deming's guidance and supervision, and considered the Father of TQM. Deming's quality management philosophies were first developed in the prior to World War II. The total quality concept is based on the following steps i.e., "chain reaction" they are as below:

- Improved quality results to decrease costs because of less rework fewer mistakes, fewer delays, and better use of time and materials. As a result productivity improves.
- Better quality output capture to higher market share and allows the company or organization to raise prices. This increases the company's profitability and allows it to stay in business.
- Quality output capture the market for this purpose the company creates more jobs.
- It involves the problem solving, and defining and satisfying customer expectations.

Implementing TQM

TQM requires close cooperation among all functions in the pursuit of the common goal of improving quality of output. Implementing total quality management function as listed below:

- **Build organizational commitment to quality:** It refers to training of employees to build organizational commitment to improve the quality of the output this is the major performance of the company.
- **Focus on customer:** TQM focus on customers as the starting point it raised the whole quality philosophy for customers to identify major role in market role. It needs to identify what the customers want from the good or service the company provides.
- **Find ways to measure quality:** TQM program is to create some metric that can be used to measures quality. It is simple to measure quality in manufacturing companies, quality measured by defects per million parts. It is more difficult to measure quality in service companies. Top management should take primary responsibility for formulation different metrics to measure quality.
- **Set goals and create incentives:** Once a quality metric has been devised, the next step is to set a challenging quality goal and to create incentives for reaching that goal.
- **Solicit input from employees:** Employees can be an important source of information regarding the source of poor quality. Some framework must be established in the organization for soliciting employee suggestions for improvement of the quality. Self-managing teams are involved in discussing quality improvement tasks.
- **Identify defects and trace them to source:** TQM main function is to identify defects during the work process and trace them to their source. Manufacturing and materials management typically have primary responsibility to find out what caused them and make corrections. So that, if any uncover defects, the use statistical procedures to pinpoint variations in the quality of goods or service. One variation identified, and traces to their source and eliminated and easily traces defective parts in manufacturing process.
- **Supplier relations:** A company must work closely with its suppliers if it is going to introduce different inventory system to manage materials flows from them. Organization plan to implement good relations with suppliers even maintain good interaction with suppliers. Organization or company is not depending single suppliers due to lack of supply of inventory which are required for manufacturing of outputs. TQM required two steps are necessary for implementation of quality in company or organization. They are as below:
    - The supply has to be rationalized to manageable; therefore, the number of suppliers is reduced to manageable proportions.
    - There is a need to commit to building cooperative long-term relationships with the suppliers that remain strong focus on supplier relationships.

- **Design for ease of manufacture:** Designing products with more parts should make assembling complex and result in larger defects. Designing products with fewer parts should make assembly easier and result in fewer defects. Both R&D and manufacturing functions need to be involved in designing products that is easy to manufacture of outputs.
- **Break down barriers between functions:** Implementing TQM requires organization, it wide commitment and substantial cooperation among functions of the organization. R&D has to cooperate with manufacturing to design products that are easy to manufacture of outputs. Marketing has to cooperate with manufacturing and R&D. Organization has identified customer problems in quality output and act to solve marketing problems. Human resource management has to cooperate with all of other functions of the company or organization in order to devise suitable quality training for employees of the organization.

Principles Guiding TQM

Implementing TQM requires company/organization wide support. Several principles are guided to how to successful of TQM. Various principles are guided the TQM philosophies are as outlined:

A Sustained Management Commitment to Quality

- An organization's personality and culture will ultimately reflect its management's value credentials in TQM.
- If organization / company planning to implement TQM, commitment is starting from the top management and ready drive implementation of TQM concept into business process.
- Any manger or senior can be claimed the responsibility to commit to work and implement to quality and how they act in entire organization.
- Management is willing to let a defective product. And make sales in order to make about quality. It won't make a difference to the people making the product.
- In the case, management is willing to take a sales hit, if quality levels are not up to requirements in this circumstances the rest of the organization will understand the commitment to quality is real.

Focusing on the Customer

According to Lee Lacocca had made three rules which are listed below:

- Satisfy customer
- Satisfy customer
- Satisfy customer

These rules sum up the TQM perspective in organization.

Preventing Rather Than Detecting Defects

- TQM is a quality management in preventing rather than detecting defects.
- It seeks to prevent poor quality in products and services.
- It simply to detect and sort out defects in organization.
- An ounce of prevention is worth a pound of cure, this wisdom says it all from a TQM perspective.

Universal Quality Responsibility

- It is responsibility for the quality, it is not restricted to an organization's quality assurance department, and it is other basic TQM percepts in organization.
- It is responsibility to guide, monitor the quality, it is the basic philosophy of the organization and share by every one in organization.
- Every one in organization takes responsibility to improve quality, quality assurance in all departments in organization.
- Few companies are implemented quality completely in their business operation.

Quality Management

- "If you don't know where you're going, you'll probably end up somewhere". It is one of the standard quotations in TQM.
- The measurement of quality for this purpose TQM asks some of questions as where we are, and where are we going basic?
- The basic tool of TQM is quality which can be measurable commodity in organization in this way to improve quality, and its level in organization.
- TQM is an extremely important concept to organization to bring cent percent quality in all functional activities in organization.

Continuous Improvement and Learning

- It refers to continuous improvement in all areas of an organization.
- It closely ties up with the quality measurement and universal quality responsible concepts in organization.
- Quality measurement is needed in this way to achieve continuous improvements and leering in organization.
- It is part of management and applicable to all systems and process in organization.
- Well defined and well executed quality approach to bring continuous improvement and learning in this way achieving the highest levels of performance in organization.

Continuous improvement refers to both incremental and breakthrough improvement. Types of improvement as listed below:

- Enhancing value to customer through new and improved quality products and services which offered by company.
- Developing new business opportunities
- Reducing errors, defects and waste
- Improving productivity and effectiveness in the use of all resources.

Learning refers to adaptation to change, leading to new goals or approaches adapted by organization.

- Learning and improvement is the basic tool for organization to operate in business process.
- Learning and improvement are the regular part of daily work, and seek to eliminate problems at their source in organization.
- It can be driven by opportunities to do better as well as by problems that are needed to take correct action in organization.

Root Cause Corrective Action

- It refers to how to solve the problems and how to occur problems in organization.
- It seeks to prevent this by identifying the root causes of problems and to take corrective action at the time of implementing corrective actions and it address problems are started at the root cause level.

Employee Involvement and Empowerment

- Employee involvement and empowerment is another fundamental concept in TQM.
- Employee involvement refers to every employee is involved in running the business and plays an active role in helping the organization meet its goals and objectives.
- Employee empowerment refers employees and management recognize that many obstacles to achieving organizational goals, it can be overcome by employees who are provided with the necessary tools and authority to do so in organization.

The synergy Teams

- Employee involvement and empowerment taking advantage of synergy of teams which are implemented quality effectively.
- These teams effectively address the problems and challenges of continuous improvement.
- Dr. Kaoru Ishikawa first time formalized the team's synergy concept as part of the TQM philosophy by developing quality circle in Japan.

Thinking Statistically

- It is another basic TQM philosophy.
- Quality efforts often requires reducing process or product design variation for this purpose statistical methods are ideally suited to support this objective.

Inventory Reduction

- It refers to reducing the inventories in organization due to lack of natural resource.
- This concept introduced by the Japanese pioneered the concept of reducing inventories.
- It introduces to just inventory management and reduce inventory in organization.
- This concept specifically focused on material shortage this time an interesting side effect immediately emerged. It result is inventories grew smaller and quality improved.

Value Improvement

- It is very important and valuable tool to organization.
- It is closed link between continuous improvement and value improvement.
- This link is efficient and apparent and considered as the definition of quality that is ability to meet or exceed customer requirements and expectations.
- Essence of value improvement is ability to meet or exceed customer expectations while removing unnecessary cost in organization. It means simply cutting costs.
- It meets the customer requirement and satisfies the customer needs.

Supplier Teaming

- It is another way to improve quality.
- It is developed long term relationships with a few highly quality suppliers, rather than simply selecting those suppliers with the lowest initial cost.

Training

- It is the basic tool in TQM process.
- It involves training employees and enhancing skills and knowledge with quality.

In totally, TQM is not an overnight cure for organizations quality problems in organization. TQM process execution is not program. A TQM implementation effort has beginning although it implemented in a properly manner, it does not have an ending in organization. The continuous improvement process is continued indefinite in organization which successfully implemented in TQM. Patience is the basic tool for continuous improvement of quality in life cycle journey.

TQM and Traditional Management Practice

Generally, TQM is quite different from traditional practice. It requires changes in terms of organizational operational process, beliefs and attitudes and behaviors. Traditional management refers to the way in which things are usually done in most organizations in the absence of a TQM focus. Recently many of traditional oriented organization have been adopting TQM policy, procedures and principles in enterprise process. TQM is totally differs from common management practice in many respects. Some of Key Differences are outlined:

Strategic Planning and Management

- Strategic planning and management are indistinguishable in TQM.
- Quality goals and objectives are the cornerstone of the businesses plan.
- Measures in terms of customer satisfaction, defect rates, and process cycle time receive as much attention in the strategic plan as financial and marketing objectives.

Changing Relationships with Customers and Suppliers

- In TQM, the quality is defined as products and services which are beyond present needs and expectations of customers.
- Innovation is the discovering of new things, it required to meet and exceed the customer's requirement.
- In the case of the Traditional management can place customers outside of the enterprise and within the domain of marketing and sales in this way to meet customer requirement.
- TQM can be seen every one who is inside of the organization and also seen by the customers or suppliers who are belong to either internal or external.
- Marketing tools and concepts are used to assess internal customers via communication to internal supplier capabilities.

Organizational Structure

- As TQM concepts, the enterprise system of interdependent processes, linked latterly over time through a network of collaborating in terms of internal and external suppliers and customers.
- Each process is connected with the enterprise's mission and vision and purpose which meet via a hierarchy of micro and macro processes.
- In every process in enterprise contains sub process and higher process. This structure of process is valuable and repeated throughout the hierarchy.

Organizational Change

- It refers to TQM in enterprise which interacts and to be considered changing constantly in business process.
- It is management job, so it can be provided that leadership for continuous improvement and innovation in processes and systems, products and services.
- External change is inevitable in spite of a favorable future can be shaped.

Teamwork

- Quality work refers to team efforts and achievement.
- Team structure like quality circles, steering committees, and self directed work teams.
- Each departments work together toward system optimization through cross functional teamwork.

Motivation and Job Design

- It refers to managers who are provided leadership rather than overt intervention in the processes of their subordinates, if who are viewed as process managers rather than functional specialists.
- People and employees are motivated to make meaningful contributions to what they believe is an important and noble cause, it enhance value to the enterprise and society.
- Motivation and job design system that enables people to feel like winners in organization.

7.5 SIX SIGMA AND MANAGEMENT

- Six sigma is invented by Motorola Company and often related it. In eighth decade of 20th Century , Motorola invented this concept and applicable to their own business process in this way brought significantly changed in terms of quality from one where quality levels where measures in percentages (parts of hundred) to parts per million or even parts per billion.
- It clearly pointed out that modern technology is so complex and it is not acceptable old ideas relating with the quality levels in organization.
- Motorola successfully changed the focus of quality worldwide. And followed by many giants like Xerox, Boeing, GE, Kodak and in India Tata's, Wipro and Bharti's and others effectively reaping the benefits from Six sigma.
- Modern technology and new tools are used by organization in this way to enhance their quality of their products and services which are seemingly of very good quality.

- Generally quality refers to the degree of excellence and standard process used in organization.
- Always better quality correlated with the superior process and products which offered by the company.
- Good quality products meet the requirement of customer and satisfy the customer in terms of reeds and requirements.
- Some times good quality is not associated with good products.
- Another dimension of the quality, it should be restricted to satisfying the existing desires of the customers.
- It should not put boundary on quality by limiting it to the current information and perspective of customers in this way to meet customers present expectations and try to improve them in organization i.e., it should be futuristic.

What is Six Sigma?

- Primarily Six sigma refers to the maintenance of the desired quality in processes and end products.
- It means that taking systematic and integrated efforts toward improving quality and reducing cost in organization.
- Six sigma is highly discipline process which helps in developing and delivering near perfect products and services which are offered by the company.
- It efforts to meet and improve organizational goals in terms of quality, cost, scheduling, manpower, new products and so on.
- It works continuously towards revising the current standards and establishing higher ones in organization.
- It has based in the concept of probability and normal distribution in statistics in real process in organization.
- It strives that 99.99966% of products and services are defects free which are offered by the six sigma adopted company.
- It puts the customer first preference than uses facts and data to drive better solutions.

Focus Areas in Six Sigma

Six sigma targets to three focus areas are outlined:

- Improving customer satisfaction
- Reducing cycle time
- Reducing the defects

Improvements in these focus areas usually represent dramatic cost savings to businesses, as well as opportunities can be retained by customers in this way capture new markets, and buildup a valuable reputation relating for top performing products and services in organization.

- Focus areas in Six sigma involves measuring and analyzing an organization's business processes.
- Six sigma is not merely a quality initiative; it is a business initiative in organization.
- Achieving goals and objects, mission, and vision of Six Sigma requires reengineering process and dramatic improvements with changes.
- It involves and brings changes in every area of operation in organization.
- In statistical terms six sigma defined as organization process or products or services will perform almost no defects.
- Six sigma is total management that committed and philosophy in terms of excellence, customer focus, process improvement and make appropriate rule for measurement of goals, objectives, mission and vision of organization.
- Six sigma is to be making it all areas in organization able to meet the changing needs and requirements of the customer, markets, and technologies with reaping benefits for employees, customers, and share holders.

Exhibit 7.1: GE's Key Concepts of Six Sigma

GE 's Key Concepts of Six Sigma	
At its core, Six Sigma revolves around few key concepts	
Critical to Quality	Attributes most important to the customer
Defect	Falling to deliver what the customer wants
Process Capability	What you process can you deliver
Variation	What the customer sees and feels
Stable operations	Ensuring consistent, predictable processes to improve what the customer sees and feels
Design for six sigma	Designing to meet customer needs and processes capability

Source: http://www.ge.com/sixsigma/sixsigstrategy.html

Six Sigma Méthodologies

Six sigma methodologies are important to implement in organization. There are two methodologies used for implementation in organization for existing and new processes. There are methodologies are listed below:

Figure 7.2: Six Sigma Méthodologies

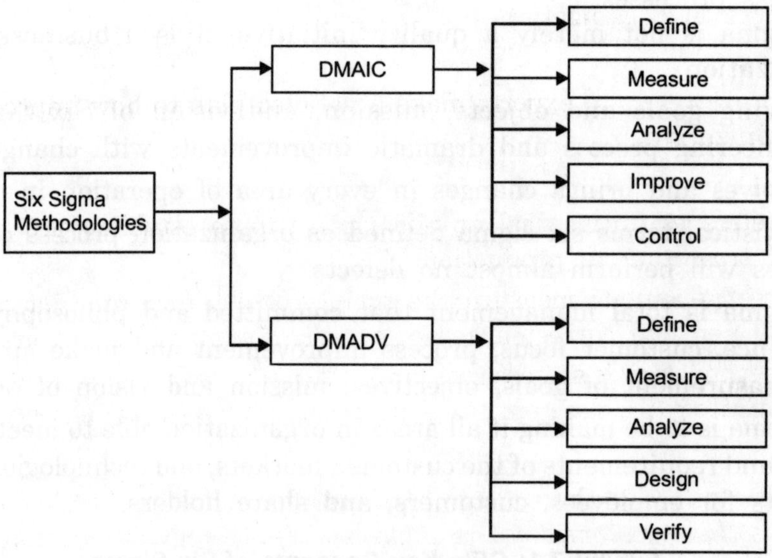

Figure 7.2 indicate the Six sigma methodologies which are used by organization as outlined below:

1. DMAIC
2. DMADV

DMAIC methodology is an acronym for five different steps used in six sigma is directed towards improvement of existing product, process or services in organization. The five steps are listed below:

I. Define

- Define refers to the six sigma experts define the process for improvement goals that are consistent to organization strategy and customer demands.
- It involves to discuss about different issues which concerns of senior managers and so as define what needs to be done in organization.

II. Measure

- It refers to the existing processes that are managed to facilities for future comparison.
- Six sigma experts collect process data for mapping and measuring relevant process in organization.

III. Analyze

- It refers to verify the cause and effect relationship between the factors in the processes.
- Experts need to identify the relationship between the factors and the relevant process.

- It involves comprehensive analyses to identify hidden or not so obvious factors in organization.

IV. Improve

- Improve refers to experts make a detailed plan to how improve process in organization.

V. Control

- It refers to initial trial or pilots are run to establish process capability and transition to production.
- Once continuous measure the process which ensures that variances are identified and corrected before experts finds results in terms of defects.

DMADV methodology is an acronym for 5 steps followed in implementing six sigma. DMADV is a strategy for designing new products, processes and services.

VI. Define

- Define refers to the six sigma experts define the process for improvement goals that are consistent to organization strategy and customer demands.
- It involves to discuss about different issues which concerns of senior managers and so as define what needs to be done in organization.

VII. Measure

- It refers to identify the factors that are critical to quality.
- It measures factors like product capabilities and production process capabilities
- It also assess risk involves in project.

VIII. Analyze

- It refers to develop and design alternatives.
- It creates high level design and evaluates to select best design from available alternatives.

IX. Design

- It refers to develop details design and optimize it.
- It verifies designs may require using techniques like simulations.

X. Verify

- It refers to verify designs through simulations or pilot runs.
- And verified and implemented processes are handed over to the process owners.

What's New About Six Sigma

Total Quality Management is popular in the 1980's. it focused on improvement program, but it affected slowly and ultimate died a slow and silent death in many companies.

Key Characteristics of Six Sigma

There are three key characteristics separates six sigma from other quality programs of the past:

I. Six sigma is customer focused

- It is one of the major characteristics in six sigma. It is almost an obsession to keep external customer needs in terms of plain sight, driving the improvement efforts.

II. Six sigma projects produce major returns on investment

- Those companies implemented Six Sigma projects which retain and save huge income to organization

III. Six sigma changes how management operates

- It involves of improvement of project.
- Senior managers and leaders throughout the business are learning the six sigma tools and concepts like new approaches to thinking, planning, and executing to achieve results.
- It is putting practices into practices the notions of working smarter but not harder.

7.6 IMPORTANCE OF SIX SIGMA IN ORGANIZATION

- It has produced some impressive numbers with help of the team members in organization and reaching them six sigma standards.
- It clearly indicates to systems which are to provide to customers what they want when they want it.
- It provides to training to employees how to tackle work challenges with using strategic tools like basic and sophisticated.
- TQM executed company wants to avoid any defects and the resulting costs in terms of money and customer satisfaction. If business organization violates that time generating defects, complaints, and costs.
- The greater number of defects in the company, it can be less greater numbers of customers from the business operation.
- The major goals of the six sigma is to help to organization and its employees and processes aim to be deliver defect free products and services to ultimate customers in business.
- It aims to produce zero defect free results to company even in the best run processes or best built product.

- Six sigma sets a performance target where defects in many process and products are almost non existent.
- It provides a goal which applies to both product and services and process activities combined under sets which are attainable in this way to achieve goals by putting efforts for long range and business objectives.

Six Sigma Act as a System of Management

A major and significant difference between the TQM and Six sigma management and it seemingly similar programs of past year Management plays a key role in regularly monitoring program results and achievement of defined goals and objectives. Jack Welch is the responsible person introduction at GE. He told senior executives that 40 % of their annual bonus would be based on their involvement and success in implementing Six Sigma.

In GE, it focused to executive attention on turbo charging with Six Sigma in their individual divisions. Six sigma training results in GE was given a huge boost, and participated thousands of teams were trained in large sessions. All the same time, executives throughout GE participated in days and sometimes weeks of Six Sigma training in GE.

- In Management system involves accountability for results and ongoing reviews to ensure results in organization. In Six sigma, both accountability and regular reviews can be used by managers and six sigma guides to executives how to lead their business process without defects in products and services in organization
- In Six Sigma system involves to find ideas, solutions for problems, process discoveries, and improvement that arises in six sigma implementing projects in the organization.
- Six Sigma companies are putting more efforts with proper responsibility into the hands of the people who work directly with the customers.
- Six Sigma systems is the combination of the strong leadership along with grassroots energy and their involvement in organization. In additionally, six sigma benefits are not just financial, it widespread core benefits to all levels of six sigma implemented companies. These companies can be finding better understanding of customers, clearer processes, meaningful measures, and powerful improvement tools make their work more rewarding.

Six Themes of Six Sigma

The critical elements of six sigma can be put into six themes

Figure 7.3: Six Themes of Six Sigma

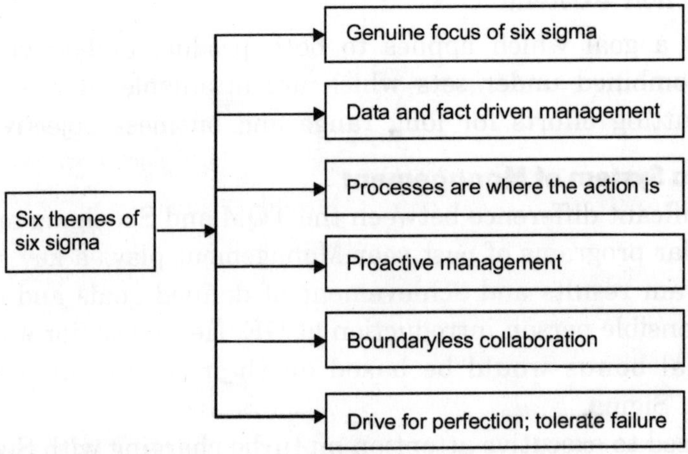

Theme One - Genuine Focus on the Customer

- It refers to six sigma executed companies have often been appalled to find how little they really understand about their customers.
- In six sigma, customers focus becomes the top priority in business process.
- Six sigma impact to customer and their satisfaction and value in business.

Theme Two - Data and Fact Driven Management

- It refers to six sigma, it takes the concept of management by fact to a new, more powerful level and attention towards the recent years to improve information system in business.
- Six sigma begins by clarifying what measures are key to be gauging business performance and then gathers data and analyses key variables in business.
- In six sigma, the problems are effectively defined, analyzed, and resolved permanently at a more down to earth level.
- It helps to managers that have answers two essential questions ɔ support data driven decisions and solutions.
    - What data/information do I really need?
    - How do we use that data/information to maximum benefit?

Theme Three – Process are where the Action is

- It refers to focus on designed products and services, these measuring performances, improving efficiency and customer satisfaction or even running the business in organization.
- The process in six sigma is key vehicle for success.

- It can put efforts to date has been convincing leaders and managers. Particularly in service based functions industries that mastering processes is a way to build competitive advantage in delivering value to customers.

Theme four – Proactive Management

- It refers to the acting in advance of events rather than reacting to them.
- Proactive management refers to making habits out of what are, too often, neglected business practice in terms of defining ambitious goals, and reviewing them frequently, setting clear priorities, focusing on problem prevention rather than fire fighting, and questioning why we do things instead of blindly defending them in organization.
- Six sigma encompasses tools and practices used for replace reactive habits in terms of dynamic, responsive and involve proactive style of management.

Theme Five – Boundaryless Collaboration

- It refers to Jack Welch's mantras for business success. Six sigma implemented by GE and was working to break barriers and how to improve teamwork up, down and across organizational unit lines.
- More opportunities available to organization when improved collaboration within the companies and with vendors and customers are valuable to earn potential income from business.

Theme Six – Drive and Perfection

- It refers to how you can be driven to achieve perfection and yet also tolerate failure.
- No company will get even close to six sigma without launching new ideas and approaches which always involve some risk for accomplishment of drive with perfection.

Totally , six sigma is gradual process, it starts with a dream or a vision ; the goal of near perfect products and services and meet customer satisfaction, company is willing to and challenge to take this opportunity and to support six sigma process, definitely company can be find good results and yield much satisfaction.

CHAPTER 8

Contemporary Strategic Issues

"If we want to stay competitive, we need to be in e – commerce"
Jessica Chu, Marketing manager, Aaeon Technology, Taiwan

"Our strategy is to integrate the internet into all of our core business"
Thomas Middelhoff, CEO, Bertelsmann AG, Germany

8.1 INTRODUCTION

In this chapter, we shall discuss the contemporary strategies issues like strategies for internet economy, needed for internet technology, strategy shaping characteristics of the E- commerce environment, strategic management in nonprofit and government organization like educational institutions, medical organizations, governmental agencies and departments.

8.2 STRATEGIES FOR INTERNET ECONOMY

- Internet and E commerce is the basic tool for formulation of strategy, implementation of strategy and control the strategy in modern business environment.
- It is rapidly growing and emerging e commerce environment that applicable all firms.
- Internet and e commerce change everything day by day in business units.

- Internet is the driving force of historical and revolutionary proportions in business.
- It creates new market and new driving forces and key success factors and help to formulation of new strategic groups in business units.
- It helps to company's ready face competitive advantages in market due to new and advanced technology.
- It presents opportunities and threats that demand strategic response and that require managers to craft bold and advanced new strategies.

What Is Internet Technology?

- The term internet is an integrated network of banks of servers and high speed computers, digital switches and routes, telecommunications equipment and lines, and individual users computers.
- **The** back bone of the internet principally composite of telecommunications lines (fiber optic lines, high capacity telephone lines) cross crossing countries, continents and the world that allow computers to transfer data in digital form at very high speed.
- The bandwidth lines determine the capacity or speed of the data transfer.
- The bandwidth lines are connected to computer like digital switches which move traffic along the backbone lines in terms of many of these switches act as routers , deciding which way to direct the traffic and how to handle the requests of users computers and send or obtain data based on the destinations and line congestion.
- Internet users can gain access to the network via a local area net work (LAN) server or an internet services providers computerized switch which has the capability to route traffic to and from end users directly connected to it.
- For internet connections purpose, many different types of specialized software are required to make the internet function and infuse it with attractive e commerce capabilities.

8.3 STRATEGY SHAPING CHARACTERISTICS OF THE E-COMMERCE ENVIRONMENT

Let us we shall know the need, understand and use of internet by businesses and consumers reshapes the economic landscapes and alters traditional industry boundaries. Important features are outlined:

- **The internet makes it feasible for companies everywhere to compete in global markets**
  - Companies offer product and services throughout the world, internet market will help to company to enhance its market into different geographic locations and it's allow to firms to create new technological developments and make cutthroat competition from similar products offered by the similar companies in global.

- **Competition in an industry is greatly intensified by the new e commerce strategic initiatives of existing rivals and by the entry of new, enterprising e- commerce rivalry.**
  - Internet an important new distribution channel that allows to sellers to reach vast numbers buyers relatively inexpensively but the use of online systems afforded by internet also holds considerable potential for improving business efficiency and lower operation costs. It is innovate tool to companies for development of new technology and its products and services.
- **Entry barriers into the e commerce world are relatively low**
  - It consists of many activities which are created value chains of e commerce business can be outsourced.
  - The software necessary to establish a Website which is readily available and it particularly provided service based functions and industries that mastering process in this way buildup competitive advantage in delivering goods and services to value customers.
- Online buyers gain bargaining power due to they confront far fewer obstacles to comparing the products, prices, and shipping times of rival vendors.
  - Online buyers will get 24 hours website services provided companies for selling products and services.
  - Using the online which captured online buyers worldwide.
  - Online buyers make order and pay bills via online.
- The internet makes it feasible for companies to reach beyond their borders to find the best suppliers and further to collaborate closely with them to achieve efficiency gains and cost savings.
  - Internet technologies provided companies supplies internet with high speeding products and services and reducing the cost of services.
  - It market through online, supply through online and make payment through online and make competition through online and offer different products and services to customers.
- Internet and PC technologies are advancing rapidly, often uncertain and unexpected directions in business.
- Internet results in much faster diffusion of new technology and new idea across the world.
- The e commerce environment demands that companies are movies swiftly throughout the world.
- E commerce technologies open up a host of opportunities for reconfiguring industry and company value chains for formulation of strategy and execution of strategy.

- The internet can be economical means of delivering customer service throughout the world.
- The internet requires capital for funding potential profitable e commerce businesses is readily available in market.
- The needed e commerce resource are short supply in human talent in the form of both technological expertise and managerial know how by companies.

8.4 STRATEGIC MANAGEMENT IN NON PROFIT AND GOVERNMENT ORGANIZATION

Figure 8.1: Classification of Business Organization

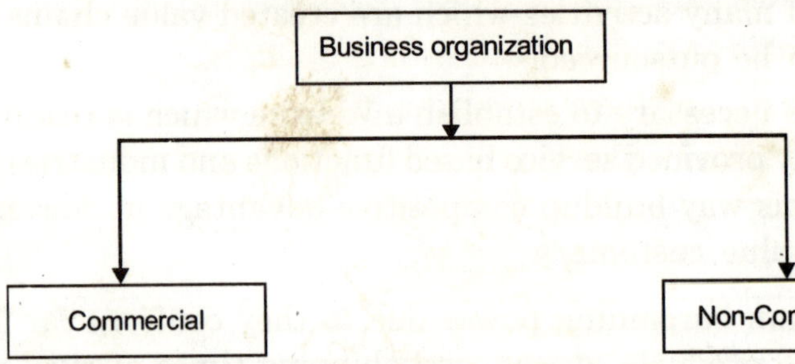

Figure 8.1 indicates the classification of business organization into two broad categories as listed below:

- Commercial Business organization
- Non commercial business organization

Commercial organization is one type of organization which main aim is to earn profit from business of an enterprise.

Non commercial business organizations are those organizations which are not doing commercial business activities. These are providing services like social, charitable, or educational purposes. This type organization main motive is not making and earning profit.

The strategic management process is being used by effectively by countless non profit governmental organizations. Non profit organizations like schools and college and industry and government organizations which are outperform for private firms and corporations on innovations , motivation, productivity and strategic management.

Educational Institutions

- Educational institutions are non profit business organization.
- Education institutions are using strategic management techniques and concepts more frequently in an organization.
- Strategist helps to academicians how to get project and how to close project with help both of them.

- Internet facilities provided to school and college for growth and development of college.
- Offer to online degree to students and convince to do any module in sap.

Medical Organizations

- Medical organizations are also non profit organization.
- It renders service to hospital management.
- Strategic leaders are creating new strategies for formulation, implementation and control of data.
- Hospital offers services to patient and effectively utilized the strategies and analysis and measures the strategic issues for business.
- Pathological department have started and collected door to door services.
- Chronic care will require day to day treatment facilities, electronic monitoring at hospital and decentralized net works.
- A successful strategy in hospital pursuing include acquiring facility which require by hospital.
- It estimation of services and analysis budget requirement.
- The most successful hospital strategies today are providing freestanding outpatient surgery centers, outpatient surgery, diagnostic centre , physical rehabilitation centers, preferred provider services, industrial medicine services, women medicine services, skilled nursing homes.

Governmental Agencies and Departments

- It consists central, state, municipal, public sector units, departments are responsible for formulation; implementation and evaluating strategies that are use taxpayers money in the most cost effective to online buyers.
- In this case, less autonomous for formulation of strategy for this purpose .
- Govt. strategist has more freedom. to take decision.
- It clearly defined mission , objectives for decision purpose.